D1470944

To Be a Jew

*Joseph Chayim Brenner
as a Jewish Existentialist*

Avi Sagi

Translated by Batya Stein

מכון שלום הרטמן
SHALOM HARTMAN INSTITUTE

continuum

Published by Continuum International Publishing Group
The Tower Building, 11 York Road, London SE1 7NX
80 Maiden Lane, Suite 704, New York, NY 10038

www.continuumbooks.com

British Library Cataloguing-in-Publication Data
A catalogue record for this book is available from the British Library

ISBN: 978-1-4411-9583-8 (hardback)
ISBN: 978-1-4411-0973-6 (paperback)

Typeset by Free Range Book Design & Production
Printed and bound in Great Britain by
CPI Antony Rowe, Chippenham, Wiltshire

This book is dedicated to the memory of Eliezer Goldman:
thinker, pioneer, man of truth

Contents

Preface

Brenner thought Jewish existence, struggled with it, and sought relevant meaning in it. His literary works, his criticism and journalistic writings and, above all, his personal life, are a prolonged voyage in search for meaning and substance in Jewish existence in the here and now, for him and for people like him.

This book is an attempt to examine Brenner's approach from an existentialist perspective. My central claim is that Brenner's understanding of the meaning of Jewish existence is definitely existentialist. In many ways, his affirmation of Jewish existence is a conclusion warranted by his overall existentialist outlook.

This perspective is reflected in the structure of this book: Chapters 1 to 4 analyse Brenner's existentialist views, whereas Chapters 6 to 8 analyse these views insofar as they touch on the meaning of Jewish existence. Chapter 5 serves as a transition, bridging Brenner's existentialism and the discussion on the meaning of Jewish existence. This structure clarifies that at the start and at the end of the Brennerian voyage is the individual contending with existence as a person and as a Jew.

Although Brenner is among the Hebrew authors about whom much has been written, a detailed analysis of his Jewish spiritual world is still missing. The myriads of words written about him, particularly on the meaning of Jewish existence, include also endless slogans. Brenner's exciting and challenging *oeuvre* inspired a tempestuous outpouring of writing, not all of it critical. As a result, one of the more significant and relevant options on the meaning of modern Jewish existence gradually vanished. Brenner confronted the question of Jewish existence and the problem of how to survive as a Jew without committing himself to an entire set of ideas that condition Jewish life.

Beyond the intrinsic significance of acknowledging the possibility of a concrete, non-ideological, non-metaphysical Jewish existence, Brenner's stance is important due to its profoundly critical character. One of my deepest motivations in writing this book was the wish to redraw the Brennerian Jewish stance as a living, challenging option. This book is an attempt to listen to Brenner, to tread in his footsteps so as to learn in detail the meaning of Jewish existence as he had traced it.

Two fundamental obstacles hinder the course of this book, both a result of its having been written by a philosopher who resorts to philosophy for a set of basic tools and for the dispositions that shape the encounter with the Brennerian text. The first is the reliance on philosophical method to discuss a work that is not philosophical; and the second, which follows from the first, concerns the risk that a philosophical study will turn Brenner's complex, contradictory, and dialectical *oeuvre* into a monolithic, organized, and coherent corpus. The first obstacle is not specific to the concern with Brenner but is typical of the prevalent philosophical concern with literature, given that literature is of interest not only to scholars of literature but also to philosophers. And yet, the use of philosophical methods and approaches is not supposed to create a special problem. Philosophical positions, as well as philosophical tools, shape the world of the philosopher as a person, hence also the philosopher's attitude to literary texts. Literary texts, like texts in general, do not appear with reading instructions, and even if they had, such instructions would not have compelled anyone. The way we read texts ultimately reflects the interest, the style, the questions, and all the other presumptions, in Gadamer's formulation, we bring along as readers. Honest readers learn not to overpower the text, to restrain themselves, and to listen to it. A balanced encounter, then, takes place between the text and the reader. This is true of all readers, and certainly also of philosophers.

The second obstacle is more problematic and is related to a feature typical of the philosophical disposition. Philosophers may be trapped into ignoring the contradicting, the dialectical. Their philosophical disposition could lead them to see literary works as philosophical works, usually purported to be coherent, clear, structured, and so forth. They could play the role of riddle solvers when the riddle is actually supposed to be preserved.

In Chapter 3, I point out the gap between philosophy and literature. Awareness of this gap, however, does not ensure that the philosophy trap will be avoided. I know that readers of this book could end up thinking that Brenner is indeed a philosopher, a partner to the traditional philosophical discourse that offers a coherent stance built layer upon layer and integrating all the genres of his *oeuvre*: literature, criticism, and journalism. The multivocal tumult of major and minor literary characters could appear as a harmonious uniform whole. But although I am aware of this danger, I cannot think of another way of exposing and explicating Brenner's views. This is true not only for the philosopher reader but also for all of Brenner's readers who, ultimately, seek to understand him. Human understanding is shaped by a desire for clarity and coherence; indeed, only because this is the starting impulse do we become aware of the contradictory element, the one that fails to join others.

In my view, two mechanisms help to preclude shallowness and uniformity in the understanding of Brenner. The first is the constant awareness of this danger and the recognition that accompanies the reader, as it accompanied me, that the coherent, clear, argumentative construct is related above all to the exposition but not to the actual experience that underlies it. The Brennerian experience, as an existentialist experience, remains packed with dialectical and complex nuances surging forth implicitly or explicitly in various places. This constant awareness may prevent readers, as it prevented me, from trying to exhaust the complex Brennerian experience. It creates a kind of distance between the text and its referent.

The second mechanism, in many ways the antithesis of the first, comes to the fore in the meticulous care I invested in remaining attached to Brenner's texts. This anchoring ensures that the structured text does not depart too far from the basic experience that underlies it, if we indeed assume that a basic experience is behind the entire literary endeavour. I confront this challenge in the first three chapters, and the reader should judge whether the book met it successfully.

The recourse to different literary genres, to quotes from various characters, and their linkage to Brenner the man, is not a simple matter. A writer's art rests on poetic imagination, on fiction, and not necessarily on the direct or indirect representation of the author's inner world. I did take this challenge into account, and Chapters 1 to 3 reflect an effort to confront this question.

This book, like all my books, is an invitation to a dialogue, the opening rather than the conclusion of the discussion. Its beginning is my dialogue with Brenner, and its ending, the book's dialogue with its readers. Hence, as in all my books, I made sure to cite at length and to enable the constant shift between the texts in order to enable the reader's participation.

This book was written in one stroke but matured slowly within me for many long years, as part of an ongoing project offering a new presentation of existentialist literature. Two of my previous books, on Kierkegaard and on Camus, in many ways paved the way to it, and the insights I yielded from them shaped my basic attitude to Brenner's work.

This book would not have been written without the ongoing encouragement of my colleagues and students at Bar-Ilan University and at the Shalom Hartman Institute in Jerusalem. Some of the chapters in the book were discussed at a seminar on 'Traces of the Past in the Present' at the Hartman Institute. My colleagues' responses helped to refine my ideas, and I am grateful to them. My students at a seminar I conducted at the Shalom Hartman Institute were also intensively involved in the reading of the book, and our joint discussions greatly enriched my understanding. Three colleagues read the manuscript with great care: Avi Lipsker, Moshe Goultschin, and Shraga Baron. Their illuminating comments helped me to remove several stumbling blocks and to clarify my formulations. My assistant Yakir Englander was tirelessly involved in the research and in the thoughtful reading of the text. I doubt I could have completed this work without his extensive help, and I am indebted to him.

As usual, I am grateful for the privilege of being a research fellow at the Shalom Hartman Institute, where I have spent more than two decades. The spirit of friendship, the mutual attentiveness, the constructive criticism, and the shared study have in large measure shaped my writing, my research, and my teaching.

My students at Bar-Ilan University, at the Philosophy Department and at the Hermeneutics and Cultural Studies Program 'suffered' from my initial attempts to formulate the ideas that inspired this book. It has been my great honour to teach at this university for more than thirty years and to have headed this programme for more than ten. The generous assistance of the Rappaport Center at Bar-Ilan University made this book possible, and I am grateful to my colleague and research partner Zvi Zohar, who heads the Center, for his support and encouragement.

This book, like all my other Hebrew writings, was rendered into English by Batya Stein. I have been fortunate to benefit from her flawless translations, her wisdom, her friendship, and her commitment to her work for over twenty years. For all of them, I thank Batya deeply. Her contribution is particularly special in this book where, unless noted otherwise, she translated into English the many citations from Brenner and from other early 20th-century Hebrew authors. The difficulty of pouring this wine into new casks is clear to anyone familiar with the Hebrew literature of the times, and her superb translations will allow English readers to appreciate its beauty.

Finally, I wish to pay tribute here to the memory of my teacher and friend Eliezer Goldman (1918–2002), who was a central figure among contemporary Jewish philosophers. The publication of Goldman's writings has begun only recently, and works about him are already beginning to appear. As his student for many long years at Bar-Ilan University, I feel blessed to have encountered a man whose mark was sincerity and modesty, a genuine Renaissance figure at home in the treasures of Western and Jewish culture. He contemplated all of them deeply and critically, invariably seeking truth and transparency. He was a philosopher but also a man of action, a pioneer, a member of Kibbutz Sde Eliyahu. This book is dedicated to his memory, with endless longing and appreciation.

July 2010

ONE

A Preliminary Outline of Brenner's Approach

Brenner's multifaceted endeavour, covering prose, criticism, and columns on topical affairs, poses a question: is there one fundamental problem that sets it all in motion, one exclusive cornerstone for his entire *oeuvre*? Isaiah Berlin distinguished between two types of thinkers and works – centripetal and centrifugal. Centripetal thinkers 'relate everything to a single central vision, one system, less or more coherent or articulate, in terms of which they understand, think and feel – a single, universal, organising principle in terms of which alone all that they are and say has significance.'[1] By contrast, centrifugal ones – 'their thought is scattered or diffused, moving on many levels, seizing upon the essence of a vast variety of experiences and objects for what they are in themselves, without, consciously or unconsciously, seeking to fit them into, or exclude them from, any one unchanging, all-embracing, sometimes self-contradictory and incomplete, at times fanatical, unitary inner vision.'[2] Berlin refers to the former type as 'hedgehogs' and to the latter as 'foxes'. Berlin acknowledged that this distinction describes a syndrome rather than a dichotomous structure of style, thought, and writing and, therefore, we may talk about 'more' or 'less' regarding each of these two characteristics: more or less hedgehog, more or less fox.[3]

Relying on Berlin's distinction, we could ask whether Brenner is a fox or a hedgehog. Specifically, however, my concern is primarily the question or questions that trouble Brenner, and less the fullness of his *oeuvre*. The problem, then, is whether Brenner asks one basic question, which makes him a kind of 'hedgehog', or many different questions, which makes him a kind of 'fox'.

My question does not rest on an a priori assumption claiming that an author's entire *oeuvre* necessarily reflects one fundamental problem. An author active in a broad field could definitely raise a series of questions and even offer a spectrum of answers. A varied and multifaceted endeavour, however, is what allows us to ask this question in the first place, though answering it requires a detailed analysis of the author's entire range of creativity.

Generations of Brenner's readers and critics who returned time and again to his works have identified, each in his or her way, the core common to all. S. Y. Penueli assumed that 'the essence in Brenner hits your mind. His essence is the artist, the chagrined realist artist…

Brenner saw and lived, was kicked and lived… realism is his only course.'[4] According to Penueli, the constitutive element of Brenner's work is artistic expression *per se* or, more precisely, realistic artistic expression rather than an inclusive world view. Penueli further asserts:

> Will we look for a world view in Brenner's stories? When the artist's spirit is not there, we will occasionally find topical passages approaching life through a contemporary perspective, through the movements and political parties of his times. But this is not the gist of Brenner. The core in him, what hits the mind, is the artistic story without method or conception, only scooping out essences from the bosom of life.[5]

The essence of Brenner's *oeuvre* for Penueli, then, is artistic expression as such, not extra-literary contents. But this approach is problematic on several counts. First, it sets up a wall between Brenner the artist and Brenner the literary critic and journalist. Although possible, is this wall indeed necessary? Is there no way of bridging across the span of Brenner's creativity? Second, as the following chapters will show, Brenner is opposed to this perception of art as a separate realm. Art for Brenner is intertwined with the web of life and directed towards it, an approach hardly compatible with the pure aestheticism of artistic expression suggested by Penueli.

Another common perception of Brenner transcends artistic expression and claims that his works represent the response of an individual and a generation that have lost their old world. Faced with the ruins of traditional Jewish life, these individuals confront an uprooted existence, devoid of meaning or identity. In this view, Brenner's creativity is a reflection of this negative experience. The experience of a tradition in crisis is the very element that connects Brenner's writings to the past. The link with the past, then, is not established through continuity but through a constant struggle with it. Gershon Shaked sensitively describes and sums up this stance, and states:

> One of the most common constructs in 'Brenner's generation' is that of 'exit' and 'return'… The main focus of this construct is the wandering from place to place that grows from the soul's malaise… The protagonists try to escape the yoke of their society, but their flight does not unravel the spiritual entanglement… The uprooted hero, suicidal or losing his mind, is a frequent protagonist in the Hebrew fiction of Brenner's generation. Only by understanding this figure will we understand Brenner's

characters. More than any other writer, he had a share in devising this construct, which leads heroes through a convoluted path to the hidden vicious circle of their existence.[6]

The approach that views the uprooted individual as the constitutive archetype of Brenner's work reached culmination in Kurzweil's interpretation. For Kurzweil, uprootedness in this case is not from the culture, from the social structure, and from Jewish tradition; Brenner's problem was not a consequence of the social-cultural rift. The fundamental crisis that has led to the experience of uprootedness is the detachment from Jewish religion: Brenner contends with the death of God – he experiences this death, and his work is a reaction to this experience:

> The religious problem is unquestionably central, even if negatively, in Brenner's stories... Lack of faith in God did not result in the same changes and transformations in world literature as in our literature, for the simple reason that the dependence of Jewish existence on the religious element is entirely different from the existence of all other nations... And whoever fails to grasp the special problematic of a Jewish existence without God in Brenner's writing misses the essence.[7]
>
> The pathos of negative religiosity hints at its source. Brenner's heroes will apparently never forgive God for not existing for them.[8]

According to Kurzweil, religiosity can be present in two modes: affirmation or denial. Paradoxically, however, the denial of religiosity is its affirmation, since denial reaffirms religiosity as a permanent element of literary creativity.

If valid, this claim ostensibly applies also to anyone who denies religiosity, since denying religiosity reaffirms it as a pillar of existence. Kurzweil appears to have relied for this claim on his teacher Paul Tillich,[9] who unhesitatingly stated (indeed, only about existentialism) that the source of this tradition's answers to life's questions is either explicitly religious – making existentialism a distinctly religious philosophy, as is true of Pascal or Kierkegaard, for instance – or implicitly so, as in the thought of Nietzsche, Heidegger, and Sartre.[10]

Kurzweil is probably aware of the problem entailed by Tillich's sweeping assertion, given that secularization does not necessarily rest on the denial of religiosity. He therefore narrows the claim and confines it to Hebrew writers and to modern Jewish history. In his view, secularization in Europe developed as a complex, extended process, which turned it into a real option. By contrast, the Jewish people have not experienced secularization for long enough, and the crisis of religiosity is therefore a permanent element in Hebrew literature, which views existence without God as absurd. In his words:

> By the first half of the eighteenth century, existence without God was already a basic assumption in most of European literature, without this change leading to a deep upheaval in the way that life, suffering, and existence in general are perceived. The culture of European nations was by then mostly secular, and these nations lived in their lands and in their states. Their existence without God, in other words, is not absurd. The situation is different for the Jewish people, and the process of detachment from religious faith carries a special, different, and more fateful meaning in our literature.[11]

This analysis leads Kurzweil to reject another interpretation, which views Brenner's *oeuvre* as an expression of Hebrew existentialism: 'Attempts to view Brenner as a forefather of the Hebrew "existentialist" writers of today, a kind of merry desperate, are actually funny. Brenner does not need this honor. He would have found this literary "continuity" revolting – what did he care about pseudo-aesthetes? He hated aesthetes already then, and even his most daring heresy is so essentially Jewish!'[12] Kurzweil, therefore, set Brenner's work squarely within the tradition of Hebrew literature. His work is not a breakthrough, but an additional chapter in the ongoing Jewish discourse. Unlike the old literature, however, this literature is stamped with the seal of crisis and collapse.

Kurzweil did not make religious existence the centre of Brenner's world on the basis of what he found in Brenner's writings. What Kurzweil found in Brenner's writings could – and should – have led him to interpret them in entirely different terms, as shown below. His views rest on assumptions about Jewish life in Brenner's times. According to Kurzweil, Brenner's work cannot be secular because a secular Jewish existence lacks historical depth. But even if this were not the case, literature can hardly be secular since Kurzweil doubts the possibility of secularism concerning the Jewish people.

Even if we endorse Kurzweil's assumptions, however, a question still remains open: is it possible and fitting to understand a writer's project and the meaning of a literary creation through historical 'circumstances'? Kurzweil's approach relies on a historical-deterministic hermeneutical approach – a writer who functions in a given set of conditions cannot escape them, and examining a writer's work outside these conditions is therefore improper.

Furthermore, to assume that religious and existentialist perspectives are antithetical ignores the split between religious and secular versions of existentialism. In the religious branch of existentialism are thinkers such as Kierkegaard, Shestov, Berdyaev, Marcel, and Tillich. In the secular branch are thinkers such as Nietzsche, Heidegger, and Sartre. Even if we accepted Kurzweil's assumptions, therefore, religiosity and existentialism could still be mediated without creating an artificial dichotomy.

Beyond these critiques, the question should still be asked: are secularism and secular creativity necessarily contingent on secularism's historical depth? Ahad Ha-Am is a distinctively secular thinker who proposes a comprehensive secular Jewish identity representing an alternative to Jewish identity and Jewish religious life. His work is, *inter alia*, an attempt to place religion itself within a broader cultural-historical context. Religion does not pose a particular problem to him. He addresses it as a specific historical manifestation, one in a series of manifestations determining Jewish heritage and explained through the same elements that explain Jewish existence as a whole,[13] although Ahad-Ha-Am grew up in a religious family and did not experience a crisis that led him away from this life.[14]

Kurzweil negates the possibility of secular Jewish creativity in principle, since he assumes that a Jewish work must take a stand either for or against religion. He failed to pay attention to the new Hebrew culture, or indeed to Brenner. Brenner's work, as I will claim, is secular in the deep sense of this term: the death of the Brennerian God, like the death of the Nietzschean God, is not an expression of what should have been and is not, but a profound articulation of God's irrelevance to life. A secular life is one where the focus has shifted from the transcendent to the immanent, from the metaphysical to the real. In this life, a religion based on the transcendent has no meaning. The restoration of religion requires what I have called the subjective shift.[15] This shift implies that the source of faith is the subject's inner religious disposition rather than a real event in the world – God's revelation. The subjective shift reconstitutes religion on immanent foundations with the subject at the centre.[16] The first one to make this pivotal change was Kierkegaard.[17] And yet, choosing this course is altogether unnecessary. All it means is that religiosity seeks its course in a world from which the transcendent has been removed.

The starting point, of Brenner the man and of his work, is wholly immanent, and he does not seek to restore religiosity within this immanent context: 'The beginning of the twentieth century, which is a period of time, became in Brenner's story an existence-without God, which needs to find an exit for the existence-of-man. This necessity could well be the core meaning of Brenner's stories.'[18]

The death of the Brennerian God is a shift from God to the individual. The Jewish individual is now caught within an immanent existence, aware that escape from it is impossible. Although conscious of the mystery of existence – 'the riddle of life' in Brenner's terms, which I consider in Chapter 4 below – the individual must remain within concrete existence and contend with it within its limits. The development of these claims is at the focus of this book.

The widespread claim that the constitutive experience of Brenner's work is uprootedness does not fit Brenner's life either. Uprootedness, as a kind of absolute detachment and severing from the old life, from the parental home, from family tradition and memory, does not pass muster in this regard. As Dan Miron showed, writers of Brenner's generation do experience uprooting from the parental home – but:

> The tragic problematic of the 'rift' entailed by this rebellion does not play a central and significant role in their spiritual world. Indeed, most of them leave their homes with their parents' blessing... The father of Yirmiyahu Feuerman, Brenner's autobiographical hero ('*Ba-Horef* [In Winter]) shows, at least externally, remnants of the traditional father's typical attitude toward a son who has 'let him down.' In the end, however, he only asks his son to maintain the lifestyle of a 'God-seeking *maskil*,' that is, to pray and observe the main commandments performed in public. He boasts about his son's education in ways inconceivable in a fully traditional father... *Shtetl* youths who endorse secular culture and Hebrew literature at the beginning of the century do not leave behind the reality from which their predecessors, the writers of the 1880s and 1890s, had come out.[19]

As shown below, Brenner the man and his work express a primal and unquestionable attachment to Jewish existence. The abandonment of religion is accompanied by a stronger sense of belongingness, conveyed in a return to the actual language of the tradition. The meaning of this language, however, undergoes a transformation: rather than a religious language, this is the language of Jewish existence. Consider the following passage from '*Hu Amar Lah*' [He Told Her], which represents a kind of manifesto justifying self-defence at the time of the pogroms in Russia:

My mouth had already ceased reciting Psalms. The belief that whatever God does is for the good had been wiped out from my heart.

Indeed, I ceased reciting Psalms. My heart did cry out through the day: 'Why are the nations in uproar'. My spirit moaned and would not cease: 'How many are my enemies become'… My soul endlessly begged, 'O Lord, heal me!' since 'I am weary with my groaning,' mother; 'All the night I make my bed to swim; I water my couch with my tears. My eye is wasted because of grief…' Yes. But I am dumbstruck, my tongue has no words. I only responded to those in hiding, who lied in caves and called out, each one separately: 'O Lord my God, in thee do I put my trust: save me from all them that persecute me and deliver me.'

But their prayer was lost, lost. Not like lions… did they tear their souls; like dogs they dragged their carcasses, and no one saved them! And from dogs, there is a savior. With accursed dogs, no old charms will help. They must be shown wonders with the rod.

Hear O Israel! Not an eye for an eye: two eyes for one and all their teeth for any shame![20]

This text embodies the transition from a religious to a secular way of life: in this transition, the language itself is not lost. Even when the Book of Psalms ceased to function as a book of prayers, as the channel connecting Jewish individuals to their God, it remained the language of discourse. Indeed, losing the ability to 'recite Psalms' exposes the language in all its power. The heart of one who no longer recites the Psalms 'cries out through the day'. In biblical language, the Hebrew word *shu'a* that appears in this verse is a kind of prayer: a call for help addressed to God.[21] But in the new secular viewpoint, the prayer is addressed to human beings, not to heaven. The wording of the traditional prayer does not change dramatically. The change is in the addressee – no longer God but human beings. The prayer is a call to assume responsibility for Jewish existence. Those who had turned their prayers to heaven – 'their prayer was lost'. By contrast, those engaged in a new prayer addressing humans are supposed to mobilize into action.

The wording of the new prayer opens with 'Hear O Israel'. In the language of prayer, this verse means 'accepting the yoke of the heavenly kingdom' and acknowledging divine rule. In secular language, however, it means preparedness, readiness for action. The wording of the prayer is therefore the required action – 'not an eye for an eye: two eyes for one'. The prayer will be the catalyst of the change. What remains of the religious prayer is the language, which joins the son to his mother. The son reciting a new prayer informs his mother that he has ceased reciting Psalms but he has not ceased to pray, and this prayer comes from an affirmation of Jewish existence and for its sake. This new prayer, not the traditional one, embodies responsibility for Jewish fate.[22] The abandonment of religion exposes the prior affirmation of this existence by resorting to the language of traditional discourse.[23] Rather than the experience of rift and uprootedness, therefore, it is this basic attachment to Jewish existence that determines the Brennerian call and critique.

Ada Tzemah, who shed light on this matter, writes:

> Indeed, decentralization rather than uprootedness is the chief hallmark of Brennerism.[24]
>
> The essence of a Brennerian life… conveys a great effort to engage in action, a struggle with the logic of death, a ceaseless search for something that will fill 'the space… with something.' With what? With what 'something'? This is the one important question that constantly confronts Brenner and his protagonists; this is the big question of Brennerism… In the answer to this question lies the foundation of necessity inside him, the foundation that marks him as belonging rather than uprooted, held and connected through all the strands of his soul.[25]

Those who considered uprootedness the core of Brenner's creativity failed to draw a proper distinction between the socio-cultural experience of uprootedness and the existential experience of the absurd that, as shown below, is the foundation of Brenner's work. The absurd is a metaphysical experience, not necessarily related to socio-cultural uprootedness.[26] Although the literary formulation of these two experiences may be similar, they should not be confused. A person may experience socio-cultural uprootedness without necessarily experiencing the metaphysical absurd, that is, without losing the meaning of existence. At most, one's specific socio-cultural existence may become meaningless.

Simon Halkin suggests a more complex perception of uprootedness. He estimates that modern Hebrew literature offers at least three versions of uprootedness and uprooted characters. The first type, 'the ostensibly uprooted', denotes 'one who is only socially uprooted'.[27] These individuals, whose social status has changed due to their university education, experience uprootedness because they return to the place they had left. Yet, they cannot find themselves in their original environment and they experience social alienation. The second kind, or the 'second type' that Halkin presents, is

> the 'uprooted' who is always 'between worlds'… Berdyczewski presents a type of person who not only shifts from place to place and returns to his own, but one whose entire life remains a kind of perpetual tribulation… highlighting the deep spiritual and cultural rift… This is a person who never reaches his place and remains forever 'between worlds'… He draws sustenance from two sources and finds no rest. This is a life without joy.[28]

The third kind of uprootedness reflects an individual radically detached from his surroundings: 'When the hero is no longer connected to his society, he encloses himself within his soul, as it were, and lives what he lives as if he had done so forever, without undergoing any change.' This uprooted character expresses 'despair from the human world after separating from it'.[29] Halkin points out that this uprootedness develops in European literature among such writers as Joyce, Proust, and Kafka, and is also found in the work of Uri Nissan Gnessin.[30]

Although some dimensions of this uprootedness do appear in some of Brenner's works,[31] Chapter 4 will show that Brenner's *oeuvre*, if such generalizations are at all possible, is not characterized by uprootedness from Jewish existence in any of the meanings that Halkin presented. Rather, the focus of Brennerian creativity is the experience of the metaphysical absurd, which does not negate a prior and unconditioned attachment to Jewish existence. Indeed, this sense of priority is in many ways a manifestation of the absurd. The third type of detachment is extremely close to the experience of the absurd, which also materializes in a turn inward and in a persistent effort to find meaning in existence.

In his critical article '*Me-Hirhurei Sofer*' [A Writer's Reflections],[32] Brenner examines modern Hebrew literature. Words he ascribes to a Gnessin character, Nahum Hagzar, appear to fit him: 'The sorrow of the nation, the death of the gods, the pulling of the rug from under his feet, the loss of existing values, the depletion of forces, the tedium of life, the lack of content, the emptiness of emptiness, the ridicule in the tragic and the tragic in the ridicule…'[33]

These basic experiences are no longer experiences of uprootedness; rather, they transcend to the metaphysical dimension and come together under the conceptual category of the absurd. As will be shown, Brenner copes with this basic experience while unconditionally affirming Jewish existence. What appears as uprootedness, then, is but a more profound existentialist-metaphysical experience.

If neither uprootedness nor religion are the basic conceptual frameworks for understanding Brenner's world, the existentialist option that lends meaning to the absurd and to the various manifestations of uprootedness is worth considering.

To examine this option, we must first clarify the main characteristics of existentialist philosophy and consider whether Brenner's work fits these categories. Kurzweil's vague statement whereby 'Brenner's daring heresy is so essentially Jewish', even if correct, does not dismiss the possibility that his work is a deep expression of the existentialist position. Existentialism and Judaism are not mutually contradictory, and Jewish philosophy includes existentialist thinkers such as Franz Rosenzweig, Joseph B. Soloveitchik, Abraham Joshua Heschel, and others.

The main thesis of this book is that existentialism is the constitutive foundation of Brenner's work and serves to clarify his view on the basic question posed in this book: the meaning of Jewish existence. Isaiah Rabinovich argued many years ago that existentialism is the suitable perspective for considering Brenner's work:[34]

> Brenner had to hew the solution to the problem out of himself... He had to turn his denial of God, of religion, of history, as well as his individual and social uncertainties, into sources of a survival vision. In Brenner's stories, one should indeed trace the signs of an existentialist process guided by Kierkegaard. Brenner's heresy, like Kierkegaard's, is meant to 'settle all accounts' and to remove, at the same time, all the disappointments, flaws, deceits, and distortions, from society and from the individual... It ascribes any sanctity, if any is possible, only to man, crowning every human action with the distinction of creation and ascribing morality solely to human creativity... Only 'breakdown and bereavement' lie in wait for one who seeks an a priori solution and a vision of the entire chain, busy with empty dreams and engaged in illusions of 'history', 'prophecy', and 'tradition'. But if he begins to see each link in the chain as self-contained, and if he sanctifies separate humane action as such and seeks only for it the 'good' and 'humane' solution, he is revealed to himself as his own master. The protagonists of Brenner's fiction, and particularly *Breakdown and Bereavement*, strive for an existentialist (almost Sartre-like) solution of this type.[35]

Many years after Rabinowich, Yosef Gorny returns to the existentialist thesis and writes:

In various formulations and with cruel consistency, Brenner strongly conveyed the meaninglessness of individual existence in a purposeless, irredeemable world. By negating the rational meaning of existence; in his belief in the death of God; by stressing the priority of actual existence over metaphysical problems; by emphasizing the individual's spontaneous will; by negating reliance on objective processes – through these ideas, which are the foundations of existentialist thought, Brenner followed F. Nietzsche, whom he had admired in his youth.[36]

Gorny was also the first to point out the connection between Brenner's positions and Camus' thought, and to identify the link between Brenner's existentialism and his views concerning Jewish existence:

Like Albert Camus' heroes, who stood up to fight death in *The Plague*, without raising their eyes to a godless heaven and despite their knowledge that the plague could not be wiped out, so Brenner stood up to fight the danger of destruction threatening his people, despite his awareness that he would not find full redemption.[37]

Gorny then analyses in great detail the differences between Brenner and Camus,[38] while adopting an existentialist perspective.[39]

In principle, I accept the existentialist orientation suggested by Rabinowich and Gorny, because it is well supported in Brenner's work. It also supplies the key for an understanding of the subject of this book – Brenner and the meaning of Jewish existence. An explication of the existentialist dimension as a constitutive element of Brenner's literary endeavour and as a basis for understanding his attitude to Jewish existence is the main concern of this book. Chapters 2 to 4 will be devoted to the existentialist aspect, and Chapters 5 to 7 to the implications of the existentialist viewpoint for the meaning of Jewish existence.

In my hermeneutical perspective on Brenner's work, I will attempt to trace in all the genres of Brenner's extensive *oeuvre* the existentialist characteristics of human existence, and to examine whether they fit the tradition of existentialist thought. My analysis of existentialist tradition does not rely on the view of one specific thinker, even when I rely at length on several existentialist philosophers. My method relies on a general existentialist phenomenology that presents human ontology in general terms. Excellent illustrations of the general phenomenological move are the works of Calvin Schrag[40] and Frederick Olafson,[41] who outlined the characteristics of existence in general terms, relying on existentialist tradition and without commitment to a particular view. As I will show, the existentialist characteristics clearly present in Brenner's work also explicate his views in the Jewish realm. Brenner, then, is a Jewish existentialist. The existentialist foundation will thus serve as the pivot of Brenner's entire *oeuvre*.

The chapters of the book follow this basic outline. The next two chapters deal with Brenner and his work, and examine the relationship between the writer and his *oeuvre* along two courses. In Chapter 2, I present the thesis that Brenner's writings should be seen as personal, as his contest with the fundamental questions of his existence. Despite the personal imprint, his work should not be viewed as a kind of confession and should not be analysed in reductionist terms, which consider the work through its creator's personality. Chapter 3 seeks to substantiate this claim, and reformulates the relationship between literature and life in Brenner's approach. In Chapter 4, I present in detail Brenner's view of existence, a view that again reflects the standing of literature as an organon for contending with life.

These three chapters create the basic framework of Brenner's world, which is also supposed to guide us in understanding his ways of coping with and interpreting Jewish existence. Brenner's existentialism, as I will show, is also Jewish existentialism. Brenner's perception of Jewish existence reaffirms his starting assumptions. Chapters 5 to 7 are devoted to the existentialist analysis of Jewish existence. Chapter 7 sums up Brenner's stance, clearly presenting Jewish existentialism and all its cultural-practical conclusions.

Notes

1   Isaiah Berlin, 'The Hedgehog and the Fox: An Essay on Tolstoy's View of History', in *The Proper Study of Mankind: An Anthology of Essays*, ed. Henry Hardy and Roger Hausheer (London: Pimlico, 1998), 436.

2   *Ibid.*, 436–7.

3   See also Shoshana Zimerman, *From Thee to Thee: The Underlying Principle in H. N. Bialik's Poetry* (in Hebrew) (Tel Aviv: Tag, 1998), 25–48.

4   S. I. Penueli, *Stages in Modern Hebrew Literature* (in Hebrew) (Tel Aviv: Dvir, 1953), 114.

5   *Ibid.*, 118.

6   Gershon Shaked, *Dead End: Studies in Y. H. Brenner, M. J. Berdyczewski, G. Schoffman and U. N. Gnessin* (in Hebrew) (Tel Aviv: Hakibbutz Hameuchad, 1973), 58. See also *idem, Hebrew Narrative Fiction 1880–1980*, vol.1, *In Exile* (in Hebrew) (Tel Aviv: Hakibbutz Hameuchad, 1978), 21–2; David Aryeh Friedman, 'The Cellar Man or the Hebrew Apostate' (in Hebrew), in *Yosef Haim Brenner: A Selection of Critical Essays on his Literary Prose*, ed. Yitzhak Bakon (Tel Aviv: Am Oved, 1972), 71–2.

7   Baruch Kurzweil, *Between Vision and the Absurd: Chapters in the Path of Our Literature in the Twentieth Century* (in Hebrew) (Jerusalem: Schocken, 1966), 272–3. See also Baruch Kurzweil, 'Between Brenner, Weinninger, and Kafka', in *Yosef Haim Brenner: A Selection of Critical Essays on his Literary Prose*, ed. Yitzhak Bakon (Tel Aviv: Am Oved, 1972), 145–7, 151.

8   Kurzweil, *Between Vision and the Absurd*, 272–3.

9   See Moshe Goultschin, *Baruch Kurzweil as a Commentator of Culture* (in Hebrew) (Ramat-Gan: Bar-Ilan University Press, 2009).

10   See Paul Tillich, *Systematic Theology*, vol. 2 (Chicago: University of Chicago Press, 1967), 25–6. *Cf.* also Roger Troisfontaines, *Existentialism and Christian Thought*, trans. Martin Jarrett-Kerr (London: Adam and Charles Black, 1949), 40–44.

11   Kurzweil, *Between Vision and the Absurd*, 272–3.

12   *Ibid.*, 268.

13   On the secular character of Ahad-Ha-Am's work see Rina Hevlin, *Coping with Jewish Identity: A Study of Ahad Ha-Am's Thought* (in Hebrew) (Tel Aviv: Hakibbutz Hameuchad, 2001), chs. 4, 6.

14   Kurzweil seems not to have heard the distress call of Nahman, the protagonist of Feierberg's *Le'an* [Whither]: 'I am wretched – he thinks – because I am the son of a people that has nothing in the world, except for religion. Only two ways are before you: to fight for religion or against religion – and I myself, I want to be a free man. This is not my life's aim, to fight for religion or against it…My heart has other aspirations, and I seek to do other things in this world, for my people.' Mordecai Ze'ev Feierberg, *Whither? and Other Stories*, trans. Hillel Halkin (Philadelphia: Jewish Publication Society of America, 1973), 127.

15   See Avi Sagi, *Tradition vs. Traditionalism: Contemporary Perspectives in Jewish Thought*, trans. Batya Stein (Amsterdam and New York: Rodopi, 2008), 21. On a construct for the religious restoration of Jewish thought, see *ibid.*, 111–13.

16   On this issue, see also Peter Berger, *The Heretical Imperative: Contemporary Possibilities of Religious Affirmation* (New York: Anchor Press, 1979), 125–38.

17   On this turning point in Kierkegaard's thought see Avi Sagi, *Kierkegaard, Religion, and Existence: The Voyage of the Self*, trans. Batya Stein (Amsterdam-Atlanta, GA: Rodopi, 2000), particularly ch.4.

18   S. Y. Penueli, *Brenner and Gnessin in Early Twentieth-Century Hebrew Fiction* (in Hebrew) (Tel Aviv: Students' Association at Tel Aviv University, 1965), 41.

19   Dan Miron, 'Hebrew Literature at the Beginning of the Twentieth Century' (in Hebrew), *Anthology of Literature, Criticism and Philosophy*, vol.2 (Jerusalem: The Hebrew Writers Association in Israel, 1961), 447–8.

20   Yosef Haim Brenner, *Writings* (in Hebrew), vol.1 (Tel Aviv: Hakibbutz Hameuchad, 1977) (henceforth and throughout the book *Writings*), 599–600.

21   Menahem Zevi Kaddari, *A Dictionary of Biblical Hebrew (Alef-Taw)*, under *shu'a* (Ramat-Gan: Bar-Ilan University, 2006), 1068.

22   *Cf.* also Moshe Yitzhaki, 'From Apostasy to Prayer: Religious Elements in Breakdown and Bereavement by Y. H. Brenner' (in Hebrew), *Alei Siah*, 55 (2006), 25–6.

23   Shaked, *In Exile*, 53–4.

24 Ada Tzemah, *A Movement at the Spot: Joseph Chaim Brenner and His Novels* (in Hebrew) (Tel Aviv: Hakibbutz Hameuchad, 1984), 217.

25 *Ibid.*, 219.

26 For an analysis of the absurd and its sources, see Avi Sagi, *Albert Camus and the Philosophy of the Absurd*, trans. Batya Stein (Amsterdam and New York: Rodopi, 2002), chs. 1, 4–6.

27 Simon Halkin, *Introduction to Hebrew Literature: Lecture Notes* (in Hebrew) (Jerusalem: Students Association at Hebrew University, 1960), 344.

28 *Ibid.*, 344–5.

29 *Ibid.*, 345.

30 See also Nurit Govrin, *Alienation and Regeneration*, trans. John Glucker (Tel Aviv: MOD, 1989), 20–30.

31 See Avner Holtzman, *Hebrew Fiction in the Early Twentieth Century, Unit 1* (in Hebrew) (Tel Aviv: Open University, 1993), 87.

32 *Writings*, vol.3, 270–94.

33 *Ibid.*, 284,

34 Rabinovich may well have been the target of Kurzweil's critique.

35 Isaiah Rabinovich, *Yezer Vyezirah* (in Hebrew) (Jerusalem: Bialik Institute, 1951).

36 Yosef Gorny, 'There is no Messiah: To Work!' (in Hebrew) *Notebooks for the Study of the Work and Endeavor of Y. H. Brenner*, ed. Israel Levin, vol.2 (Tel Aviv: Tel Aviv University and Workers' Federation, 1977), 20–21. See also Israel Levin, 'A Few Notes By Way of Introduction', in *ibid.*, vol.1, 14–15.

37 Gorny, 'There is no Messiah', 23.

38 *Ibid.*

39 Yitzhak Tabenkin, 'Brenner in the Perception of his Contemporaries' (in Hebrew), *Notebooks for the Study of the Work and Endeavor of Y. H. Brenner*, vol.2 (Tel Aviv: Tel Aviv University and Workers' Federation, 1977), 18–19, denies any connection between Brenner and existentialism. Tabenkin's view, however, can hardly be considered a critical analysis because the characteristics he ascribes to existentialism do not fit the literature.

A slightly uninspired attempt to read Brenner through an existentialist perspective is the book of Gila Ramraz-Rauch, *Y. H. Brenner and Modern Literature* (in Hebrew) (Tel Aviv: Aked, 1970). The weakness of her existentialist analysis of Brenner is twofold: first, the description of existentialist thought is minimal, and second, she neither offers a detailed analysis of existentialist characteristics in Brenner's *oeuvre* nor shows them to be the foundation of his work.

Boaz Arpali, in several works, offers a deep reading of Brenner's existentialist dimension. See *The Negative Principle: Ideology and Poetics in Two Stories by Y. H. Brenner* (in Hebrew) (Tel Aviv: Hakibbutz Hameuchad, 1992); '*Ba-Horef* by Brenner: An Existential-Psychological Point of View' (in Hebrew), *Eleventh World Congress of Jewish Studies*, Division C, Vol.III (Jerusalem: World Union of Jewish Studies, 1994), 151–8; 'Asymmetrical Contrasts – Between the Truth of Death and a Life of Falsehood: Ideological, Existential, and Psychological Crossroads in Y. H. Brenner's *Misaviv la-Nekudah*' (in Hebrew), *Sadan: Studies in Hebrew Literature at the Outset of the Twentieth Century*, 4 (2000): 211–65. See also Ortzion Bartana: *Caution,*

Israeli Literature: Trends in Israeli Fiction (in Hebrew) (Tel Aviv: Tel Aviv University, 1989).

40 Calvin O. Schrag, *Existence and Freedom: Towards an Ontology of Human Freedom* (Evanston, IL: Northwestern University Press, 1983).

41 Frederick A. Olafson, *What is a Human Being? A Heideggerian View* (Cambridge: Cambridge University Press, 1995).

TWO

Brenner the Personal Writer

A suitable starting point in the understanding of Brenner's existentialism is his location in the map of existentialist literature. This literature splits into two main genres, which Jacques Maritain called existential existentialism and academic existentialism.[1] Existential existentialism refers to the thinker's personal contest with his or her real, concrete life, with the various forms of artistic creativity reflecting the ongoing personal voyage to the self. This literature is not an expression of cold concern with metaphysical questions, and what drives it is the self, the anxieties of the self and of concrete existence. Nietzsche successfully distinguished between this kind of philosophy and its antithesis, and wrote: 'It makes the most telling difference whether a thinker has a personal relationship to his problems and finds in them his destiny, his distress, and his greatest happiness, or an "impersonal" one, meaning he is only able to touch and grasp them with the antennae of cold, curious thought.'[2]

Nietzsche, whose thought is a classic example of this kind of personal philosophy, emphasizes:

> We are no thinking frogs, no objectifying and registering devices with frozen innards – we must constantly give birth to our thoughts out of our pain and maternally endow them with all that we have of blood, heart, fire, pleasure, passion, agony, conscience, fate, and disaster. Life – to us, that means constantly transforming all that we are into light and flame, and also all that wounds us; we simply *can do* no other.[3]

A work belonging to this genre is neither an autobiography nor a fictional autobiography,[4] not even an attempt at self-psychoanalysis, since it does not focus on the facts of the writer's life, on what was or could have been. Above all, it is an interpretive effort. It represents the writer's attempt to endow his life with meaning, to knead anew the raw facts of life within an interpretive context that is not derived from these facts but from the author's imagination and creative freedom[5] and, in Nietzsche's terms, to draw 'light and flame' from them. In this voyage, it is not the facts that are the essence but the creative interpretation that confers new meaning upon them. It has a therapeutic aspect, although healing is not attained by analysing the data of life but by reshaping the meaning of existence.

This philosophy, then, is not cast by the past but born from the present, from the perspective that the thinker projects on the past and on her being. The artist never returns to the past that was, but relocates it within the present. The past itself changes from a point along the linear axis of time to an element in the present, where artists contend with the meaning of their lives.

Repetition, a leitmotif of Kierkegaard's thought, means restoring the self and healing its rift, never returning to the past. Kierkegaard, who did sense at certain moments of his life and work a restoration of the harmony with his existence,[6] writes: 'I am myself again… The split that was in my being is healed. I am unified again… Is there not, then, a repetition? Did I not get myself again?'[7] The return to the self is never a return to what was, since it is loaded with a new perspective – the interpretive perspective bearing within it possibilities and meanings flowing from a free imagination.[8] Hence, a work belonging to this genre bears within it the facts, but also the imagination and the free creativity that endow the facts with meaning. Personal writers do not wallow in their past, they locate it within a context of meaning that is itself creative and gives their lives sense and reason.

Existentialist existentialism is an expression of care and self-concern.[9] The artist duplicates himself – he is the object but also the subject of the work, since the literary activity is itself the active expression of this concern. The rhetoric of sincerity typical of this genre conveys the fact that this is a genuine effort, flowing from the depth of the writer's personality, to decode her own being, 'to understand himself in existence'.[10] It is close to concrete life but also far from it, as is interpretation from the brute facts that constitute its platform. It was Camus who stated that a literary creation, as any artistic or philosophical creation, is far from experienced existence, since it creates a world.[11] It is a stance *vis-à-vis* the world, *vis-à-vis* the self, and therefore 'marks…the death of an experience'.[12] Ultimately, existential existentialism is personal in the sense that it seeks subjective truth, that is, the truth that will grow from the writer's being and will answer the writer's questions. In Kierkegaard's term, this truth is the 'truth *for me*'.[13]

But personal thinkers are not concerned only with their personal existence, since they do not focus on the incidental and the ephemeral, that is, on all that touches the individual's closed interest in himself. Their thought, which follows from their concrete distress and yearns for meaning and sense in existence in light of it, transcends their contingency. This transcendence is attained through the very recourse to reflection, which drives and shapes the actual work. In this sense, personal existentialist thought is not part of the confessional genre.

Writers do not create a personal monologue in which they expose their own world to their readers,[14] resembling believers confessing their sins to the priest. Personal existentialist thinkers do not return to their past and do not explicate it; they transcend it into interpretation, where the past and its factual data are only material from which the personal creation will emerge. This creation is personal because it reflects the creator's interest in himself and in the options of his life, but it is not private, since it does not return to the private raw material of the author's life. Thought is driven by reflection which, like judgment and evaluation, transcends the datum and is not dependent on it.

Kierkegaard claimed that this reflection, which turns life into an object, points to the dual meaning of the compound 'single individual': universality and particularity – everyman and the one and only. In his view, 'this dialectic is precisely the dialectic of "the single individual"'.[15] Thought about life necessarily fluctuates between factual units and explication, which naturally resorts to a universal language. The universal aspects of the explication process expose generalized basic constructs. Writing is itself a kind of invitation to self-reflection extended to the reader, the very reflection that the writer performs on his world and his being. Personal writing is supposed to function, in Heidegger's terms, as a kind of conscience that awakens the other to thought and self-criticism. Thus, even what is personal is not private and belongs to all readers, who may and perhaps are indeed meant to hold on to this tortuous personal voyage and draw on it for their own sustenance. Many existentialist writers wrote within the conventions of this genre, including Kierkegaard, Nietzsche, Gabriel Marcel, and Camus.[16]

Other existentialist thinkers, however, offered a different model of writing. For them, existentialism is a new method for solving classic metaphysical questions. The most significant figure in this context is Martin Heidegger who, in *Being and Time*, strives to contend with the question of being. For various reasons he raises in his book, he holds that the proper way to understand being is through an analysis of the human creature.[17] In his wake, Sartre wrote *Being and Nothingness*, where he suggested a phenomenological-ontological analysis of human existence, including the practical implications compelled by this analysis. These writers, and others, are not troubled by personal existential questions or by their own concrete distress, and its solution is not the intended purpose of the philosophical discourse. Their personal anxiety, if it exists, will find an answer within the context of the general systematic analysis. The individual at the centre of their thought is the universal individual and not the personal one, the actual writer. They ask the big metaphysical questions about Being in general or about the human being, and are part of the classical tradition in the history of philosophy. Their partners to the dialogue are the great philosophers.

My central claim here is that Brenner's writing belongs to the former genre of existentialism. He is a personal writer seeking an answer to the personal existential question, even if the contents of his writing do transcend him. Brinker writes:

> Brenner uses biographical materials, changes them slightly, or fuses them with other materials until they are unrecognizable. From the perspective of autobiographical reading, the only decisive question here is: does he strive to create, with the help of the general categories mentioned in his stories, a plausible picture of his overt and concealed life, or does he resort to his life story to convey a specific vision of Jewish and human reality? In my view, there is no room for ambiguity on this matter. In most of his stories... Brenner uses his life and his history just as he uses other materials that reached him through listening, reading, rumor, and imagination. The diversion undergone by the 'original' biographical materials... almost invariably points to the adaptation of these materials to a non-autobiographical intent.[18]

Brinker endorses the dominant theories in literary studies, which for many decades have been emphasising the poetic function of the means that authors use in their work. In his view, therefore, features such as 'autobiographical' and 'fragmentary' are literary means meant to intensify the association between literature and life; the work is supposed to express and reflect life itself. This theoretical approach, which I discuss in Chapter 3 below, leads Brinker to the following assertions:

> Brenner's stories recurrently send us to his life as a potential source for what happens in them. But since they never develop a consistent and reliable model for a representation of the author's life, this hint at the writer's biography remains undefined... [This hint] is not meant to enable the reader to compose a reliable picture of Brenner's life from his stories. Its only intent is to plant in him the understanding that the sources of Brenner's story are in life and not in literature.[19]

The basic outline that Brinker suggests for reading Brenner's work ostensibly subverts the possibility of locating it within the tradition of personal existentialism, since Brinker holds that the seemingly personal dimension is merely a literary technique. This approach contrasts with the personal existentialism anchored in the life of the concrete person – Brenner, whose writing is a personal, particular voyage.

On closer scrutiny, however, not only do Brinker's assertions not contradict the suggested classification of Brenner's work, but they are definitely compatible with it. Personal existentialism, as noted, is not autobiographical and never aspires to offer a picture of the artist's life. Rather, it conveys an effort to cope with the fundamental questions of concrete life. Life's questions and anxieties are the things that connect this genre to life, not the description of real life in the writing. Indeed, real life is merely one of the options of existence. Through the power of freedom and imagination, the writer, and indeed any person, can transcend the facticity, the givenness or 'thrownness' within which individuals find themselves. The imposed facticity loses its coercing power through the very process of creativity and is no more than one option, not necessarily the most worthy one.[20] This is the first step in the distancing of personal existentialist thought from the autobiographical.

The second and complementary step is shaping the meaning of life, which also transcends the coerced givenness and expresses a kind of free decision. This decision is an expression of reflection and of consideration, unbridled and unlimited by personal life. The aim of subjective truth – 'the truth for me' – is what returns the distant writing to life. Before us, then, is a voyage[21] that begins with the personal and private, transcends into the general, and returns to the personal and private. The start of the voyage is a reflection that grows from life and transcends it, and its end is a return to the domain of practical life. This dialectical movement of reflection and life makes existence dialectical and restless.[22]

Brenner explicitly traces the contours of this type of existence, though not always in relation to himself but in his evaluation of the other. Beyond this evaluation, however, his inner voice resonates. In an essay he wrote on Moshe Leib Lilienblum, Brenner notes:

> In Lilienblum, we saw no contradiction between world view and action. His world view was, literally, his beacon. His truth was never something outside him... the truth of the surroundings or even only a rational truth, but a rational-temperamental one. His world view derived mainly from his essence, his quality, his character. He was not Lilienblum because he held such and such views, but rather – since he was Lilienblum, he held such and such views.[23]

Brenner draws a clear contrast between various kinds of truth. In the equation he offers, he places two kinds of truth on the one side: truth as a social convention and rational truth. Despite the clear differences between them, these two kinds of truth share a common denominator – both are external to the person, they do not follow from the person's self, and they do not reflect it. As a balance to these two types of truth, Brenner places a third one – 'rational-temperamental truth'. This truth is complex: like any reflection, it has a rational aspect, but this rationality is turned inwards rather than outwards, to the world or to the human surroundings. The characteristics of this truth are those of subjective truth as described by Kierkegaard or Nietzsche, that is, it is enclosed within and stamped by the seal of concrete life. As Heidegger described it, its meaning is exposure and revelation, above all, of the self.[24]

This truth, which grows from the self, does not crystalize narcissistically nor does it appear in a mysterious *Augenblick* (decisive moment). It is accompanied by a complex process of reflection, which Brenner calls self-evaluation. Like other existentialist thinkers, Brenner points to the stages of the process that unfolds parallel to maturation. The beginning of human existence becomes manifest in experiences of fullness, originating in the person's inability 'to think about himself satisfactorily, to evaluate himself properly... he is so full of his own "self" that this, as it were, does not fall at all under the category of evaluation'.[25] This stage of life, which thinkers such as Hegel and Kierkegaard viewed as the original stage of existence, dissipates 'when it [the self] leaves the limited circle of the sensorium, as it draws further and further away from primitiveness'. This stage occurs when the self coalesces and reaches a higher stage of existence: 'When he starts to see the other, and as the relationships between him and the other become increasingly complex, as metaphysical doubts and mental ponderings awaken in all their strength – that is when the need for evaluation in general and personal evaluation in particular begins.'[26]

Self-consciousness, or 'self-evaluation' in Brenner's formulation, crystalizes *vis-à-vis* the other and *vis-à-vis* the self. A plausible assumption is that Brenner was aware of Hegel's statement whereby 'self-consciousness exists in and for itself when, and by the fact that, it so exists for another; that is, it exists only in being acknowledged'.[27] The encounter with the other poses all the questions related to being with the other, questions involving obvious implications for the self's own consciousness. Self-consciousness does not evolve *ex nihilo* but from the contact with the other. The other can function in various ways: he can be the mirror where the self sees only itself – since the self cannot perceive itself, the other functions as a kind of object through which the observing subject is exposed. The other can also be an object shaped by the subject, who views him as no more than raw material kneaded according to the self's construct. Be it as it may, the other is a kind of alter-ego to the self, who observes him or acts upon him.

Brenner rejects these options, since for him the other is distant from the self and is present as an other with whom the self must shape a relationship. Brenner's stance of rejection is not only theoretical, and he points to two models of artists – narcissistic artists who see only themselves, and Mendele as the antithesis:

> Mendele writes only about us, that is, he is not one of those artists who draw everything from their personal, inner experience, who in all the others around them are capable of seeing only themselves and what is inside them, and whose judgment of others, about everything, invariably depends on their mood and their relationship to themselves.[28]

Self-evaluation or self-consciousness, then, is not meant to become manifest in epistemic solipsism. Since a conscious existence unfolds *vis-à-vis* the other, the possibility that the self-evaluation that will guide the person will be detached from any association with the other appears implausible.

Increasing awareness of the complexity involved in the relationship with the other will evoke or, more precisely, is supposed to evoke, metaphysical and existential reflections. Brenner, like Hegel, ties self-evaluation or self-consciousness to the other's consciousness of the self, in the negative, since he then writes: 'When an old man or a long living nation lack any need for genuine self-evaluation, it augurs badly for their essential value when they come to be evaluated'.[29] The attitude of the other to the self discloses the self's self-value: did his consciousness come together and did his existence become valuable, or did his consciousness shrivel and, with it, his existence.

Brenner's assertions are not part of some abstract theory of existence, but carved from the surrounding Jewish reality. In his view, Hebrew rabbinic literature 'hardly knew any self-evaluation since everything was clear and known to it and essentially received. In its view, everything is compatible, and within it – all are words of the dead God'.[30] The basic questions, then – 'what we are and what our lives are, what is our nature and what is our character, what is our appearance and what are the visions of our lives, what is our value in our eyes and what impression do we make on others' – never came up in this literature.[31]

The absence of self-consciousness at both the personal and the general-Jewish levels originates in the same source – turning the gaze outwards to God or to the external, non-personal reality. Brenner targets not only Orthodoxy in this critique but also *Haskalah* literature that, beyond exceptions such as Smolenskin, Gordon, and Lilienblum, focuses its concern, in Heideggerian terms, on the ordinary person (*Das Man*),[32] that is: 'The "rational" person, who understands worldly success, who understands how to adapt to conditions for his profit, who speaks clearly in several languages... and knows how to mingle.'[33] This person has replaced the living, actual person, seeking life and self-realization.[34] Brenner, argues Penueli aptly, was not opposed to the *Haskalah* movement,

> so long as it did not become an 'ideology,' was not corrupted through obsequiousness, and was not defiled by the abominable desire to please... so long as it did not beg for emancipation as a handout. Because to ask for emancipation is despicable. Man does not receive freedom as a handout but earns it with his blood, his toil, and his creativity... Freedom is not acquired for free and is given only to one who created it with his blood.[35]

The refusal to deceive, the demand of self-transparence and autonomous standing are the pillars of the Brennerian stance. The demand of self-evaluation is not only a theoretical position, to become manifest merely in a transparent self-consciousness. Quite the contrary – this consciousness is supposed to guide the meaning to be ascribed to life and the action compelled by it. Kierkegaard writes in his journal: 'What I really need is to get clear about *what I must do*, not what I must know, except insofar as knowledge must precede every act. What matters is to find a purpose...; the crucial thing is to find a truth which is truth *for me,* to find *the idea for which I am willing to live and die.*'[36] Similarly, Brenner never tired of claiming that consciousness or self-evaluation has a role in life: it is ultimately meant to guide life, to reshape it so that consciousness can reconnect to existence itself. In his story *Mi-Saviv la-Nekudah* [Around the Point], Abramson engages in self-evaluation and says:

> I, Yaakov Abramson, a simple man, really simple, I'm indeed not afraid of metaphysics... I'm not a philosopher... and indeed, I ask and ask about the value of my life. Very good: not everyone asks, everyone is sure, everyone knows, or they do not need to know. But I ask and I cannot but ask: I face life and I ask. I do not seek pleasure, I do not seek satisfaction, I do not seek happiness, I do not seek non-suffering, but I do seek value, content...[37]

Brenner, then, traces a complex picture of the relationship between self-consciousness and existence. Self-consciousness, even if it is self-concern, cannot by nature close itself up within the privacy of self-existence. Self-consciousness is also simultaneously self-transcendence. Nevertheless, the truth exposed through the complex process of consciousness formation is a personal truth that touches on concrete existence.

Brenner understood that the very characterization of this truth as truth turns it outward as well – to the other. He preceded Heidegger in the deep insight that subjective truth, which touches on the life of the individual, may act as a guiding, path-breaking element for the other. He therefore writes: 'There is no Lilienblumism – there is Lilienblum – a man who sought paths in his life, sought truth, with his entire essence – and therefore, unwittingly, paved ways for others.'[38]

Elsewhere, Brenner relates to 'Maupassant and his followers' and says: 'They grab your heart and compel you by their force; by force of their simplicity; by force of the life in them; by force of their truth, to live what they themselves lived.'[39] Brenner, like Kierkegaard or Heidegger, emphasised that 'a certain vision of human reality', in Brinker's formulation, is not necessarily antithetical to self-concern. This concern, embodied in a life of ceaseless self-search, may also radiate to the other, opening him up to himself and to the truth that his life can engender. Other and self are thus integrated, both in the process of self-consciousness and in the finding of the truth that constitutes the value of their lives.

The fact that Brenner raises the basic questions of existence in his work while shifting from the personal to the general provides an important key for the understanding of his readers' attitude towards his work:

> This element [the 'eternal' element in Brenner's influence], which is the true and main topic in all of Brenner's works, is the individual who seeks his path to himself, asks ceaselessly about the reason for life, stands always on the edge of the abyss, but nevertheless remains attached to life. Thus, in the story of his life, he also raises different lives, different spiritual and mental problems as interesting today as they were when he wrote about them, which can concern people who are very different from Brenner, who live outside that defined reality where he and his characters lived, and who are not familiar with the topical issues that concerned them.[40]

Apparently, this element in Brenner's writing is also what impressed his readers. A full analysis of this approach requires us to focus on Brenner's perception of literature and its meaning in life.

Notes

1   See Jacques Maritain, 'From Existential Existentialism to Academic Existentialism', *Sewanee Review*, 26 (1948): 210–29.

2   Friedrich Nietzsche, *The Gay Science*, ed. Bernard Williams, trans. Josefine Nauckhoff (Cambridge: Cambridge University Press, 2001), §345, p.202.

3   *Ibid.*, §3, p.6 (emphasis in original).

4   For an analysis of this genre, see Menachem Brinker, *Normative Art and Social Thought in Y. H. Brenner's Work* (in Hebrew) (Tel Aviv: Am Oved, 1990), ch.1.

5   On this issue, see Avi Sagi, *Kierkegaard, Religion, and Existence: The Voyage of the Self*, trans. Batya Stein (Amsterdam-Atlanta, GA: Rodopi, 2000), chs. 1 and 4.

6   *Ibid.*, particularly chs. 6 and 9. As I show there, Kierkegaard offers more than one approach to the problem of the split self.

7   Søren Kierkegaard, *Fear and Trembling: Repetition*, ed. and trans. Howard V. Hong and Edna H. Hong (Princeton: Princeton University Press, 1983), 220. For an analysis of the concept of repetition in Kierkegaard's thought, see Sagi, *Kierkegaard*, especially 19–24.

8   See also Charles E. Winquist, *Homecoming: Interpretation, Transformation, and Individuation* (Missoula, MT: Scholars Press, 1978), 9.

9   Heidegger developed this claim at length because care (*Sorge*), self-concern, is constitutive of human existence. See Martin Heidegger, *Being and Time*, trans. John Macquarrie and Edward Robinson (New York: Harper and Row, 1962), 225–74.

10   See Søren Kierkegaard, *Concluding Unscientific Postscript to Philosophical Fragments*, trans. Howard V. Hong and Edna Hong, vol.1 (Princeton: Princeton University Press, 1992), 351.

11   See Albert Camus, *The Myth of Sisyphus*, trans. Justin O'Brien (Harmondsworth, Middlessex: Penguin Books, 1975), 91–2.

12   *Ibid.*, 87.

13   See Sagi, *Kierkegaard*, 7. On the concept of subjective truth in Kierkegaard's thought, see *ibid.*, 23–4, 137ff.

14   See Northrop Frye, *Anatomy of Criticism* (Princeton: Princeton University Press, 1957), 365. On confessional literature, see Hannah Naveh, *The Confessional Narrative: A Description of a Genre and Its Practice in Modern Hebrew Literature* (in Hebrew) (Tel Aviv: Papyrus, 1998).

15   Søren Kierkegaard, *The Point of View for My Work as an Author*, trans. Walter Lowrie (New York: Harper and Row, 1962), 124.

16   On his philosophy, see Avi Sagi, *Albert Camus and the Philosophy of the Absurd*, trans. Batya Stein (Amsterdam: Rodopi, 2002), particularly ch.2.

17   Heidegger, *Being and Time*, 21–35. Heidegger explicitly rejected Sartre's attempt to view his thought as an existentialist philosophy interested in the question of human existence. See, for instance, 'Letter on Humanism', in Martin Heidegger, *Basic Writings* (London: Routledge and Kegan Paul, 1978), 193–242.

18   Brinker, *Normative Art*, 42–3. Compare Boaz Arpali, *The Negative Principle: Ideology and Poetics in Two Stories by Y. H. Brenner* (in Hebrew) (Tel Aviv: Hakibbutz Hameuchad, 1992), 166–7.

19   Brinker, *Normative Art*, 64.

20   See also Sagi, *Kierkegaard*, 60–63.

21   For my discussion of the voyage motif, see Sagi, *Kierkegaard*, and Sagi, *Albert Camus*.

22   See Sagi, *Kierkegaard*, 53–4.

23   *Writings*, vol.4, 1217.

24   See Heidegger, *Being and Time*, 256–73.

25   *Writings*, vol.4, 1225.

26   *Ibid.*

27   G. W. F. Hegel, *Phenomenology of Spirit*, trans. A. V. Miller (Oxford: Clarendon Press, 1979), 111.

28   *Writings*, vol.4, 1229.

29   *Ibid.*, 1225.

30   *Ibid.*

31   *Ibid.*, 1226.

32   For Heidegger's analysis of this type of existence, see Heidegger, *Being and Time*, 149–68.

33   *Writings*, vol.4, 1227.

34   On the disappointment with Haskalah literature in Brenner's times see Iris Parush, 'The Conception of Literary Canon in Brenner's Criticism', in *Yitzhak Bakon Volume: Belles-Lettres and Literary Studies*, ed. Aharon Komem (Beer Sheva: Ben-Gurion University, 2002).

35   S. Y Penueli, *Brenner and Gnessin in Early Twentieth Century Hebrew Fiction* (in Hebrew) (Tel Aviv: Students' Association at Tel Aviv University, 1965), 36–7.

36   *Søren Kierkegaard's Journals and Papers*, ed. and trans. Howard V. Hong and Edna H. Hong, 2 vols. (Bloomington, IN: Indiana University Press, 1967), §5100. I analyse this passage at length in Sagi, *Kierkegaard*, ch.1.

37   *Writings*, vol.1, 519–20.

38   *Ibid.*, vol.4, 1218.

39   *Ibid.*, vol.3, 255.

40   Matti Megged, 'Y. H. Brenner: Two Episodes' (in Hebrew), in *Anaf: An Anthology of Young Literature*, ed. Dan Miron (Jerusalem: Schocken, 1964).

THREE

Brenner and the Existentialist Meaning of Literature

How to write a literature that deals with life? How does existentialist literature differ from other literary genres? Can we say that existentialist literature has specific characteristics? These questions exceed the scope of the present book, but one claim bears emphasis: some literary works do belong to an existentialist corpus. The claim that literary works by Sartre, Camus, or Unamuno are part of this corpus is not new, and their literary *oeuvre* is adapted to and complements their philosophical writing. But Dostoevsky, Kafka, or Max Frisch – who was deeply influenced by Kierkegaard – are also considered part of the existentialist corpus.[1] Indeed, John Macquarrie claimed that Kafka 'must be reckoned the greatest existentialist writer of all'.[2]

This affinity between existentialist philosophy and literature is not accidental: a philosophy seeking to capture concrete existence will find abstract philosophical formulations wanting, and will necessarily seek a path to life. Better than philosophy, literature can capture the *Augenblick* that enables us to grasp life. Better than philosophy, literature can offer a complex phenomenology of life, which encompasses its contingencies and its latent possibilities and describes situations, actions, and events in ways close to life itself. Its time is the time of life itself.[3] All unlike philosophy. For philosophy, said Franz Rosenzweig, 'thinking is timeless and wants to be timeless',[4] since its essence is the general abstract claim. 'The new thinking', in Rosenzweig's terms, referring to a philosophy concerned with life, must forge a path to life, to its temporality and its historical essence, to its contingency and fragility, to human discourse and human solitude. Literature, not philosophy, offers a path to life, and the significance of the phenomenological description of life in existentialist philosophy is not merely a fortuitous coincidence. This charged depiction is meant to open up a path to life, regardless of whether it is systematic, as in Heidegger's or Sartre's philosophy, or presented through situations and feelings, as in the work of Nietzsche and Kierkegaard. The latter hold that their fragmentary, non-systematic writing is precisely what enables life to surface in language. Language does not exhaust life, but life bursts into it.

This association between literature and existentialist philosophy has led some scholars to argue that existentialist philosophy must express itself only through literature, because any other form turns existentialism into a system resembling those it struggles against.[5] This stance, however, is patently implausible and represents a romanticization of existentialist discourse. Well-known existentialist philosophers – Kierkegaard, Heidegger, Jaspers, Sartre, and others – have successfully formulated their philosophical thought relying on traditional philosophical tools without in any way renouncing its uniqueness. The use of the term 'system' as the absolute antithesis of existentialism, and hence to be rejected at all costs, is but a myth promoted by existentialist thinkers such as Kierkegaard, and then unquestioningly accepted by certain scholars. These scholars, who held that existentialist philosophy is not rational in any sense of this term, enhanced this myth.[6]

This myth, however, should not mislead us: existentialism is a chapter in the history of philosophy and should therefore be written as philosophy is written. Due to the emphasis on the concrete and contingent character of the real person's existence, however, many philosophers and writers have resorted to two powerful tools in order to connect the abstract to the concrete. The first is phenomenological writing, meaning a detailed description of concrete reality and an interpretation of its meaning, its constitutive 'idea'. Kierkegaard, Heidegger, Sartre, and other existentialist writers have extensively resorted to this method. Kierkegaard's writing reflects reality, shifting in complex ways between the concrete and the abstract, the personal and the universal, the datum as it appears to the observer and its meaning. Whereas Kierkegaard's writing leans in a literary-poetic direction, Heidegger's writing reflects a more rigorous use of the phenomenological method and has influenced such writers as Sartre, Merleau-Ponty, and others.

The second tool is literature, which plays a crucial role in mediating between the concrete-particular dimensions of human existence and its depth insight. Many existentialist thinkers view literature as a suitable organon for expressing the existentialist dimensions of human reality, without suggesting it could or should replace philosophical discourse. Writers such as Sartre, Simone de Beauvoir, Camus, Pirandello, and others wrote literary works that were recognized as phenomenological narrative, with the writer described as a metaphysician.[7]

Literature is especially important from the perspective of personal existentialism, since it assumes a particularly extensive and flexible scope for expression. Personal existentialism, stemming from the artist's concrete world, requires a literary tool for conveying the personal. Philosophy, however, transcends the personal by definition, and its language is universal rather than particular. Hence, it was only natural that an author like Kierkegaard, who set personal existentialism on its course, writes philosophy like a novelist.

By contrast, Milan Kundera warns us against any attempt to bring philosophy, meaning philosophy in general, closer to the novel: 'The novel's wisdom differs from that of philosophy…. The art… does not by nature serve ideological certitudes… it undoes each night the tapestry that the theologians, philosophers, and learned men have woven the day before.'[8] Philosophy and theology do well with transparence and the light of day. Art in general and the novel in particular, says Kundera, need the cover of night, which leaves room for ambiguity. Novelists or poets are not supposed to develop systematic metaphysical positions. The power of literature lies in its ability to capture what existentialists have called the '*Augenblick*', the fundamental experience that exposes existence in all its fullness. This exposure, however, is only fleeting, and its price is the barrier that hinders the transition from experience to its methodical, reflective, and conscious structuring.

This condensed experience may indeed merge into a philosophical reflective insight. The '*Augenblick*' surging in a poem or a story in succinct and rhythmical lines that distil the vital essence of a sober consciousness could become an object of philosophical reflective study. What the artistic experience captured in the *Augenblick* now becomes the object of thematic philosophical criticism. What is implicit, polysemic, and dark in the experience is opened up, sharpened, and illuminated in the philosophical analysis. A complex relationship thus prevails between literature and existentialist philosophy. Literature provides this philosophy with a powerful means of expression, whereas existentialist philosophy provides this literature, its writer and readers, depth insights evident in the writing and then reinterpreted in the reading.

Brenner's *oeuvre* responds to this complex tension between literature and existentialist insights. As the chapters that follow will show, Brenner rejects large conceptual theses as a basis for understanding existence. He assumes that comprehensive philosophical theories fail to penetrate life and its complexity. Philosophical ideas are ideas detached from life. Following Russian tradition, Brenner sees a special role for literature because of its power to make inroads into existence that are unthinkable to abstract philosophical thought. As Menachem Brinker notes, Brenner's enormous admiration for Mendele rests precisely on this aspect: 'Brenner credited this brilliant prose writer with an intuitive penetration of reality that could never be attributed to abstract thinkers.'[9]

Literature for Brenner, or at least modern literature, is concerned with individual life, with the individual's predicament and inner mood: 'All our literature is now individual…one cannot live otherwise….Only individuals are left, European-Hebrews who have a special psyche, each one with his soul, his despair, and his dreams.'[10]

Literature is a kind of self-'reflection' of the 'shattered soul',[11] concerned with the artist's ongoing attempt to pierce the darkness and distress of life.[12] The purpose of writing is to attain self-clarity and redemption, in the words of a Brenner character: 'Who knows, perhaps through my writing I will be redeemed.'[13]

In the existentialist world view, literature does not create an autonomous field of artistic form. Its concern is real life – it draws on life, is guided by it, and meant to influence it. And when life loses meaning, or when the work does not change attitudes to life, writing becomes problematic. In a letter to Micha Josef Berdyczewski, Brenner writes: '"To abandon writing altogether" – that's the thing to do. Clearly, I have nothing more to say or to cry about, and indeed – why? Why? We dwell within a rotten egg. Let us sit alone and be still.'[14]

Berdyczewski, who understands Brenner, formulates their shared view for him in his response: 'To abandon writing – for whom and why? You must understand that I am very well aware of the nature of things, and this is the curse that hangs over us. But one thing – we do not write for others but for ourselves. Better to spit it out than to swallow it.'[15]

Writing is an existential need; it wells up from the depths of personal existence, pushing out from the depths of the individual's life onto the space of the world. Thus, the imperative of living joins up with the imperative of creativity. In this view, the core of the work is clearly the content rather than the artistic form:

> Indeed, we cannot imagine a proper form without a proper content, since what is the purpose of a proper form but to deliver in the best way the content seeking outlet and expression? Without it, without an important content, beautiful expressions and elegant turns of phrase are unnecessary, only a heap of nutshells – and what is the beauty in a heap of nutshells?[16]

Quite astonishingly, and although his social and cultural background is so very different from Heidegger's, Brenner independently develops a position that Heidegger would formulate years later in theoretical and thematic terms. According to Heidegger, the beautiful is a feature of the ontological truth that is exposed in the artistic act: 'When truth sets itself into the work, it appears. Appearance – as this being of truth in the work and as work – is beauty. Thus the beautiful belongs to the advent of truth.'[17]

Just as for Heidegger the form – the beautiful – is revealed as such with the exposure and discovery of the truth, so, for Brenner, artistic form emerges as such only if it bears a content. It does not appear by itself and, in his formulation: 'Form and content... are not two separate worlds.'[18] According to Brenner, the content of the artistic work is life in all its manifestations and depth, as shown below. Brenner, then, locates literature at the core of life, as a reflective tool of the consciousness exposing life.

This theoretical position is concretized in Brenner's literary *oeuvre*, which is a steady effort to capture life and contain it within a literary form without allowing it to lose its vitality. Brenner's work is an attempt to overcome the dichotomy between life and writing. Kurzweil who, as noted, vigorously rejected the possibility of locating Brenner within the existentialist tradition, appropriately described the Brennerian mode of writing: 'Brenner's greatness as a narrator lies in the optimal congruence between his perception of reality and the modes of composition, the structure of the chapter, the paragraph, the phrase – up to the punctuation. All serve one sole supreme aim: to give voice to an unredeemed, almost dead-end reality.'[19]

This approach, pointing to the connection between literature and life, is one Brenner himself clearly emphasises when writing to his friend Uri Nisan Gnessin:

> As for the theory in that letter of yours about 'literature for literature's sake,' the purpose of man, and so forth, I do not agree with it at all. My view of life is entirely different; in brief – we must sacrifice our souls and lessen evil in the world...We must understand everything, understand and move away from mysticism and fantasies; we must intensify the reality and the holiness of the world....You are writing a historical poem – and I don't understand that at all. Can we indeed put aside the present even for a moment? Do you know the plight of our youth?...Do you know that our people are going to die? Do you know that the world is sick? Do you know that despair is devouring souls? Do you have eyes?![20]

Brenner rejects a purely aesthetic perception of literature as unacceptable. Literature must be related to life and the harsh, pressing reality leaves no room for writing 'historical poems'.

According to the classic taxonomy of M. H. Abrams,[21] the category most suited to describe Brenner's *oeuvre* is pragmatic theory, which claims that literature has an external purpose, beyond the work itself.[22] According to this theory, a literary work is a tool for influencing the readership. In the Brennerian context, literature should focus on concrete problems of existence. Iris Parush articulates this idea as follows: 'A literature that avoids relating to concrete reality and refrains from accounting for it is bad literature. It is bad not only *per se*, but also because of its negative influence on the readers.'[23]

Brenner denies that aesthetic value is the supreme value for examining art, since 'what did the aesthete know about life?'[24] Literature does not ensure a connection with life, since literature can create an autonomous world of books entirely divorced from existence. In a critical view of Tolstoy, Brenner writes:

> He wrote books about life and about 'the books'… and his books also became 'the books' and one of life's assets… and on these books they write more books… and Fishman and Kleinstein review them… Brandes reviewed Tolstoy as well… Max Nordau also wrote about him… and life goes on, goes on, goes on – forever, endlessly…shocking![25]

In rejecting the independent value of an aesthetic existence unconditioned by concrete life, Brenner joins writers such as Kierkegaard, who rejects aesthetics because it presents imagination as an alternative to actual reality.[26]

Brenner's literary writings, however, go beyond the pragmatic stance and include a prominent personal dimension that will not be ignored here. Indeed, Dov Sadan holds that Brenner's writing belongs to the confessional genre,[27] which is associated with concrete existence but is also an attempt to expose the personal, inner, hidden life. In Sadan's view, Brenner belongs to a category of writers

> characterized by an exaggerated measure of narcissism, whose works are tied and bound to the external unfolding of their experience, who are vastly interested in themselves, and who place their own selves at the center of issues and events so that all will pay attention to them, admire them, be happy with their joys and involved in their sorrow… In these types, the artistic personality is definitely less restrained than that of their fellows, who take many liberties when 'ordering' and shaping the materials of their own experience.[28]

Kurzweil also argues that Brenner's writing points to the 'increasing importance of the inner monologue, originating in a new psychological and anthropological perspective resting on a re-evaluation of the relationship between life and the spirit'.[29]

This reading of Brenner's *oeuvre* rests on impressive evidence. In his assessment of Mendele, as noted, Brenner describes him as an artist whose sources of inspiration are neither derived from nor bound by his internal experiences. He says:

> Although Mendele tells about others, to others, and for others, when the artist in him reached the supreme echelon, he could not but feel that the purpose of artistic creativity is mainly to soothe the author. The artistic word is uttered not only to shock but rather, and mainly, so as to be uttered, to come out, to surge, as if it were a contained fire that must break out.[30]

Brenner, then, views literature, the linguistic utterance, as an expression that erupts from the inside against the person's will. In Heidegger's terms, writing is an organon for disclosing the truth hidden inside.[31] Brenner often uses terms that approach literary works as a 'pouring out of one's soul'[32] or 'description and confession'.[33] In his view, linguistic expression is instrumental in the emergence and clarification of self-consciousness.[34] The expressive function is not unique to literature, and may also come to the fore in philosophy. In open admiration, Brenner quotes Breinin and states that his claims, 'even if not really new, deserve the attention of the Hebrew reader because none like them have so far appeared in our literature':

> Philosophers everywhere became humanity's teachers and educators, influencing many generations, but only when their philosophy was their inner confession. The books of Schopenhauer and Nietzsche are confessions, the history of their spirits. The inner life of the great writer or of the artist, the contradictions of his soul and the pangs of his creation, are outstandingly formulated in Breinin's concise words.[35]

If Brenner's work is an inner monologue or a confession, it has a therapeutic purpose. Zach describes it as follows:

> Brenner is a very conscious writer, exceptionally self-conscious. The ceaseless criticism of weakness and the constant concern with the flaw – his and others' – stems from a powerful passion to analyze himself, to identify himself, to locate his own self in every situation, and certainly also to alleviate his pain in this 'psychoanalytic' fashion.[36]

Zach's view is widely accepted in the scholarly literature.[37] Yosef Lichtenbaum went a step further and pointed to the correspondence between Brenner's life and his works: 'In a description of Brenner's life, his works in chronological order, their unfolding, and their reality contents serve as concrete material. Observing their continuity, we come to learn about the writer's personal development... From one text to another, Brenner's psychological make-up becomes livelier, stronger, and more aware.'[38] And yet, reading Brenner's entire literary *oeuvre* as a kind of confession and inner monologue that reveals his personal life and thereby mitigates his suffering is problematic on various counts. First, it is an autobiographical-psychological reduction of art. Even if we assume that a literary work contains autobiographical-confessional elements, perceiving it as a transcript of inner experiences is problematic because it disregards the artistic element that impels it beyond the personal.[39]

Isaiah Rabinovich expressed reservations about the application of this method to Brenner, when he related to Menachem Poznansky's comments about the autobiographical element in the story *Mi-Saviv la-Nekudah* [Around the Point]:

> Poznansky identifies all the characters in the story: he calls them by their real names and places them within Brenner's biography... Poznansky's testimony... does add to the study of Brenner's personality and his literary work. At the same time, however, it effaces the artistic objective foundation, the aesthetic narrative dynamic that is not entirely dependent on the 'known' individual and social conditions of the life that Brenner lived with a particular intensity of his own. Textual study, which addresses the functional processes of the narrative genre, must go beyond the biographical material to assess the narrator's artistic domains and the personal-individual longings latent in them.[40]

Reduction as a hermeneutical method is possible, but its drawbacks override its advantages: it negates the autonomy of the creative texture and turns the work into a kind of guide or medium that leads to what is beyond it – the writer's inner life.

Friedrich Schleiermacher did present a hermeneutical approach meant to lead the reader to the writer.[41] According to Schleiermacher, interpreters engage in a transposition that leads them from their world to that of the writer. The interpreter, so Schleiermacher maintains, reproduces the work. Schleiermacher, however, did not formulate a reductive thesis, and did not pretend to pin a writer's entire *oeuvre* on a specific psychological make-up presented as final and sealed. He described understanding as an ongoing process mediated by two elements: one linguistic and one psychological, whose role is mutual criticism:

In order to complete the grammatical side of the interpretation it would be necessary to have a complete knowledge of the language. In order to complete the psychological side it would be necessary to have a complete knowledge of the person. Since in both cases such complete knowledge is impossible, it is necessary to move back and forth between the grammatical and psychological sides, and no rules can stipulate exactly how to do this.[42]

Understanding, therefore, is an ongoing process that is always temporary rather than leading the interpreter, in a kind of 'leap', to the writer's personal psychology: 'A text can never be understood right away. On the contrary, every reading puts us in a better position to understand.... Only in the case of insignificant texts (i.e. those of the market place) are we satisfied with what we understand on first reading.'[43] Focusing the hermeneutical process on the writer does not mean focusing on the writer's private life but on the writer as the creator of the work. Interpreters do not use the text as a medium for accessing the author's private psychology, but focus instead on psychological dimensions that shed light on the work.[44] In Hans Georg Gadamer's incisive formulation, the aim of hermeneutics according to Schleiermacher is not to understand the author's thoughts as part of understanding another person's life, but as part of understanding the truth. Hermeneutics is a tool for exposing the truth concretized in the author's work.[45]

This schematic depiction explicates the obstacles lurking on the path of any attempt to reduce a work to its author's biography. The reduction pretending to create a fit between the literary and the autobiographical fields ignores the complexity of the hermeneutical process, its temporariness, and above all, the dual nature of the leap from the linguistic to the psychological field. The first step is a leap from an objective datum – the linguistic field – to a subjective one – the author. The second step is a leap from the author as author to his concealed subjectivity as a particular person, living at a given time in specific circumstances, whose biographic and psychological existence does not come together easily within a linguistic field that, by nature, has universal characteristics. Schleiermacher's warning about the impermanence of understanding, then, precludes any unequivocal assumptions about a direct connection between the literary and autobiographical fields.

The autobiographical-psychological reduction imposes on the interpreter too the implausible burden of finding correspondences between the written text and what truly took place in the confessant's inner experience, leading to distortions and mistakes. Brinker, who opposes the application of the autobiographical confessionary method to Brenner's work, sums up this critique:

> Brenner's stories repeatedly send us to the author's life as a potential source of what happens in them. But since they never develop a consistent and reliable model for representing the author's life, this hint at the author's life remains undefined, up in the air. It can distort and mislead the reader in various directions, whenever he understands it as more than a vague and unspecified hint.[46]

A problem no less serious concerns the meaning of confession in a literary work. As a literary creation, a confession is, at most, part of the work's poetic form. Contrary to what Brenner writes, even if the writer does confess, the confession does not surge directly from the author's inner recesses without mediation, organization, or re-creation within a literary context. In other words, the creative subject is not a passive entity functioning as a medium of the inner self, but an active subject whose action comes forth in the artistic scheme.[47]

Asher Beylin, Brenner's friend, describes Brenner's conscious investment in his writing: 'Before setting out to write anything, he would cull and collect strong, isolated words from books, which he would then include in his work.'[48] Beylin then adds: 'Brenner would write everything twice before publication. Before writing, he would look at many scraps of paper where he had written out many unrelated words, single sentences, fragments, conversations, and descriptions. The content and the form were almost entirely clear to him before he began to write.'[49] Brenner's writing, then, is intent and deliberate, and unfolds within the context of an evident poetic outline. The Brennerian text is not the confession of Brenner the man but of the literary figures he created. Brenner is aware of biographical aspects in his work, but points out that his writing is not biographical:

> I wanted to do what you[50] said, but I simply cannot sit down and write 'autobiographies'! I have, after all, outlined my life in my stories: 'In the Winter,' 'Around the Point,' 'From A to M,' 'Beyond the Border,' 'One Year,' 'Out of My Distress,' 'Travel Impressions,' 'Nothing,' 'Evening and Morning,' and many many more, although not with biographical precision but actually – necessarily and intentionally – with external changes[51] in the details. Whatever in my life that is not worth sharing with my friends and acquaintances, for whom I write, or whatever is a

secret that I would not share with strangers – I could not use in a biography.[52]

We can hardly ignore this testimony by the writer, and one exceptionally self-conscious at that, and impose on the work a hermeneutical perception that views it as a confession. Even if Brenner's work has autobiographical aspects, and it does indeed have many, these are only raw materials, changed and adapted through creative imagination and artistic form. This process of elaboration reshapes the raw autobiographical facts, embedding them within a creative web and re-interpreting them. The past is determined by the present, by the new context wherein it assumes its meaning. The past that was is not the past that is created. This is a new past, one to which we return from the present and from the future. The attempt to capture the past as it was seeks to prevail over the interpretation that is part of any creative process. We might retrieve remnants, traces, or stubs of the past by reshaping it, but these remains cannot be the foundation of the literary *oeuvre*.[53] Vladimir Nabokov offers an informative account of the complex relationship between the autobiographical shift and the literary construction:

> I have often noticed that after I had bestowed on the characters of my novels some treasured item of my past, it would pine away in the artificial world where I had so abruptly placed it. Although it lingered on in my mind, its personal warmth, its retrospective appeal had gone, and, presently, it became more closely identified with my novel than with my former self, where it had seemed to be so safe from the intrusion of the artist.[54]

Ultimately, two problems hinder a view of Brenner's work as a personal confession. First, the texts do not fit the actual facts of Brenner's life. Second, the confession is part of the artistic design, a creation of Brenner the conscious writer. As various scholars have indicated, Brenner's pseudo-confessional writing is typical of a literary genre that was widespread in the 19th century.[55] Its meaning, however, is not autobiographical-confessional. Brenner, as noted, has one of his characters ponder: 'Who knows, perhaps through my writing I will be redeemed.'[56] Writing is thus part of a therapeutic process. But what is this process? The view that writing is self-redemption is not alien to the existentialist tradition. Kierkegaard too argued that his literary endeavour had saved his life.[57] Yet, the way through which writing or speech redeem is not straightforward. Joseph B. Soloveitchik, whose thought was deeply influenced by existentialist tradition and whose work at times conveys a passion to confess, writes:

'All I want is to follow the advice given by Elihu the son of Berachel of old who said, "I will speak that I may find relief" [Job 32:20]; for there is a redemptive quality for an agitated mind in the spoken word and a tormented soul finds peace in confessing.'[58]

According to Soloveitchik, spoken or written philosophical discourse plays a therapeutic role. This discourse does not redeem through a metaphysical method that provides answers to theoretical questions. The redemptive, healing power of speech or writing lies in the self-explication of the person's inner world, which leads to inner harmony and understanding.[59]

Brenner's negative paraphrase of a verse in the Book of Job suggests he does not trust the redemptive power of confessional speech: 'I said, brethren and companions, I will say to you what is in my heart, I will pour out my words, I will speak… so that I may sink into my sorrow and so that I may never be relieved, forever and ever.'[60] In Brenner's understanding, confessional speech may not only fail to heal but may even intensify pain and sorrow. This, rather than self-redemption, may indeed be its purpose, although Brenner was the one who, in the passages cited above, had held that the purpose of the 'artistic word' is 'to ease the pain' of the writer. In what way does the 'artistic word' ease or redeem, if not through confession? And what is the meaning of the emphasis on confession in Brenner's writing?

Gershon Shaked suggested that Brenner's writing belongs in a literary genre of 'authentic' writing, meant to 'create an "authentic" impression that will draw it closer to the documentary'.[61] This technique, however, is ultimately a literary device. Shaked, who analyses the nature of the Brennerian art, compares it to that of writers such as Scholem Aleichem and André Gide,[62] and sums up its characteristics:

> We thus learn that 'non-fictional' art resorts to artistic ways in order to persuade us of its closeness to reality. In the interplay of distance and closeness or structure and life that is typical of narrative art, it chooses closeness and life over distance and structure. All art puts life into a structure and draws away from what is close by placing a muddled world into an organized frame. The more the structure overwhelms life, the less reliable the story, until the world might appear as 'a play of correspondences and structures.' On the other hand, the more the 'world' overwhelms the structure and the more purposeful closeness to the world is preferred to purposeless distance, the less the aesthetic sense and the more muddled the work appears, as life itself.

In all his works, Brenner tries to draw close to the threshold of chaos typical of life. Hence, he tends to renounce the omniscient author's point of view and confine himself to the more limited perspective of narrator-witness, or to the techniques of the narrator protagonist, from autobiographical notes and up to the confessional monologue.[63]

Similarly, Brinker suggests that the purpose of the autobiographical hints is to 'plant in him [the reader] the understanding that the sources of Brenner's narrative are in life and not in literature'.[64] This thesis, however, offers no explanation for Brenner's own emphasis on confession and on the redeeming role of writing. According to Brinker, this is merely a literary device whose meaning is altogether different – it is supposed to lead the reader to the idea of an association between literature and life. I agree with Brinker that, for Brenner, literature is rooted in life. Contrary to Shaked and Brinker, however, I will argue that confession for Brenner is more than a literary device.

The confession signals a displacement from the world to the person, from the objects to the subject, to emphasize the centrality of self-reference. This self-reference is part of the individual's attempt to contend with existence, with the question of meaning in life. In an approach stating that finding meaning in the world is no longer possible, individuals are directed to turn to themselves and to their existence.

Lichtenbaum, who, as noted, tends to an autobiographical-biographical interpretation of Brenner, offers a better formulation of the relationship between Brenner and his work: 'Brenner sunk his heart in his writings, his compassion, his whole self, the limbs of his soul, as living fluttering limbs.'[65] Brenner's writings are the place where Brenner struggles with and confronts his thoughts, his doubts, possible and rejected ideas, and above all, the fundamental questions of existence posed by the individual Jew. The field of literature is the inner battle zone, though not the private one. Lichtenbaum therefore states: 'The fable of his [Brenner's] stories unfolds in the inside, within the space of the soul; the events, the circumstances of external life are only landmarks, merely a framework for show. Brenner's art always aims for the center and for the psychology, for the person in the person, for the absolute, the concrete beyond all the guises and the cultural layers.'[66] In this internal self-confrontation, events that took place in the past do not play a decisive role and the work is an expression of the author's freedom when facing givenness. Redemption or salvation will be found in the individual's effort to interpret his existence and find in it new meanings and possibilities. Rather than a return to the past, confession involves the past speaking anew in the present, which already reflects a new interpretation. This claim is valid not only concerning Brenner's work, but concerning personal confession in general. Confession is a deliberate act of speech, which judges and evaluates past events. Thus, what appears as the voice of the past is truly the voice of the present. Brenner the confessant is thus Brenner the creator and interpreter. Here and now. The present and its options are the focus of the confessing discourse.

Brenner expressed these insights, at least implicitly, when relating to Berdyczewski. He claimed that the importance of Berdyczewski's endeavour is that he taught 'inner freedom, the freedom to think about our responsibility and to be free men, at least within ourselves'. Berdyczewski set up the model of the 'man who thinks deeply by himself, who looks not only to one side but sees many sides'. Berdyczewski's creative force comes forth in the fact that 'he composes everything he says from what is kept inside his soul and from the foundation of his soul. The angel in Berdyczewski's life is all eyes, with which it sees and looks into the visions, through and through.' Berdyczewski's creative force, the anchoring of his work in his soul, leads his work to be rich and varied, free. Hence, Brenner sums up: 'Will he refrain from making up phrases as he wishes, according to his unique vision?'[67] A literature that is anchored in the writer's soul is not exhausted by a confession but will also be linguistically rich, shaping varied literary options.

If literature is indeed anchored in life, then literary richness attests to the richness of life since, so Brenner holds, literature is a kind of seismograph attesting to the human condition. This close association enables Brenner to affirm:

> Whoever is dissatisfied, for instance, with our literature not only in a technical sense, whoever finds it has fundamental flaws, meaning it has no life, should probe further and will then find he is dissatisfied with our life in general. He will find that ours is not a genuine life. A life that does not have, let us say, one complete language is not a life and, in a life like that, there is no room for a complete literature either, for a literature that is an absolute need.[68]

With the erosion of certainties and the acknowledgement of the absurd in human existence, a topic that will be at the focus of the next chapter, literature becomes increasingly important for the discovery of concrete, relevant options of human existence for someone experiencing the collapse of Jewish life: 'Well, all the foundations are collapsing, but we are still alive. However that may be, we live. And life has many worlds, and various hues, and infinite combinations of forces. And these worlds of ours and these hues, some of the hues, we want to put into the vessel of our literature in the new Hebrew language.'[69] Unrealized possibilities, potential visions, are crucial. Turning to the self is thus the beginning of a voyage to discover and shape these possibilities. The fixation of life leads to literary fixation.

This analysis points to the closeness between Brenner's view of literature and those of existentialist authors, for whom turning to the self was not a return to a past datum, to what had been, but a return to the self and to the existentialist possibilities it can create by virtue of its freedom. This creativity, which fluctuates between the coerced and the possible, between facticity and imagination, rescues and redeems the individual through its very insights about existence, even if it never affects the suffering of life.[70]

The beginning of this writing is in the authors' turn to themselves. Brenner presents the contrast between this type of literary writing and Mendele's work: 'The pondering, the reflection, the ignorance of the Hebrew narrators of this generation are altogether alien to Mendele. The broken, noble, superior soul of our new artists is entirely strange to him and, therefore, so are their brief and intensely subtle traces, which they draw not for the audience but for themselves.'[71]

This turn to the self, however, is not a sinking into an unmediated confession and an unreflective monologue, not even into autobiography. The turn is expressed in an attempt to understand life, to reach conscious transparence regarding concrete human existence. In existentialist terms, literature strives to expose human ontology. This exposure has a practical implication – it has the power to rescue us from coercion, from 'the fall', from perceiving ourselves as objects. Transparent self-consciousness overcomes the datum by identifying the individual with the ability to transcend it. This self-transcendence is redemption.

Brenner formulates these insights almost explicitly. He supports bringing into our 'humble abode' the 'literary figures who have ostracized us' (referring to writers such as Dostoevsky, who was critical of Jews and was also claimed to be an anti-Semite) because 'bringing them in will help our true self-evaluation... will redeem us in a certain sense and place us above them, since nothing elevates and liberates like true self-evaluation. Art in general may release us from flaws because it expresses them and rises above them.'[72]

The redeeming power of literature, like that of art in general, lies in its ability to express and surpass the raw material of life, an act that represents the deepest expression of human existence.

The work turns to the self rather than to the 'audience', but its mode of turning transcends the personal in two senses. The first sense, as Brenner himself understood, is that the exposure of subjective truth[73] creates a possibility that is also open to others.[74] At times, the writer's turn to the self opens up the way to the other:

> Everyone experiences the depth of life and all human creatures have a need to express. Artists, however, have not only the need but also the power to express, to convey in a few or in many words, sounds, colors. Through his expression, the artist fulfills primarily his own need, he finds in this satisfaction for his soul. But his fellow creatures, those who share his life, see this as if he were doing for them what they themselves cannot do.[75]

The writer is thus the transparent consciousness of every person as an individual creature, and is thus able to impart to others what they cannot provide for themselves.

The second sense is manifest in the fact that the literary product, as noted, transcends the personal. The self at the foundation of the literary work is everyman or, more precisely, every addressee of the literature, as a human creature who experiences existence. Through the act of creation, authors transcend their own existence and detach themselves from the biographical, psychological, factual bonds that confine them to their concrete reality. They transcend from the given to the possible, from necessity to freedom.

This analysis clarifies the connection between Brenner's approach to literature and that of Aristotle, who describes the connection between poetry and reality as follows:

> It is also evident from what has been said that it is not the poet's function to relate actual events, but the *kinds* of things that might occur and are possible in terms of probability or necessity. The difference between the historian and the poet is not that between using a verse or prose....No, the difference is this: that the one relates actual events, the other the kinds of things that might occur. Consequently, poetry is more philosophical and more elevated than history, since poetry relates more of the universal, while history relates particulars.[76]

As Josef Ewen shows, Brenner is definitely aware of the Aristotelian approach and applies it to narrative fiction as well.[77] Thus, for instance, Brenner writes: 'They will fail to notice that the poor belletrist at times imagines special situations – including such that have not actually happened but are contingent on the circumstances, or such that might happen – so that he may thereby reach the aims he has set for himself.'[78]

In Brenner's interpretation, Aristotle's claim highlights the pivotal role of possibility within reality. Possibility liberates us from the coercion of the 'personal', of concrete reality. In literature, the author transcends beyond the coerced datum into the possible, and from it into the universal. Brenner, then, pours Aristotle's approach into the existentialist format of literature, which is concerned with the self.

The deep association between literary creativity and selfhood explicates Brenner's cleaving to Hebrew. His association with Hebrew, rather than conceptual or contingent, rests on selfhood and real existence. Hebrew is a language 'that can express the whole of our inner world – we cannot help at all in this! We cannot change it! In any event, Hebrew is one of the languages that grasp our soul the most, a language we cannot erase without thereby erasing ourselves.'[79]

A literature written in Hebrew, then, is *the* way to confront concrete existential questions. We approach experienced reality through it and learn from it about the wealth of human existence and its possibilities. Brenner assigns literature a role in life. It is no longer a theory created by those 'engaged all their lives in discussions'.[80] The antithesis of theories is 'the literature of life',[81] which grows out of life, contends with givenness, and outlines the possibilities of existence. The literature of life is neither a confession nor a monologue, but an ongoing account of the struggle with life. Literature is a central moment in self-consciousness. Through it, real life becomes aware of itself and the roots of human existence become exposed. Brenner formulated this insight through a new approach that mediates between a realistic and a symbolist stance in literature: 'A deep, genuine reality is one where everyday life is elevated to the rank of a symbol, until it succeeds in discovering the core and foundation of life.'[82]

Brenner, then, holds that literature is embedded in the ontological construct of human existence.[83] It grows out of real life and strives to understand its ontological truth and meaning. Since it grows out of real life, it must grow out of self-experience.[84] Hence, the writer starts from himself, 'tells about himself',[85] and 'withdraws into his soul; only into his soul'.[86] This introverted move at times leads to a perception of the literary work as a confession and an outpouring of the soul. The outcome of this self-withdrawal, however, is self-transcendence, because understanding existence means understanding not only the personal and the contingent, but grasping the most profound foundations of concrete human life.[87] Brenner allows us a glimpse of this insight. He describes the writer that focuses on the individual,

> and, against his will, turns wholly toward the individual, only to the individual, to his mood, to the life of his soul, to his sorrow and pain, to the lack of solid ground beneath him... Indeed, we need not repeat that no individual is a desert bloom, and when literature comes to describe the Hebrew individual, it thereby also – deliberately or unwittingly, directly or indirectly – necessarily touches on the national problems.[88]

Understanding of the individual's life, of the writer's life, expands in concentric circles. It begins with the concrete life of the writing individual, transcends to the life of the individual as individual, and becomes manifest in the self-understanding that 'no individual is a desert bloom'. Self-understanding, then, is the understanding of the broader surrounding human space that is its backdrop. It is also the symbolic meaning of the work of art.

The role of literature in the exposure of existential truth is thus decisive. It is part of an existential dialectic that shifts between givenness – the circles of facticity within which the individual functions as a private person, as an individual *vis-à-vis* a collective, and as part of a cultural-historical collective – and freedom – the possibilities that transcend facticity. This dialectic becomes clear and aware of itself through literature, which mediates between freedom and real life. It is literature that exposes the *is* and the *possible*.

From Kierkegaard to Heidegger, human existence has been traced as a course extending between factual givenness and possibility, or between finitude and infinity. Givenness includes the imposed facts, such as the physical data and the social-historical contexts into which the individual is born. Facticity is the past within which we find ourselves, one we can transcend through the power of freedom to shape new possibilities of existence. These possibilities are created by the imagination, which provides us with new pictures of existence beyond the given concrete situation. If givenness is ruled by the past, possibilities are ruled by the future. But the two poles of facticity and possibility do not exhaust human life. Kierkegaard claimed that 'a human being is a synthesis of the infinite and the finite... of freedom and necessity, in short, a synthesis. A synthesis is a relation between two. Considered in this way, a human being is still not a self.'[89]

The third constitutive element is the attitude of the self to facticity and possibility. The attitude of the self organizes and mediates the relationship between the two ontological foundations of human existence. The concrete human creature is formed through the relationship between past and future, between givenness and possibility.

In Brenner's view, literature plays an important role in the process of shaping human existence. Although it strikes root in real life, in the facticity imposed on the individual or on society, it does not give in to it. Through the power of creative imagination, it transcends to the realm of possibilities, to the future, it anticipates what as yet is not and what could have been and never was. Literature plays a key role in the dialectic of existence, in the tormented voyage of life as such. It is not free from life, but not bound by it either.[90] It thereby adds a critically significant dimension to the self-consciousness of human existence and to the delineation of its possibilities. The well-known Brennerian statement about 'the literature of life', which is contrasted with 'literature and life',[91] clearly reflects the location of literature within existence rather than as a useless addition.

In Chapters 2 and 3, I set out the existentialist framework of the Brennerian *oeuvre*. In Chapter 4, I will analyse the characteristics of existence that Brenner lays out in his work. This analysis, as noted, will not focus on the study of specific literary works, on the characters, or on the narrative plots, but on the characteristics of human existence as he formulates them in various contexts. Brenner, as well as his characters, speak in an existentialist language that shapes their experience of existence. This language and these characters will be at the centre of the discussion.

Notes

1   William Hubben, *Dostoevsky, Kierkegaard, Nietzsche, and Kafka: Four Prophets of Our Destiny* (New York: Macmillan, 1952).

2   John Macquarrie, *Existentialism* (Harmondsworth, Middlesex: Penguin Books, 1973), 265.

3   Iris Murdoch *Existentialists and Mystics: Writings on Philosophy and Literature* (New York: Allen Lane, 1998), 3–30.

4   Franz Rosenzweig, '"The New Thinking": A Few Supplementary Remarks to The Star [of Redemption]', in *Franz Rosenzweig's 'The New Thinking'*, ed. and trans. Alan Udoff and Barbara E. Galli (Syracuse, NY: University of Syracuse Press, 1999), 86.

5   Murray Krieger, *The Tragic Vision: Variations on a Theme in Literary Interpretation* (Chicago: University of Chicago Press, 1966), 247.

6   For a paradigmatic rendition of this approach, see William Barrett, *Irrational Man: A Study in Existential Philosophy* (Garden City, NY: Doubleday, 1962).

7   Murdoch, *Existentialists and Mystics*, 101–107.

8   Milan Kundera, *The Art of the Novel*, trans. Linda Asher (New York: Harper and Row, 1988), 160.

9   Menachem Brinker, 'Brenner and the Workers' Movement: A Critic from Within' (in Hebrew), in *Hebrew Literature and the Labor Movement*, ed. Pinhas Ginossar (Beer Sheva: Ben-Gurion University Press, 1989).

10   *Writings*, vol.3, 456.

11   *Ibid.*, 148.

12   *Ibid.*, 316.

13   *Ibid.*, vol.2, 1366. See also Yitzhak Bakon, *The Lonely Young Man in Hebrew Literature 1899–1908* (in Hebrew) (Tel Aviv: Tel Aviv University, 1978), 58–60.

14   Shlomo Bartonov, ed., *Micha Josef Berdyczewsky, Yosef Haim Brenner: Letters* (in Hebrew) (Tel Aviv: Hakibbutz Hameuchad, 1962), 29.

15   *Ibid.*, 30.

16   *Writings*, vol.4, 1065.

17   Martin Heidegger, 'The Origin of the Work of Art', in Martin Heidegger, *Poetry, Language, Thought*, trans. Albert Hofstadter (New York: Harper and Row, 1971), 81.

18   *Writings*, vol.4, 1065.

19   Baruch Kurzweil, *Between Vision and the Absurd: Chapters in Our Twentieth-Century Literature* (in Hebrew) (Jerusalem: Schocken, 1966), 263.

20   Y. H. Brenner, *Collected Writings* (in Hebrew), vol.3 (Tel Aviv: Hakibbutz Hameuchad, 1967), 222.

21   M. H. Abrams, *The Mirror and the Lamp: Romantic Theory and the Critical Tradition* (Oxford: Oxford University Press, 1971), ch.1.

22   *Ibid.*, 14–20.

23   Iris Parush, *National Ideology and Literary Canon* (in Hebrew) (Jerusalem: Bialik Institute, 1992), 262.

24   Yosef Haim Brenner, *Breakdown and Bereavement*, trans. Hillel Halkin (Philadelphia: Jewish Publication Society of America, 1971), 145.

25   *Writings*, vol.1, 192–3.

26   Avi Sagi, *Kierkegaard, Religion, and Existence: The Voyage of the Self*, trans. Batya Stein (Amsterdam-Atlanta, GA: Rodopi, 2000), 75–6.

27   On this literary genre, see Hannah Naveh, *The Confessional Narrative : A Description of a Genre and its Practice in Modern Hebrew Literature* (in Hebrew) (Tel Aviv: Papyrus, 1988).

28   Dov Sadan, *A Psychoanalytic Midrash: Studies in Brenner's Psychology* (in Hebrew) (Jerusalem: Magnes Press, 1996), 31.

29   Baruch Kurzweil, *Our New Literature: Continuity or Revolution* (in Hebrew) (Jerusalem: Schocken, 1965), 241. See also Nathan Zach, 'Sickness and the Allure of the Concealed' (in Hebrew), in *Yosef Haim Brenner: A Selection of Critical Essays on his Literary Prose*, ed. Yitzhak Bakon (Tel Aviv: Am Oved, 1972), 200. Naveh includes Brenner among the representatives of this genre.

30   *Writings*, vol.4, 1240.

31   See also Yeshurun Keshet (Yaakov Koplewitz), *In Bialik's Times: Essays* (in Hebrew) (Tel Aviv: Dvir, 1943), 263.

32   *Writings*, vol.3, 315.

33   *Ibid.*, 277.

34   *Ibid.*, vol.4, 1244.

35   *Ibid.*, vol.3, 209. See also *ibid.*, 75, 277.

36   Zach, 'Sickness and the Allure of the Concealed', 200. Note that a similar approach
       was suggested regarding Kierkegaard. See Sagi, *Kierkegaard*, 68–9.

37   See the excellent bibliography in Avner Holtzman, *Loves of Zion: Studies in Modern
       Hebrew Literature* (in Hebrew) (Jerusalem: Carmel, 2006).

38   Yosef Lichtenbaum, *Yosef Haim Brenner: His Life and Work* (Tel Aviv: Niv, 1967),
       28–9.

39   *Cf.* Rene Wellek and Austin Warren, *Theory of Literature* (New York: Hartford
       Brace, 1949), 72–3.

40   Isaiah Rabinovich, *Hebrew Narrative Seeks a Hero: Directions in the Artistic Development
       of Modern Hebrew Fiction* (in Hebrew) (Ramat-Gan: Hebrew Writers Association in
       Israel, 1967), 70.

41   Besides the philosophical-theoretical context, these questions are also part of the
       discourse of literary criticism. For an exhaustive analysis, see Wayne C. Booth, *The
       Rhetoric of Fiction*, 2nd ed. (Chicago: University of Chicago Press, 1983), 23–43,
       211–64. This book considers in detail the relationship between the writer and the
       literary work, and its implications for the interpretation of the literary text. I have
       adopted a philosophical perspective, however, and examine Brenner relying on
       the course of philosophical hermeneutics from Schleiermacher to Heidegger.

42   Friedrich Schleiermacher, *Hermeneutics: The Handwritten Manuscripts*, ed. Heinz
       Kimmerle, trans. James Duke and Jack Forstman (Missoula, MT: Scholars' Press,
       1977), 100.

43   *Ibid.*, 113.

44   *Ibid.*, 223.

45   Hans Georg Gadamer, *Truth and Method*, trans. Joel Weinscheimer and Donald
       G. Marshall (New York: Crossroad, 1989), 163. For an additional analysis of
       Schleiermacher's view, see Anthony Thiselton, *New Horizons in Hermeneutics*
       (Grand Rapids, MI: Zondervan, 1992), 204–27.

46   Menachem Brinker, *Normative Art and Social Thought in Y. H. Brenner's Work* (in
       Hebrew) (Tel Aviv: Am Oved, 1990), 64. Yitzhak Bakon, in *The Young Brenner*
       (in Hebrew) (Tel Aviv: Hakibbutz Hameuchad, 1975), carefully pointed out the
       gap between biographical elements and the autonomous literary work. Yet, see
       Samuel Schneider, *The Traditional Jewish World in the Writings of Y. H. Brenner* (in
       Hebrew) (Tel Aviv: Reshafim, 1994), 37–9.

47   On this question, I differ from the view of David Aryeh Friedman, *Y. H. Brenner:
       The Man and his Work* (in Hebrew) (Berlin: Judischer Verlag, 1923), 24, who writes:
       'If a grieving man cannot be judged, all the more so an artist. As long as real pain
       or actual pleasure have not been suitably refined and have not elapsed, the artist
       cannot create a complete work of art. Yet Brenner always hastens to bring out
       his life experience! That is why we are not surprised when, reading his writings,
       we sometimes find ourselves thinking that this is valuable literary material that is
       unpolished, and could have become important had the author enjoyed sufficient

peace of mind. This is how it seems to me. The truth, however, is that Brenner lacks not only external peace of mind but also inner serenity, which is the main thing.' Needless to say, Friedman failed to identify the meaning of Brenner's fragmented style, which is the artistic form he gave to life.

48   Asher Beylin, *Brenner in London* (in Hebrew) (Tel Aviv: Hakibbutz Hameuchad, 2006), 39.

49   *Ibid.*, 42.

50   The letter was sent to his friend M. Ginzburg.

51   The editor notes in note 4: 'Written and erased: "– including important ones –".'

52   Brenner, *Collected Writings*, vol.3, 346.

53   The analysis of these two perceptions of the past is based on Martin Heidegger, *Being and Time*, trans. John Macquarrie and Edward Robinson (New York: Harper and Row, 1962), Part 2, chs.4–6, and on Martin Heidegger, *The Basic Problems of Phenomenology*, trans. Albert Hofstadter (Bloomington, ID: Indiana University Press, 1988), §§20–21.

54   Vladimir Nabokov, *Speak, Memory* (New York: Pyramid Books, 1968), 70.

55   See, for instance, Gershon Shaked, *Hebrew Narrative Fiction 1880–1980*, vol.1, *In Exile* (in Hebrew) (Tel Aviv: Hakibbutz Hameuchad, 1978); Brinker, *Normative Art*, 117 and *passim*.

56   *Writings*, vol.2, 1366.

57   Sagi, *Kierkegaard*, 49–50.

58   Joseph B. Soloveitchik, *The Lonely Man of Faith* (Northvale, NJ: Jason Aronson, 1965), 2.

59   See Avi Sagi, *Tradition vs. Traditionalism: Contemporary Perspectives in Jewish Thought*, trans. Batya Stein (Amsterdam-New York: Rodopi, 2008), 21–3.

60   *Writings*, vol.3, 75.

61   Gershon Shaked, *Dead End: Studies in Y. H. Brenner, M. J. Berdyczewsky, G. Schoffman and U. N. Gnessin* (in Hebrew) (Tel Aviv: Hakibbutz Hameuchad, 1973), 69.

62   *Ibid.*

63   *Ibid.*, 72,

64   Brinker, 'Brenner and the Workers' Movement', 64.

65   Lichtenbaum, *Brenner: His Life and Work*, 31.

66   *Ibid.*, 77.

67   *Writings*, vol.3, 834–5.

68   *Ibid.*, vol.4, 1727.

69   *Ibid.*, vol.3, 742.

70   Gila Ramraz-Rauch, *Y. H. Brenner and Modern Literature* (in Hebrew) (Tel Aviv: Aked, 1970), 45–6.

71   *Writings*, vol.3, 148.

72   *Ibid.*, vol.4, 1075.

73   On truth as an element of Brenner's *oeuvre*, see Boaz Arpali, *The Negative Principle: Ideology and Poetics in Two Stories by Y. H. Brenner* (in Hebrew) (Tel Aviv: Hakibbutz Hameuchad, 1992), 27–9.

74   See, for instance, *Writings*, vol.3, 255.

75   *Ibid.*, vol.4, 1538–9.

76 Aristotle, *Poetics*, ed. and trans. Stephen Halliwell (Cambridge, MS: Harvard University Press, 1995), ch.9.

77 Josef Ewen, 'Cathartic and Anti-Cathartic Elements in Brenner's Work' (in Hebrew), in *On Poetry and Prose: Studies in Hebrew Literature*, ed. Zvi Malachi (Tel Aviv: Tel Aviv University, 1977), 102–104.

78 *Writings*, vol.3, 575.

79 *Ibid.*, 743.

80 *Ibid.*, 116.

81 *Ibid.*, 104.

82 *Ibid.*, vol.4, 1068.

83 On this question see also below, 136–43.

84 See *Writings*, vol.4, 1352.

85 *Ibid.*, vol.3, 745.

86 *Ibid.*, 315.

87 *Ibid.*, 177, 846, and elsewhere.

88 *Ibid.*, 316.

89 Søren Kierkegaard, *The Sickness unto Death*, trans. Howard V. Hong and Edna Hong (Princeton: Princeton University Press, 1980), 13.

90 I suggested a similar analysis of Kierkegaard's work in Sagi, *Kierkegaard*, 46–56.

91 See *Writings*, vol.4, 1727.

FOUR

An Existentialist Analysis of Life

The 'Riddle of Life' and the Absurd

Kierkegaard often relates to his experience of anguish and alienation. In one instance, he writes: 'alone with torments... alone in anguish unto death, alone in the face of the meaninglessness of existence'.[1] In his journal, he notes: 'All existence makes me anxious, from the smallest fly to the mysteries of the Incarnation; the whole thing is inexplicable to me, I myself most of all.... My distress is enormous, boundless.'[2] In *Repetition*, he expands on the questions evoked by the encounter with existence: 'Where am I? What does it mean to say: the world? What is the meaning of that word? Who tricked me into this whole thing and leaves me standing here? Who am I?... How did I get involved in this big enterprise called actuality? Why should I be involved?'[3]

Existence is experienced as a sequence of meaningless events – the individual is lost and lives through anxiety and alienation. This sense of estrangement is a key element of existentialist thought, and Kierkegaard, Sartre, and Camus approach it as the cornerstone of human life.

Two trends are easily discernible in the interpretation of this experience. For Sartre, it is a deep expression of the meaninglessness of life. Existence is revealed as contingent and lacking any compelling justification. Its apparent unity crumbles: 'Existence had suddenly unveiled itself. It had lost the harmless look of an abstract category... all that had vanished: the diversity of things, their individuality, were only an appearance, a veneer. This veneer had melted, leaving soft, monstrous masses, all in disorder – naked, in a frightful, obscene nakedness.'[4] Given the inability to explain what exists, everything remains in its raw concreteness, in the incomprehensible contingency wherein we find ourselves. This is precisely the experience of the absurd, as Sartre proceeds to describe it:

> The world of explanations and reasons is not the world of existence. A circle is not absurd, it is clearly explained by the rotation of a straight segment around one of its extremities.... This root, on the other hand, existed in such a way that I could not explain it. Knotty, inert, nameless.... The function explained nothing.... This root, with its color, shape, its congealed movement, was... below all explanation.[5]

Fundamentally, then, the absurd is a negative experience – casting doubt on the order and meaning of existence and confronting the datum directly in all its meaninglessness.

By contrast, Camus describes the absurd as a dual experience, both negative and positive. The negative experience is as Sartre describes it – the collapse of what is understandable and the confrontation with its absence, that is, the recognition of the irrationality of life. The positive experience is the yearning for clarity and rationality or, in Camus' terms: 'This world in itself is not reasonable, that is all that can be said. But what is absurd is the confrontation of the irrational and the wild longing for clarity whose call echoes in the human heart.'[6] The experience of the absurd, then, combines the recognition of the world's meaninglessness and the unfulfillable yearning for metaphysics. We must live with immanence and can never transcend it, even if we long to do so. This tension between the negative and the positive creates the experience of the absurd and ultimately directs us inwards, away from the world.

Sartre's approach denies any option of viewing reality as bearing a mystery or a riddle. Reality is meaningless and is meant to remain so. This lucid understanding is the supreme expression of conscious transparence. But for Camus, as for Kierkegaard, recognizing the mystery of life complements the experience of meaninglessness. The yearning for metaphysics or the discontent with reality thus leads human beings to the border of an immanence that cannot be transcended, while it also acknowledges that immanence as such remains opaque and enigmatic. Camus acknowledges the mystery of life in his autobiography, *The First Man*. In a voyage that Jacques attempts in his dead father's footsteps, he experiences the fragility of order and the collapse of existence:

> The statue every man eventually erects... into which he then creeps and there awaits its final crumbling – that statue was rapidly cracking.... All that was left was this anguished heart, eager to live... still struggling against the wall that separated him from the secret of all life, wanting to go farther, to go beyond, and to discover, discover before dying, discover at last in order to be, just once to be, for a single second, but forever.[7]

Like Kierkegaard, Camus maintains that 'the secret of life' will not be found in immanent reality but 'beyond', in a mysterious, transcendent one. Only the revelation of the mystery will establish existence as such, will allow a person 'to be'. Unlike Kierkegaard, however, Camus held that the mystery is doomed to remain so, a mystery. Lucid clarity cannot transcend the immanent reality that dictates its borders. The passion for transcendence and the ontological knowledge that immanence is not total are manifest in the recognition of a mystery that cannot be deciphered. Recognizing the mystery, or the passion for the metaphysical, means that, together with the clarity of self-recognition that identifies limits, we experience darkness – what we do not and cannot understand will nevertheless remain a yearning. We experience immanence, but also its borders and limitations.

Yitzhak Bakon[8] holds that a story where Brenner emphasises the absurd, such as 'From A to M',[9] leaves no room for the riddle of life because recognizing the riddle of life goes beyond the experience of the absurd. My analysis shows that this approach is correct only from Sartre's perspective of the absurd, but mistaken within the context proposed by Camus. Camus and, as shown below, Brenner too, view the absurd as an experience shaped by the tension between the passion for solving the riddle of life and the knowledge that this is impossible.

In sentences amazingly similar to Kierkegaard's,[10] Brenner writes:

> This life-matter is a strange, mysterious thing, sealed up within us. At every step, wonder besets us; at every step, our eyes widen in a shudder: What is this? Where are we? What is creator and what is creature? Everything is so incomprehensible, everything is hidden from us. The various worlds, the various combinations, the various processes, the various attributions, the various powers, the various creatures – all bear a mystery within them, some inner side, powerful, invisible… For sensitive people, everything is mysterious, everything is wonder and bewilderment… Fear comes and sinks us into it… sinks us…[11]

Terms such as 'wonder', 'bewilderment', 'fear', denote the deep experience of crumbling meaning that Heidegger called anxiety. As Heidegger describes it, this anxiety is not related to a particular object in the world; rather, it is characterized by the undefined and unspecified character of the threat. Anxiety is the absolute collapse of meaning in the world.[12] This collapse leads us to lose faith in existence and to an experience that can be characterized as ontological insecurity.[13]

Rollo May articulated the psychological implication of the distinction between anxiety and fear: 'The difference is that the anxiety strikes at the central core of his self-esteem and his sense of value as a self, which is the most important aspect of his experience of himself as a being. Fear, in contrast, is a threat to the periphery of his existence; it can be objectivated, and the person can stand outside and look at it.'[14] Anxiety is metaphysical, the person experiences absolute estrangement.

The protagonist of *Breakdown and Bereavement* experiences it as nausea, which for Brenner has a meaning similar to that which it has for Sartre: a strong bodily experience of split.[15] Life becomes hard and intolerable:

> Why is it hard? You do know, friend, it is hard for man that he was created at all, hard that he was created altogether! This man, who does not know from where and to where, why, and what for; to whom what all this means, what is the world, where is the haven from all the pains and horrors, and where light will be found is entirely concealed. Furthermore: this man who is born without knowing what is light, what is light and what is not-light and why this is light and this not-light; yes, yes, this man who is born to ignorance – will forever clearly know only one thing: that a secret ending, brief and not too rational, will soon come, must come, to all these misfortunes and horrors, one that will swallow everything and cover everything as if it had never been, as if nothing had ever happened.[16]

Brenner, like Camus, understands that estrangement and anxiety are anchored in an expectation of meaning. The experience of emptiness, of the nothingness denoting a void that cannot be filled, is related to the absolute push to the existential extreme – to the borders of transcendence. This is exactly the Brennerian life riddle, the experience of the border of life or, more precisely, of an immanent life that remains unfulfilled. Meaning as an endless question epitomizes this standing at the edge. One of the characters in the story 'Nerves' says the following:

> Like all those who had ever thought about their own lives, I too had long come to the usual conclusion that its riddle, the riddle of this life, 'will never be solved,' that I would not grasp or apprehend what would be after my life up to my last moment… and including it…. that is: there would be nothing… Worse: not only what would be after my life – I would never understand what my life is either… I would not understand what the world is, or what I am within it and what I had been before, and what I would be after – … who had thrown me into this universe to breathe, to live, to see the sky and the earth…[17]

'Thrown' is a special term in this text. The experience of 'thrownness', as Heidegger analyses at length, is the basic human experience of 'being in the world'. Above all, it denotes the facticity imposed upon us, which is not outside our existence but is indeed our very being.[18] The transparent consciousness that exposes the human being as creature rather than creator is accompanied by the negation of any possibility of ever knowing the source and purpose of this thrownness: 'The pure "that is" shows itself, but the "whence" and the "whither" remain in darkness.'[19] Like Brenner, Heidegger understood that the facticity of existence, which has no rational explanation, does not remove the darkness but leaves it in place as a riddle. A facticity accompanied by the inability to transcend beyond immanence leads to a life of emptiness filled with anxiety:

> All that totality of shapes and voices, of visions and shudders, all that we label with names that mean nothing: life, existence, world; all these manifestations within which we breathe, that we are impressed by, moved by – all is so diverse, mixed, multifaceted, so entangled in situations, acts, relationships, ties, so contingent, variable, detached from the real, that telling about it gradually, painting from it some actual, real picture, is indeed impossible. However you put it on a page, however you pass it on, in the end you come to realize that it is not truly so, that there is some flaw here, that the actual reality, the spirit of reality that cannot be missed, is absent, that there is some lie here... The general process of all we call 'life' is not clear to me, I cannot apprehend it, I cannot grasp it. Its very essence eludes me, drifts away from me... and the anxiety of emptiness overtakes me.[20]

Brenner is aware that confronting the nothingness, facing up to the lack of meaning, is an essential part of the maturation process. Childhood is a time of innocence, when we have no experience of the loss of values, of doubt, and of fundamental existential questions.[21] But when we become adults and our consciousness matures, the fundamental questions of existence emerge, not as an event breaking into life from the outside but as a part of being alive – we become 'lost in the ways of the world'.

Brenner attests about himself, in a personal note, that he cannot be a light to others precisely because of his deep personal experience of the loss of meaning:

> Let me hear new things this time... new and concealed. Although I am not very modest, I have never pretended that 'I showed him the light and it was good... I began to teach him... I showed him and taught him,' and so forth and so forth (his actual words). Indeed? I? I, who always thought of myself as one of the lost? I, who myself never knew anything, how could I

release myself from jail? I, lost in the ways of the world – could I
have solved problems for others?[22]

This existential personal experience cannot find answers in rationalist
metaphysics. Like many existentialist thinkers, including Kierkegaard
and Nietzsche, Brenner acknowledges that rational consciousness
is incapable of a profound confrontation with existence. He mocks
rationalist trends mainly concerned with 'inventing ideas' to understand
existence. Like Nietzsche, Brenner emphasises that this approach fosters
a 'special psychology', implying that a rationalist concern with existence
shapes a type marked by artificiality and stagnation, a personality seeking
absolute avoidance of existence *per se*. A fundamental understanding of
this personality is that knowledge about the world

> can be attained almost exclusively through the rational method,
> which is so artificial, so crooked! Theoretical analysis is always
> forced to freeze and stop what is fluid and flowing in life; the
> conceptual world aspires to picture the entire world as a series
> of isolated visions, although these visions are always inextricably
> mixed, tied together, inseparable. Every ideology offers gross
> and specific definitions around the subtle nuances of real life so
> as to introduce formal order into a place that is truly nothing but
> change, transformation, and chaos. Thought requires a specific
> system for everything, while able to grasp only a fraction of the
> infinite universe.[23]

With great sensitivity, Brenner identified the link between empiricism
and existentialism. Existentialism, particularly in its Nietzschean version,
inferred from David Hume's epistemology that consciousness falsifies
reality and builds an unsuitable construction.[24] This structuring is not
dictated by reality but by psychology. Whereas Hume argued that the
source of the development of consciousness is a cognitive-mechanistic
psychology, Nietzsche strove for a depth psychology and sought the
hidden motives for presenting reality as static and rational. Rational
consciousness develops because of the will to explain and give meaning
to what is essentially meaningless and should be quashed. When human
beings cannot function as a creative, moulding power, they turn to reason
so as to remove the threat:

> The familiar means what we are used to, so that we no longer
> marvel at it; the commonplace; some rule in which we are stuck;
> each and every thing that makes us feel at home: – And isn't our

need for knowledge precisely this need for the familiar, the will to uncover among everything strange, unusual, and doubtful, something which no longer unsettles us? Is it not the *instinct of fear* that bids us to know? And isn't the rejoicing of the person who attains knowledge just rejoicing from a regained sense of security?... Take the philosopher who imagined the world to be 'known' when he had reduced it to the 'idea'; wasn't it precisely because the 'idea' was so familiar to him and he was so used to it? Because he no longer feared the 'idea'?[25]

Brenner, following Nietzsche, identified the motivation behind the development of a rational worldview: to avoid the threat, to make the infinite finite. And yet, it is precisely clear and transparent consciousness that must valiantly confront enigmatic, unexplained reality. Unlike Nietzsche, Brenner was not satisfied with immanence and did not celebrate liberation from the gods. Like Camus, Brenner understands that we are doomed to live mid-way between immanence and what is beyond, and remain with eternal questions. Metaphysical passion and the search for answers we cannot find represent recognition of the oppressive borders of immanence. Together with his great admiration for Tolstoy and Tolstoy's influence on his life,[26] Brenner accuses him:

In what vicious circle do Tolstoy's main characters move and ask themselves the ultimate questions – what for and why, questions that have no answers – and then immediately tell themselves: in order to live we must know the answer to these questions, and if it is impossible to know, it is impossible to live.... What answer is there [in the altruistic theory that Tolstoy's characters endorse] to Tolstoy's ultimate questions, to the questions that every thinking person asks?[27]

This, then, is the mystery and the riddle of life – the recognition of the tension between immanence and its discontent, the recognition that individuals often experience the border and what Jaspers called 'boundary situations', which block them and force them to remain within immanence.[28]

The 'Riddle of Life' and Mysticism

My call to search for what Brenner called the mystery of life could be countered with another stating that, when using terms such as the 'mystery of life' or the 'riddle of life', Brenner is hinting at mysticism as an organon focused on the mystery of life. Brenner does lend credence to the possibility of such a reading in several instances discussed below. In a letter he sends to his friend Hillel Zeitlin,[29] he emphasises that his mood 'inclines slightly toward mysticism'.[30] In two manifestos, Brenner resorts explicitly to Kabbalah and to mysticism:

> We want the Hebrew man… to find in his language – the language of sweet hymns and of storytellers, the language of poets, of kabbalists, and of the early pietists, the language of '*Ha-Mahshavah ve-ha-Kinor*' and '*Me-ever la-Nahar*', the language of '*Be-emek ha-bakhah*' and '*Masa Nemirov*' – all that is close to his heart, all that touches on his *Weltanschauung*, all the burdens of his soul, all the sparks of his spirit, all the echoes of his ideas, all the rays of his imagination, all the words of his God that rise from the earth.[31]

Similarly, he states:

> The prayer of *Ha-Me'orer*: May they all gather at my academy, all those who have a share in the visionaries of Judah and its prophets and in the prayers of the afflicted, in the burly heroes of the rebellion and in the diligent Mishnah scholars, in the poets Halevi and Ibn Gavirol and in the followers of R. Shlomo Yitzhaki and R. Solomon Luria, in those who gather behind R. Yitzhak Luria and in those drawn to the grave of R. Nahman of Bratslav. May they all come here, all who have the word of the God of Israel and the God of man in their hearts and in their lips, and may they all join together in one glorious, sublime, sacred whole![32]

In these two manifestos published in *Ha-Me'orer*, Brenner devotes special attention to Kabbalah and to Hasidism, and we might conclude that he views them as major channels for solving the riddle of life. A more critical reading, however, shows that Brenner's aim is entirely different: he wishes the literary corpus to include all those who have a share in the Jewish public space, those who believe in the 'God of Israel' and those who believe in the 'God of man'; those interested in kabbalistic literature and in Hasidism and those interested in contemporary literature. Brenner is not interested in creating a canon preserving continuity between the new literature and traditional Jewish culture, as Ahad Ha-Am and Bialik had proposed. Both of them had assumed that the national character of the new Hebrew literature and culture would only emerge through an association with the past, making this connection imperative.[33] In this passage, Brenner is not at all interested in establishing a canon, but in mustering all the creative forces of the people. He saw literature – the writing *per se* and its standing in the world – as a form of 'divine worship'.[34] The concern with all literary genres as a sacred pursuit reveals his desire to gather all Jewish forms of literature and not only Kabbalah and Hasidism. Brenner did not view Kabbalah and mysticism as a special variety paving the way to the mystery of life.

True, Brenner does show deep empathy with the Baal Shem Tov and prefers him to Lilienblum:

> The souls of the Baal Shem Tov and those like him, as they are revealed to us in the various verses, are closer to us than the souls of, say, Lilienblum and others. The Baal Shem Tov was indeed a miracle man who knew nothing of the laws of nature and the philosophy of nature as taught at schools, a man full of prejudices, a God-fearing man who willingly observed the commandments, who had never read Simmel on Friedrich Nietzsche. And yet, we clearly see that, in the life of his soul, in his keen understanding of the mystery of life, the world, existence, beauty, light, in his joy and sadness, in his wanderings in the Carpathian mountains and in his lonely thoughts on the Carpathian mountains, he is closer to the soul of the modern Jew than the author of *The Path of Repentance* and so forth.[35]

Ostensibly, this is Brenner's own testimony declaring his deep closeness to the Baal Shem Tov, the mystic, and preferring him to Lilienblum, whom Brenner deeply admired. Brenner finds an affinity between the modern mood and Hasidic mysticism.

But this text too requires closer scrutiny. Brenner does not identify with the mystical stance of Jewish tradition; he does not think that the mystery of creation implies an ontological claim about the existence of a hidden transcendent entity. For his contemporary, R. Abraham Kook, the mystical entity undergoes a process of personification and, from this mode of existence, turns to human beings and makes demands on them.[36] Similarly, Brenner's friend Hillel Zeitlin writes:

> Man wishes to solve the riddle of life and of the world, to understand the mystery of creation, its purpose and existence, to hear a clear answer to the universal questions that trouble him and torment him, to gain great and wonderful insights from time to time, to expand his spiritual wholeness, to climb one

step after another. Time after time, he incurs gross mistakes, offenses big and small and, to his great sorrow, sees he is still standing outside, that all is still closed and sealed to him... And the believer sees this, in his way, as if he were being pushed out, as if the heavens were hinting they do not welcome his good deeds and his yearnings and longings for God, as if his sin was so great they do not wish to place him under the wings of the *Shekhinah,* as if they were banishing him from the heavenly temple so that he might not see the treasures of the King, the King of the universe.[37]

For Zeitlin, experiencing the mystery of existence, the 'riddles of the world',[38] is an expression of the distance between man and God. What should be exposed is the mystery, which is an expression of the gap between human expectations and the human capacity to apprehend and understand. The antithesis of the mystery is the mystical experience of conjoining with God.

For Brenner, by contrast, the mystery of existence is not mediation between man and the *deus absconditum.* The mystery of existence is not an interim situation that we may hope will disappear, but an acknowledgement of the limits of immanence. This acknowledgement is a well-known philosophical outlook, that begins with Kant and culminates in the thought of Karl Jaspers.[39] This stance makes two claims – one ontological and one epistemological. Ontologically, it claims that immanence and finitude fail to capture the full entity – there is something beyond immanence or, in other terms, reality is infinite. Epistemologically, the claim is that whatever is beyond immanence is closed to human understanding. We are doomed to spend our lives on the border between immanence and transcendence. The metaphysical passion is an expression of the desire to transcend the immanence that clasps human existence in an inextricable embrace.

This view, which has gone through several formulations that will not be discussed here, is the one that Brenner supported.[40] For Brenner, the mystery of existence or the riddle of life is not a name for a transcendent entity found 'out there', but an expression of man's reflective attitude towards the surrounding reality. Brenner rejects the rationalism of the Enlightenment, or the practical *Haskalah* attitude *à la* Lilienblum. These approaches exalted the 'light' and clarity of existence. Following Spinoza, they established the identity between rational consciousness and reality. Brenner maintains that modern consciousness is shaped by recognition of the 'haze' of existence. Reality is closed and sealed to us; it neither whispers nor commands us to anything. It is a border and a barrier at which human consciousness stops. Actually, 'the shattered, complex, tragic' souls are those that 'penetrate the secret, ascend to the haze, to the mystery'.[41] These souls from the world of chaos are not endowed with a better epistemological organon; they do not expose what rational perception cannot grasp. Rather, what these souls discover is the finitude of consciousness as well as the finitude of reality, and the fact that human beings are doomed to spend life imprisoned within an immanent reality. Through the religious experience, we become aware of the duality of existence, including both immanence and what cannot be contained within it. The duality implies that immanence is not the totality, yet what is beyond it is still doomed to remain hidden. Brenner formulated this insight unambiguously:

> The various worlds, the various combinations, the various processes, the various ascriptions, the various powers, the various creatures – all bear some mystery within, some internal side, intrinsic, invisible… A mysterious, hidden soul is in every ray, every manifestation, every simple, seemingly unspiritual thing. All bear traces of light that human creatures do not imagine… For the sensitive, all is mystery, all is wonder and amazement.[42]

The experience of wonder and amazement rests on the human ability to transcend daily experience beyond the sense of fullness latent within it. Since the dawn of Western philosophy, wonder functions as an organon that raises human beings beyond their basic existence. This wonder has many manifestations, but its characteristic feature is the defamiliarization of the commonplace: what had been self-evident ceases to be so, since at the foundation of existence is an unstructured darkness that casts doubt on what is already understood. In other words, not only does what is 'there' become an object of wonder, but so does what is 'here': reality loses its obviousness.[43] Ephraim Shmueli points out the closeness between wonder and the experience of the absurd:

> Both are extreme experiences, resting on the human possibility to transcend the bolts of the 'nature imprinted' on everyday life, that is, the cage of the usual and the accepted… The root of the experience of wonder is trust; the root of the experience of the absurd is heresy, lack of trust. The former assumes the possibility of a match between the entity and meaning… whereas the latter is based on the refutation of this option.[44]

Brenner did not accept the dichotomy between religiosity and the absurd typically embraced by many existentialist thinkers, and above all Albert Camus who, in this equation, chose the absurd. In Brenner's view, wonder and amazement lead to mysticism and to a genuine religiosity that does not transcend this world and does not seek the transcendent entity, yet does elude the trap of immanence. At the core of immanence, a human being experiences its incompleteness, and this is the essence of the Brennerian wonder – it does not strive for realization in a metaphysical answer or in the rejection of the metaphysical longing. It simply recognizes the borderline quality of the immanent and of human existence, and this borderline quality becomes the constitutive foundation of human life.[45] The experience of anxiety and wonder when facing reality is what Brenner calls the mystical element. Mysticism is not the action of turning to a transcendent object, but the proper attitude towards an unintelligible reality:

> The mystical mood – this is a matter pertinent to the individual spirit, but cannot dictate the ways of public life. 'The writer of these lines,' for instance, cannot imagine what other, non-mystical, attitude could the soul assume toward the wonder that envelops us, toward the unintelligible that enfolds us at every movement and in every breath. Whoever has been endowed with the qualities of a not-insensitive soul will find it impossible not to see a mystery in every manifestation of life and not to relate to it all as an enigma.[46]

This complex approach reached unique expression in Brenner's Yiddish article 'The Meaning of Hasidism in Judaism and its Echoes in the New Hebrew Literature'.[47] As Bakon points out, the title of this article is related to the story *Mi-Saviv la-Nekudah* [Around the Point].[48] Abramson, the story's protagonist, writes an article with this title. The article takes a positive view of basic attitudes in Hasidism as a mystical movement. True, 'the superficial Jewish intellectual' rejects the mystical trend, because 'mysticism is religious and he is the European *maskil* – practiced in rational thought and sure of knowing everything – so what does he have in common with Hasidism?'[49]

But Brenner takes a stand that supports this movement against rational superficiality. The foundation of this movement is a basic disposition of 'people seeking a way to God, people who often think about their attitude to existence and about the changes in their lives and about the places they occupy in the various worlds'.[50]

In his appreciation of Hasidism, then, Brenner shifts the weight from this movement's unique patterns of worship to its new understanding of the human situation. Brenner draws a clear distinction between the 'contents' of Hasidism and the 'dry husks' represented by many Hasidic practices and superstitions.[51] In his view, the gist of Hasidism is its new spiritual stance:

> Instead of the dry Talmud with its rules and commentators, which sustain only the mind and not the heart, the dialectical need but not the metaphysical and poetic experience; instead of the revealed Torah, which commands belief and teaches forbidden and allowed – the concealed wisdom emerges that nonchalantly dismisses the entire world of action and leads directly into a thousand *Hekhalot de-Ksifin* [Silver Palaces]... The rabbis' strict and unbending Master of the Universe becomes the merciful Father-King, who sits on his heavenly throne and to whom all the nations of the world and their kings are worthless because he is fully dedicated to the liberation of the Jewish spirit, the Jewish soul... The kabbalist is free; he roams in the supernal worlds and plunges into abysmal depths. The practical commandments are external matters of trivial value to him. The gist is the content, the soul of the Torah. He becomes a partner in Creation.[52]

This detailed description clarifies how far the focus of Brenner's perception of Hasidism and mysticism shifts from God to man. Hasidism and mysticism lead to a metamorphosis in the perception of human beings, who experience themselves as free, as partners in Creation, entities whose lives are not confined to halakhic minutiae. The religious way of life is a profound affirmation of metaphysical yearnings. Brenner, therefore, does not hesitate to point out the closeness between Hasidism and the new Hebrew literature:

> For us, people of the present and the future, for whom Judaism is a living body from which we draw spiritual sustenance; we, who search for content in our lives – what is most important for us are the sublime aspirations and the leap to the heights of Jewish thought in different eras. Particularly important for us is the light with which Hasidism filled the Jewish soul, its struggle against rabbinic fossilization, the enthusiasm it evoked, its devotion, its desire, its romanticism, and its poetry. We therefore see that ever since Hebrew literature outgrew its *Haskalah* cradle, ever since it began to seek and find a national Jewish content, Hasidism is reflected in it in a unique way.[53]

This romantic appreciation of Hasidism and mysticism actually widens the gap between Brenner's perception of mysticism and its meaning in religious tradition. In religious tradition, mysticism relates to the object, the divine realm, whereas in Brenner's approach, mysticism is a human disposition that transcends the rational, normative course. Mysticism is the romantic approach that makes human beings and their metaphysical experiences the focus of existence. This is one of the meanings of Brennerian religiosity, as Penueli formulates it:

> The romantic in Brenner did not forgive the sin of 'romanticism' in *Haskalah*: the lack of religiosity in the attitude to man, the lack of 'holy passion'... The romanticism that is missing from *Haskalah* literature found a haven in Brenner's stories. Religiosity in the attitude to man is a sign of man's positive character in Brenner's stories, and its absence a sign of its negation. Brenner the secular prosaic writer seeks holiness in man. He did not sanctify its external, frozen signs. The holiness he requires is dynamic, acquired at the price of enthusiasm and devotion...[54]

According to Brenner, the turn to the self, to its world of metaphysical longings that are doomed to remain unanswered and without a transcendent object is, existentially, the appropriate mystical religiosity. Precisely because Brenner points to mysticism as the proper attitude to the incomprehensible riddle of existence, he rejects the classical mysticism that, in his view, diverts us from reality. Mysticism as an existential stance is a kind of self-deception, since even mystics cannot ignore real life: 'You will find that mystics do not take their mysticism at all into account when taking care of their everyday needs, and they try to fulfill their needs in ways that are not at all mystical. Concerning themselves and their close ones, mystical sayings are just empty and groundless.'[55]

The real-existentialist perspective precludes Brenner's adoption of an approach that creates a dichotomy between existence and consciousness, and mysticism is therefore negated altogether. More precisely: its negation is not theological or epistemological. Brenner does not deny mysticism by claiming that God is dead or that transcendental reality can never be known. He denies it in principle: the disposition that characterizes mysticism leads to self-alienation, to estrangement from concrete physical life.

By contrast, the mystical approach of religiosity towards concrete reality as mysterious is compatible with an affirmation of actual existence. Indeed, the mystical attitude to reality encapsulates the lucid acknowledgement of the borders of immanent existence on the one hand, and the entrapment of an existence that leaves no room for escape on the other. This mystical attitude is therefore the existentialist attitude to reality. 'Earth', argues Brenner, 'is the source of the mysterious, profound, basic attitude to life; heaven – the source of the conceptual, calculated mysticism, lacking vitality and blood.'[56] Brenner can therefore state:

> Enlightened, truly mystical spirits, pure and religious... are not engulfed by the sweetness of mysticism. They simply speak about the good of man, the development of all his powers, the joy of his life. Those who, 'materially,' need no more than a few carobs, are the ones who seek to ensure that human beings should be well fed, stand tall, connected to this world and unafraid of the world to come.[57]

Brenner indeed thought that the Baal Shem Tov sensed the darkness of existence and was thereby a modernist, but he did not think that penetrating this darkness and shedding light on it was in any way possible. Contrary to various mystical approaches that sought to pave ways to the other reality and mediate between it and immanent reality, Brenner thought that we are doomed to live within this haze. This stance is the cornerstone of the absurd and of the alienation inherent in existence, and is indeed what leads us to remain within existence and struggle for its concrete moulding.

For Brenner, experiencing the mystery of existence ultimately leads us to ourselves. This experience shatters the sense of security and self-fulfilment inherent in immanence but does not lead to conversion, to revelation, to the 'light'. Brenner returns to immanence, is pushed into it, and sees transcendence as seduction and deception. He lives within the tormented tension of immanence, which is aware of its limits.

Shaping the Experience of the Absurd

How is this lucid consciousness fashioned? What leads a person to the knowledge that the absurd riddle of life is doomed to remain unanswered? Brenner held that this consciousness represents, above all, a refusal to be deceived:

> Now I am necessarily wretched, because I think, and thought leads to a negation of illusions – and takes away life. Life has always loathed knowledge and philosophizing because they are its most dangerous enemies, its most terrible foes... A man

wants to live and, sensing that he depends on what is outside him, on another power doing everything 'according to his will,' he trembles and fears, he flatters, falls on his face, seeks rescue and deliverance, and believes he has found it. Be gone, then, you who deny the gods! Here is Socrates – give him the poisoned cup…[58]

Deceit and falsity appear as demands of life itself. Life requires deception, be it the religious deception embodied by the gods or that of other kinds of gods, involving elaborate metaphysics. A lucid consciousness is a struggle against the seduction of the gods. Brenner pleads with his readers: 'No rest and no self-deception, whatever it might be, no fear of any consequences, whatever they might be. No inkling of falsity and tender-heartedness… approach the haze [*arafel*], climb to the *pardes*, face existence.'[59] It was said about Moses that he drew near 'to the thick darkness [*arafel*] where God was' (Exodus 20:18), Moses alone approached God and the people stood afar (Exodus 20:15). The haze (or thick darkness) is not existence itself, but the epistemological cover or barrier of the divine. In Brenner's use, the haze is not the place of the transcendent but the place of existence, which is submerged in a haze because it is not entirely transparent. It bears an oppressive mystery, a border that cannot be crossed even if one yearns to do so. Brenner demands from all his readers, and not only from the very special ones like Moses, to face the darkness of a non-transparent existence.

The experience of the encounter with finite and limited existence, whose finitude is not its be-all and end-all, is the experience of the absurd, of the riddle of life that places us in a no exit situation. Experience is thus an expression of the reflection typical of a thinking person. Indeed, a person who reaches maturity cannot but grasp the meaninglessness of life, together with a yearning that cannot be fulfilled in a transcendent, metaphysical sense.

The lucid recognition that existence cannot transcend immanence but nevertheless continues to yearn for what is beyond – decoding the mystery of life – is an expression of religiosity, as noted. Aharon Appelfeld describes Brenner's stance in these terms:

His [Brenner' literary] weaknesses come together into some kind of thunderous force that raises him onto another sphere, one I would call the sphere of religiosity in distress. And when we speak of the sphere of religiosity, we mean the primary, fundamental stance of: 'Who am I and what am I?' … Beyond the individual's wonder at the riddle of life, the disposition of religiosity focuses on the search for the meaning of life, not as a matter of benefit, convenience, or spiritual wealth but as a distress that, barring any glimmer of hope that it will be found – make all delight, beauty, pleasure, appear feeble.[60]

Appelfeld's use of the term religiosity is uniquely accurate in the analysis of Brenner's position. Religiosity is not the type of traditional religious experience that has the transcendent entity as its object. Quite the contrary, religiosity deals with immanent existence itself. Appelfeld unerringly recognizes the Brennerian existential experience as one that strives to understand and solve the problem of concrete existence for the individual, who is the subject and the object of the Brennerian *oeuvre*.

Brenner himself often uses the term religiosity and ascribes to it different dispositions, according to the context. In one place, he describes himself and others like him as 'people characterized by religiosity, but not in the common denotation of the term, people far removed from theology, even *maskil* theology'.[61] This religiosity does not address the transcendent object, since there is 'no one to pray to',[62] as Nietzsche had already argued, 'the gods, all the gods, are dead, dead… dead to us, dead forever'.[63] Hence, religiosity cannot be the relationship between an individual and the non-existent transcendent entity. Quite the contrary, wherever religiosity turns to the transcendent in general and to God in particular, Brenner negates it.[64] Brenner does not hesitate to state that 'the seekers of God… do not seek him at all… they speak in his name'.[65]

What, then, is religiosity? As Appelfeld's analysis pinpoints, Brenner's view resembles that of other existentialist thinkers, and prominently Paul Tillich. They characterized religiosity as an experience that is ultimately focused on absolute self-concern.[66] Religiosity is expressed as devotion, as pathos,[67] ceaselessly striving to confront the dark foundations of existence within the borders of human consciousness. Religiosity is realized in self-transcendence, that is, by a transcendence that finds concrete existence as it is experienced in everyday life unsatisfactory. Hence, religiosity remains within the borders of human existence and does not turn outward – to transcendence. Religiosity is therefore distinctly atheistic.

In a letter to Menachem Poznansky, Brenner's friend Gershon Schoffman writes: 'A few weeks ago I saw Brenner in my dream – young, towering, handsome, and I said to him: "I know the secret of your youth. It is that, despite all your religiosity, deep inside you you're a skeptic, a heretic." He laughed, and was impressed by my having captured his essence so accurately. "Yes, yes, Poznansky, long live skepticism."'[68] According to the analysis I suggested, Brenner's atheism, his scepticism and heresy in Schoffman's terms, are not a denial of his religiosity but its very expression. Genuine religiosity, according to Brenner, is directed inward, to human existence.

Brenner has deep respect for this special type of religiosity. Aryeh Lapidot, the 'old man' of '*Mi-Kan u-mi-Khan*' [From Here and Here], is A. D. Gordon. Brenner describes him as a figure representing a non-mystical kind of religiosity: 'He is religious not because he is ignorant; he is religious not because he is bourgeois, and his religiosity is not mystical. Say whatever you wish: I admire his prayer. Before that kind of prayer, I too can kneel and pray.'[69]

This prayer, in which an atheist can also share, is the prayer that pours out only when the individual has a 'spiritual need for it'. Its wording is not that of the set traditional prayers, it offers 'wordings of his own, from his soul'.[70] This prayer thus flows and erupts out of 'the logic of instinct, the logic of life, the essence of life'.[71] Hence, atheistic religiosity does not do away with prayer, except that this prayer does not turn outwards. Rather, it is an in-depth voyage to life experiences founded on the mystery of life, which can only be apprehended by touching the borders of human existence.

In concrete life, the experience of religiosity is expressed mainly negatively – a discontent manifest in existential doubt, wonder, and a ceaseless effort to find an answer, an answer that will also be stamped with the seal of finality. This religiosity shapes life as dialectical and tense, unable to offer an absolute answer, a final stable anchor endowing life with meaning.[72] In Brenner's *oeuvre*, this tension arises and intensifies because of the tension between the yearning to solve the riddle of life and the thrownness into a finitude that closes and delimits the individual. The person is thus led to experience the absurd, the fruit of an epistemological clarity that exposes the ontological foundations of human existence.

But the absurd results not only from a critical consciousness. What strengthens it is the experience of death. In the Brennerian *oeuvre*, the certainty of death is a stable, unavoidable element. This certainty, evident in many of his works, led David Aryeh Friedman to state: 'Throughout Brenner's work, death accompanied him, but he would bless life, both bless it and curse it.'[73] Like other existentialist thinkers, Brenner raises in several of his writings the thought that death, or more precisely the dread of death, destroys the option of a metaphysical-rational response to questions of existence.[74] Death removes the mask of self-deception from all metaphysical theories. Brenner says about Tolstoy: 'He who knew how to describe with such brilliance the anxiety of death and the process of dying, was himself terrified of death; throughout his life, therefore, he imagined many things in order to soften the anxiety, and in the end was not released from it.'[75] Brenner criticized this approach and demanded attachment to the certainty of death, which lays bare human finitude and limitations.[76]

Brenner's contemporary, Franz Rosenzweig, chooses the motto '*In philosophos!*' [Woe to philosophers] as the epigraph of *The Star of Redemption*. The weakness of philosophy is its attempt to dismiss the first certainty of existence – the certainty of death:

> All cognition of the All originates in death, in the fear of death. Philosophy takes it upon itself to throw off the fear of things earthly, to rob death of its poisonous sting, and Hades of its pestilential breath... each bound to die, each awaiting the day of its journey into darkness with fear and trembling. But philosophy denies these fears of the earth. It bears us over the grave which yawns at our feet with every step... – for all this dire necessity philosophy has only its vacuous smile. With index finger outstretched, it directs the creature, whose limbs are quivering with terror for its this-worldly existence, to a Beyond...[77]

In Rosenzweig's view, as in that of existentialist thinkers such as Kierkegaard, Heidegger, Sartre, and Camus, the failure of philosophy to confront the question of death is only one expression of philosophy's dismal failure in contending with the meaning of human existence. The failure to confront the question of death mirrors the failure to confront the question of life.

To understand the full depth of this critique, we must reconsider what exactly is it that philosophers confront when dealing with the question of death. Classic philosophical tradition dealt with the fear of death, whereas existentialist tradition dealt with the angst of death. Two basic assumptions determined the approach of classic philosophy to the problem of death: the first is that the problem of death is the problem of the pain it causes the individual. The second is that the remedy to this pain is to study philosophy, which reveals that this pain is only apparent, since it is irrational.

Socrates offers a classic and instructive formulation of the problem of death in 'The Apology':

> For to fear death, gentlemen, is only to think you are wise when you are not; for it is to think you know what you don't know. No one knows whether death is really the greatest blessing a man can have, but they fear it is the greatest curse, as if they knew well. Surely this is the objectionable kind of ignorance, to think one knows what one does not know?[78]

At this stage of the argument, Socrates has not yet conveyed his view on the question of whether death represents the end or a change. After he is sentenced to die, Socrates uses this very question to confront the fear of death:

> Death is one of two things: either the dead man is nothing, and has no consciousness of anything at all, or it is, as people say, a change and a migration for the soul from this place here to another place. If there is no consciousness and it is like a sleep, when one sleeping sees nothing, not even in dreams, death would be a wonderful blessing…. But if, again, death is a migration from this world into another place, and if what they say is true, that there all the dead are, what greater good could there be than this, judges of the court?[79]

Socrates' argument, as noted, is typical. It reflects most efforts throughout history and until recent times to confront what had been considered the problem of death: the pain of it. And yet, death is a topic that has troubled few philosophers. Those who assumed that death is merely transformation and transposition did not see death as painful, since change is a blessing. Most philosophers adopted these and other arguments to support this stance, which spread widely after Christianity. But even the few philosophers who adopted the opposite view and maintained that death means extinction, continued to argue that death causes no pain. They also counselled holding on to life, to friendship, and to other factors that give meaning to existence.

Underlying the discussion of death is the question about the ontological meaning of human existence. The classic formulations had assumed that human beings are rational creatures, and rational analysis can therefore heal their pains and spiritual afflictions. The understanding that the pain of death is not genuine, therefore, will suffice for it to vanish. Existentialist tradition, beginning with Kierkegaard and up to Sartre, however, takes this view to task. In the view of existentialist thinkers, philosophy has ignored death, the meaning of death, and its presence in human life. This disregard is evident in the identification of the problem as well as its solution. For existentialism, death is the fundamental problem of human existence, not because it is painful but because it negates life and exposes its fragility and finitude.

This finitude is not something occurring out there, sometime in the far-away future. Quite the contrary, in Heidegger's words – man is a 'being at an end' (*Zu Ende Sein*): 'As soon as man comes to life, he is at once old enough to die.'[80] Death, claims Heidegger, does not resemble a brewing storm or the redesign of a house, which represent events to take place in the future that are not extant in the present. Unlike them, the experience of death is the deepest experience of existence, in the present: 'Death, in the widest sense, is a phenomenon of life.'[81] The presence of death in life is in the dread of being towards death; a dread that isolates the person, takes away all assurances and guarantees, and throws him onto himself.[82] This throwing of man onto himself means that 'the world has the character of completely lacking significance'.[83] The anxiety of death threatens the self with extinction, but also reveals that he is actually an individual, an entity essentially different from any other: he is an existence. Death undermines the old metaphysics but engenders a new one – the ontology of man, which clarifies that man is different from any other entity.

Existentialism accepts the classic argument that we have no experience of death. But death is nevertheless present in human life through the very discovery of the constant possibility of extinction, which may either paralyse us or redirect us to ourselves. For existentialist thinkers, therefore, death is not merely one more problem, but one that sums up the meaning of human existence. Death attacks individuality, threatens consciousness, and, at the same time, discloses its existence.

Brenner offered a similar stance, much before Heidegger. He rejects the classic approach and, conscious of the Socratic view, one of his characters says the following:

> All the philosophy about not fearing death is nonsense. It is impossible not to fear something that is so undesirable and that we definitely know will come! He who does not fear death in his heart, it is not because he has accepted it – something entirely impossible! – not because he thinks of death as a new, perhaps even more complete, form of life. That is nonsense!... It is only with his consciousness that man apprehends his own death, not with his feeling. Hence, he appeases the feeling, 'is not afraid,' and as long as the powers of life are there, even negligibly, they will burst out and seek room to materialize, despite consciousness.[84]

Death is dismissed because cognitive consciousness does not penetrate our being. We can thus elude the confrontation with the fragility of our existence of which we become aware, according to Brenner, only when close to death. In Heidegger's terms, life unfolds in a 'fall', that is, in an existence that blurs consciousness. But whereas Heidegger, like Nietzsche, held that consciousness muddles and leads to deceit, Brenner argued that consciousness is too weak to create a deception. Rather, once we acknowledge that we are 'beings at an end', we find ourselves at a fundamental crossroads and facing the decision of how to shape our lives. In the next section, I examine the options that Brenner proposes.

Reactions to the Absurd

How to react to the clear understanding that there is no meaning, given what Brenner calls the 'removal of illusions'?[85] His *oeuvre* reveals there is hardly an option that existentialist literature offers that Brenner failed to consider. In the context of this critique, Brenner presents his rejection of the religious option as self-evident. The religious option emerges as part of his negation of the rationalist stance,[86] but although he rejects rationalism as a metaphysical position, Brenner refuses to give up sceptical critical thought. Indeed, he follows Nietzsche, and holds that the critique of reason implies the triumph of consciousness, which identifies the falsity of reason. Brenner therefore understood that the possibility of a religious romanticism that has God as its object is not actually open to us: 'An enlightened, modern writer, who comes and speaks to us with a sound mind about his search for God, about his longings for God, about finding God – what will we think of him but that he is a liar, an inveterate liar?'[87]

Like Nietzsche, who referred to the herald of the death of God as a madman[88] because he understood the angst entailed by this message, Brenner too knew of the deep human need for God. In *Breakdown and Bereavement*, this dread is presented through the figure of Haim, who ponders his faith and is torn by it:

> Now that he had seen that the ways of Providence were unfathomable, that good and evil were rewarded unfairly, that the wicked prospered and the just were made to suffer, his faith in God, in a personal heavenly father, no longer sustained him as before; nevertheless, he lived in terrible dread of being left without it; he dreaded the very possibility – dreaded it so that he refused to let himself, to permit himself, even to think of it. One simply didn't think of such things! Without God one couldn't take a single step, dress a single stone, plaster a single wall.... Without faith in God one couldn't breathe even for an instant!... *to breathe is truly impossible... but there's nothing to hold on to... only empty space... and nothing, nothing can ever fill it... there isn't any God...*[89]

The Brennerian dread is the experience at the moment of the crisis, a time when sustaining faith in God, even though necessary, is no longer possible. Existential anxiety exposes the void that faith cannot fill – God is dead, even if the price of the loss of faith is terrifying.

From Brenner's perspective, lucid consciousness must block the seduction of religion. He therefore writes:

> I do know, as does every simpleton who has a soul, the short-comings and emptiness of human reason, all its mistakes and all the trickeries of our senses, as well as all the hardships and vicissitudes of life, all the bitter gloom of a Being without God… Yet – perhaps *because* this simple and elementary pain of mine enters me and pierces me to my depths – I do not understand how people who pretend to be enlightened are not ashamed to throw into this terrifying, gaping opening all kinds of trivialities and matters that will never ease anything, warm anything, or reveal anything about some fiction – fiction in all senses – that they search for and long for and find, about some fiction called Deity.[90]

From Brenner's viewpoint, the seduction of religion is twofold: religion may appear as a suitable channel for the expression of a basic religiosity when faced with existence, and it may be a remedy for the distress of a godless humanity; a remedy for confronting the riddle of life and the insignificance of human consciousness. Religion, however, neither is nor can be a solution because it is based on deceit, on uncritical thought. Brenner unequivocally renounces the theology and theodicy inherent in religion: 'He [Job] dealt with the question of the righteous and the wicked. I have no questions.'[91] Only someone entirely liberated from the seduction of religion can view the question of theodicy as meaningless.

In a paraphrase of Nietzsche,[92] Brenner sums up: 'Has the fire burning within us for liberation, for freedom in all its manifestations despite the dread of an irremediable void, come to an end? Do we not yet know that they are dead, the gods are dead, all the gods? They are dead to us, dead forever.'[93] Brenner follows Nietzsche and claims that consciousness redeems, even at the cost of anxiety and despair. Nietzsche writes:

> *But nothing exists apart from the whole!* – That no one is any longer made accountable, that the kind of being manifested cannot be traced back to a *causa prima*, that the world is a unity neither as sensorial nor as 'spirit,' *this alone is the great liberation* – thus alone is the *innocence* of the coming restored… The concept 'God' has hitherto been the greatest *objection* to existence… We deny God; in denying God, we deny accountability: only by doing *that* do we redeem the world.[94]

A redeeming consciousness releases us from submission to the transcendent, allows us to exploit our powers. In Nietzsche's terms: 'finally, our ships may set out again, set out to face any danger; every daring of the lover of knowledge is allowed again'.[95]

Similarly, Brenner too thinks that consciousness redeems: 'Because nothing raises us and liberates us like proper self-consciousness.'[96] Redemption is the very freedom that human beings discover, the liberation from the bonds of transcendent judgment and from the yoke of generations: 'the death of God' is the discovery of freedom, which becomes the 'positive religion' that replaces traditional religion.[97]

According to Brenner, however, consciousness does not bring release from the riddle of existence. Rather, consciousness discerns the riddle as well as the borderline nature of existence in its full transparence. Ultimately, religion and religiosity are mutually contradictory. Religiosity leads us to the darkness of existence and keeps us there, as the expression of a lucid consciousness that has matured. Religion seeks to overcome the riddle of existence, and to liberate human beings from their consciousness and their strenuous freedom. As Matti Megged points out, Brenner did not see 'the tragic dimension in his world view only as a weakness, or as the result of "dead-ended hesitations" but also, and no less, as evidence of man's greatness, of his freedom, of his aspiration to build for himself a rich and intensive, healthy life... [which] never seemed to him to contrast with tragic consciousness, or even with extreme despair'.[98]

Another option that Brenner examines is suicide.[99] Yirmiyahu Feierman, the protagonist of *Ba-Horef* [In Winter] thinks: 'I thought that nothing needs to be, and at least (or particularly) I and those like me.'[100] And again, in the wake of self-reflection, he tells himself: 'I know only one thing now: if I could listen to the voice of my consciousness, then I, Yirmiyahu Feierman, should not live even for one hour – and I still live today and I will also live tomorrow. I will not be free. I do not have the strong will to be free. I lack the inner freedom...'[101]

Reading the words of Brenner's character, it is hard not to return to the opening lines of *The Myth of Sisyphus*: 'There is but one truly serious philosophical problem and that is suicide. Judging whether life is or is not worth living amounts to answering the fundamental question of philosophy.'[102] Camus, like Brenner, views suicide as a concrete option. The possibility of death is clearly present in life,[103] since life is not perceived as self-evident. The basic question confronting us is the meaning of life. Without a satisfactory answer to this question, suicide is no more than the most logical conclusion. Suicide is a deep response to despair about life or, more precisely, about the meaning of life. These thoughts emerge only if life is equated with the metaphysical-conceptual meaning ascribed to it. This equation leads to the conclusion that the denial of meaning is the denial of life. Brenner formulates this thought in the story '*Bein Mayim le-Mayim*' [Between Water and Water]:

> But to end life makes no sense, even from a logical perspective. It would be logical to end a life without an ultimate purpose were this ultimate purpose not found in reality, elsewhere, in some other life. But since it is temporary in any event, always and frequently without reason and fundamentally without purpose, would it be logical to end it because he is not living the life of some Shimon Bar-Kokhba – which was actually what?... – but rather the life of some invalid, as they call it, without will, without any hope...[104]

Brenner thus assumes that, in the absence of any supreme metaphysical meaning, life, as is, is preferable to death.[105]

For Feierman, suicide is not a merely a whim. It is seen as an inference or as a flicker of consciousness, which is hindered by the lack of freedom. Through his character, however, Brenner understood that to admit that suicide could be a solution is not a kind of pure thought detached from one's mode of being human. A person's consciousness is anchored in a concrete reality. Feierman describes his circumstances when he considered the option of suicide: 'That time was for me one of wavering at the bottom of the mountain.'[106] Suicide, then, is not the conclusion of a neutral rational analysis, but the reflection of a person's response to his existential plight.

The option of suicide conveys a deep despair about existence. But when a person is corroded by despair and led as far as suicide, the implicit assumption is that meaning, if at all available, must be found in some metaphysical idea. Yet Brenner, like Kierkegaard, acknowledged that despair can play a positive role, liberating the individual from the expectation and the yearning for a generalized metaphysical insight. Despair, therefore, has a dual meaning: it expresses failure to transcend the riddle of life, but can also play a decisive role in diverting consciousness from this expectation to actual reality. Despair, like the anxiety of death, has a liberating, purifying power. It leads us back onto ourselves and to the surrounding reality, and compels us to make a change. 'I, who was dissatisfied with myself, who always felt that this is not how one should live, and there wasn't a moment when I didn't feel the need to change, to start life anew.'[107]

Brenner points to the positive power of despair to facilitate a more lucid consciousness: 'A despairing outlook at least illuminates some facts, sheds light on our surroundings, explains to us, clarifies something in the course of our lives.'[108] Furthermore: 'Indeed, despair too is a virtue and is necessary for poets…'[109] Despair and an awareness of death as the epitome of conscious transparence lead the individual to awareness of the split in human existence, which is no longer harmonious. The person is thrown into the loneliness and meaninglessness of existence. A mood of despair, as Kierkegaard had already noted, has cathartic powers.[110] It releases us from illusions and forecloses any option of return to an immediate life. Despairing reflection forces a decision, when the question is whether to choose or reject life, a question that gives rise to a special situation. We do not ask whether life has value or metaphysical meaning, but whether to choose life even if it lacks such value or meaning. And even if we choose life, we still face the question – what is the practical meaning of this choice. These questions trace the course of the existentialist search for Brenner and his characters.

Abramson, the protagonist of Brenner's story *Mi-Saviv la-Nekudah* [Around the Point] allows us a glimpse into existentialist reflection confronted with despair: 'After all the paradoxes, the understandings, and the insights, you're alive, and so-and-so is also still alive, somehow alive, but alive! So what's the conclusion? The conclusion is that man sticks to that hidden riddle, and even in all that trouble, his soul still finds some mysterious sweetness…'[111]

Confronted with despair and with the anxiety of death, consciousness becomes lucid because the affirmation of life is primary and unconditioned by any philosophical theory or metaphysical idea that grants it value. Brenner assumes that the primary affirmation of life, its contradictions and torments notwithstanding, reveals the true greatness of human beings, who struggle within life for life itself. Matti Megged, who discerned the depths of Brenner's position, noted that the tragic character of this struggle is the basis for the self-renewal that evolves from the abyss of life.[112]

Despair reveals that the human will is not to transcend life to what is beyond it, but only to transcend to life in life. Josef Ewen rightfully notes:

> In Brenner's *oeuvre*, the one who actually realizes his suicidal will is not a central character but to some extent its opposite. Thus, for instance, the suicide of Uriel Davidovsky ('*Mi-Saviv la-Nekudah*') is merely the quiet, logical, and philosophical decision of a man for whom everything is over… By contrast, Abramson, a central character, stands amazed and bewildered when faced with the power of his friend to perform his task in

light of the burning lamp – without fuss or excitement. But his [Abramson's] last step pushes him to take the opposite decision: he chooses life, even as madness.[113]

A similar reflection can be traced in *Breakdown and Bereavement*. Yehezkel Hefetz ponders: 'In his Torah, it was now written: *And it was very good* – it was Life.' Yehezkel's wisdom challenges the teaching of R. Meir, of whom the Midrash says: 'In the copy of R. Meir's Torah was found written: And, behold, it was very (*me'od*) good: and behold, death (*mavet*) was good.'[114] Against the magic of death postulated in the Midrash, Yehezkel adheres unquestionably to life: 'Life was good, the only good, there was none other beside it.' Indeed, for life to be fully realized, 'the people you were close to had to be alive, healthy, happy and contented; all your senses had to function… there had to be meaning'. But Yehezkel Hefetz, whose hold on life is tormented and full of anxiety, can move to the unconditional affirmation of existence, an affirmation that is not sustained by the fullness of life but by its very being:

> But even if there was nothing to rejoice about but only to mourn; even if Life had left you crippled and choking on your own caul; even if its treasures were barred to you and this was bad, so bad, and you had no comforter – even then, Life, your life, was good … Anyone could say if he wishes, 'This house doesn't agree with me'… but a fool alone would insist: 'I demand to know what this house is for, because until I do you can't possibly expect me to like it!'
>
> Life was good not only because it could be filled with good deeds or because there was room in it for love, happiness, ideals – in a word, not only because it offered all kinds of fulfillment – but in and of itself. True, there were times when one's suffering obscured Life's face until it could barely be made out and then one might say, 'it isn't worthwhile.' But even this – was Life; one said it only with one's lips. The truth of the matter was that everything was Life and everything was worthwhile, and only the person who understood that everything was worthwhile – yes, *everything*, even if meaningless – could appreciate Life in all its manifestations, could find meaning everywhere, could bless each radiant smile, each stone and blade of grass, the good with the bad, yes, though the bad was bad and it hurt, because it too was Life.[115]

The metaphor of the house is highly significant in the existential context, since the basic sense of one who experiences the absurd and the anxiety of existence is that of not being at home – *unheimlich.*[116] Brenner's central claim is that anxiety and despair denote the deep hold on life; we affirm life as is, regardless of the conceptual meaning assigned to it. This primary affirmation of existence, liberated of values and ideas, is proof of life's fullness, since looking at life through any perspective means diluting its fullness, reducing it to the system of meaning that endows it with value. The affirmation of existence directs the individual to this life as it is, without masks and without the deceit of ideas.

The negation of suicide does not imply a weakness of will, and Gila Ramraz-Rauch is therefore mistaken when she maintains that the affirmation of life conveys the '"un-heroism" of the Brennerian hero. [A hero who] lacks total internal freedom, a freedom that enables action and its performance.'[117] In her view, the hero (in the story *Ba-Horef* [In Winter]) is Uriel Davidovsky rather than Feierman.[118] My analysis suggests that, for Brenner, the choice of life over suicide is the deep expression of a freedom that clings to life unconditionally and without an ultimate purpose. Underlying suicide is a theological-metaphysical approach stating that life has meaning only if anchored in a transcendence beyond existence itself. This view negates freedom in favour of a metaphysical outlook. Brenner rejected this approach. Brenner's hero, writes Matti Megged,

> cannot choose this 'solution': even if he accepts the 'glory of death,' even if he knows that to remain alive means coming to terms with cowardly humiliation… he chooses life. Not only that, but he knows that he who chooses it will not tire and will not cease to seek, at any price, in every place, the reason and purpose of his choice – and will not find it but will still cling to this life, as is.[119]

Brenner formulates these insights in personal terms. In the eulogy of his friend Uri Nisan Gnessin, Brenner describes Gnessin's last visit to London. Brenner claimed he had not invited Gnessin and had actually told him: 'This place is not for you, but if you're no longer expecting anything and have nothing to lose – come!'[120] Gnessin answered, according to Brenner, that he was indeed not expecting anything since 'the next place is not for me, and where is the place that is for me? I'm coming – what can I lose?' The pessimistic tone adopted by Gnessin, whose connection to reality was rather tenuous, leads Brenner to thoughts about our unconditional hold on life: 'And he came. But on the first day of his arrival, on the first hour, I realized that, as long as a man has a soul – not all hope, not all expectations are yet lost. He still, after all, awaits and expects, and he still has – always has – something to lose.'[121] A human being, all human beings, even those who have almost lost their tie to life, have something to lose – life itself. Brenner, then, embraces life unconditionally. Embracing life means accepting it as is, without blurring or hiding the suffering, the pain, the anxiety or the despair, and acknowledging it instead as a part of life. Despair reflects the resilience of metaphysical longings. The unconditional affirmation of life suggests a reduction, a renunciation of an ideal world in the name of concrete existence, but the ideal reappears as yearning. This is the tragic dimension of Brenner's works, that Matti Megged so excelled at describing:

> Unquestionably, then, their [Brenner's characters] view of the world is essentially tragic. And it could not be otherwise: Brenner's character aspires, as noted, to be liberated from his 'existential stature' and to create for himself 'an ideal world.' His tie to concrete truth and to self-criticism, however, repeatedly impose on him the understanding that this aspiration is impossible to realize in the actual situation in which he is forced to live. And yet, this tragic consciousness is not necessarily a source of 'misery' and weakness. Quite the contrary: it is also a source of power, of spiritual superiority, even of pride... The tragic dimension of life, as expressed in Brenner's stories and in many of his articles, is not only a cause of man's weakness and of defeat by destiny. It is also evidence of spiritual freedom, of greatness, of an undeterred aspiration to fashion his world and his life.[122]

To embrace the world unquestioningly, including despair and doubt, is not just one more theoretical position. Brenner understood that the idea of embracing life might be perceived as merely another theory, and his character therefore says:

> A fine theory?
> – *Yes, a theory if I were to tell it to others...if I were to try to persuade them of it, because then it would be just another hypothesis, and they could believe in it or not, accept or reject it, as they pleased. But when you come to it from your own experience, in a house on the outskirts of town – then it's no longer a theory but Life itself.*[123]

A theory, any theory, so Brenner assumes, has a hypothetical and contingent standing: it can be rejected or adopted; it is an option available to anyone interested. But the affirmation of life is anchored in experience, in the existentialist voyage that unfolds within life and reveals its affirmation as primary and unconditional. The affirmation of life, then, does not reflect a distant stand that turns life into a conscious object. Statements affirming life are a product of self-reflection, a report that individuals submit to themselves. The affirmation of life is a person's primary experience of existence.

The voyage to the depths of one's being shows that the hold on life precedes any decision, is forced upon us, concealed: 'the veiled, hidden power of life, which rules us against our will'.[124] Free will comes after the recognition of the primary datum, which is coerced upon us. It transcends the datum and also embraces it. The famous Brennerian formula, 'voluntarily-by force', reflects this connection between coercion and will. What is coerced is what we choose and want: 'For all of us, the end is extinction, our entire globe will end in extinction, and yet we live. We live and strive to make our lives better, as far as possible.'[125] This is the existentialist repetition and the moulding of harmony with the self: the hold on life is primary, coerced like all the data of life and even more so, since it is the basis for all the rest. The option of death, which we can choose, liberates us from givenness, but self-restoration is attained by returning to the coerced datum. The hold on life, which is initially coerced, is now an expression of voluntary reflection through which we affirm what we already are – living creatures who want to live. The affirmation of life or, more precisely, the recognition of its holiness is, in Megged's words, a position of 'distinct religiosity, though radically atheistic'.[126] Brennerian religiosity, then, does not refer to the transcendent beyond existence but to existence itself in all its contradictory and complex manifestations.

As usual, Baruch Kurzweil does not abandon the thesis presented at the start of the discussion. He wishes to read Brenner as the work of a man who has lost his way, lost his faith, and hence himself. In an essay that he wrote on *Breakdown and Bereavement*, Kurzweil writes that Brenner's position is:

> An anticipation of the existential[127] plight of modern man in general, who lives without faith. … This truth is known to all of Brenner's characters, as to all of Kafka's or Camus' characters…
> In *Breakdown and Bereavement*, reality is finally abandoned by God and leaves no room for a new positive faith – it ends in suicide.[128]

Even without entering into a discussion of Kurzweil's problematic assertions about man or about Camus,[129] the passages cited point out

Brenner's resolute and unconditional affirmation of life. Indeed, Brenner's claim is that only in a world liberated from ideas, including religious faith, can we discover the original datum – the affirmation of life, which is both coerced and chosen. The closing lines of *The Myth of Sisyphus* resemble many that Brenner wrote:

> But Sisyphus teaches the higher fidelity that negates the gods and raises rocks. He, too, concludes that all is well. This universe henceforth without a master seems to him neither sterile nor futile. Each atom of that stone, each mineral flake of that night-filled mountain, in itself forms a world. The struggle itself towards the heights is enough to fill a man's heart. One must imagine Sisyphus happy.[130]

The culmination of the absurd Sisyphean voyage is the unconditional affirmation of life. But Camus' affirmation of life, and also Nietzsche's, is accompanied by a deep sense of achievement – concretized in an experience of reconciliation and acceptance – Sisyphus happy.[131] Brenner is a partner to Camus in the affirmation of Promethean man or, in Keshet's formulation: 'Bound – he is free. Promethean Jew, "*aher*" [other].'[132] Brenner, however, is not a partner to the joy of the victory over immanence celebrated by Camus and Nietzsche.[133] At times, we do find in Brenner formulations close to Camus' position. Thus, for instance, Yehezkel Hefetz has an experience of this kind:

> On the threshold. Because ultimately nothing was permanent, nothing was assured. There were only thresholds, moments. Seize the day and enjoy it! There was no straight and narrow. There was only a twisting, turning path which was sometimes easy to travel and sometimes not. And all there was to know was the old wisdom: that it was happiness to be lost on this path, happiness to live life and to cherish it, both for its infinite pleasures and for all its rude surprises.[134]

The happiness that Brenner speaks of resembles the Sisyphean happiness that represents the complete acceptance of reality. At this moment of absolute acceptance, Yehezkel Hefetz can indeed break out in a prayer:

> My Father! Father of Light and of Life, blessed are they, selah! My Father, father of orphans, be good to me: send me a gift of your sunbeams, and I, an orphan among orphans, will gather them gratefully, hopefully, lovingly. I know now to cherish your

gifts, your goodness, selah. My heart will rejoice in you, yea, will be jubilant. O Father of Life, blessed art Thou, selah![135]

This prayer, even if addressing God, ultimately expresses the fullness of the self, the harmony that Yehezkel Hefetz experiences in his own existence. Moshe Yitzhaki pointed to the traditional Jewish sources of this prayer, and interpreted it as a 'spontaneous, existentialist prayer, a prayer seeking to introduce holiness into reality, into actual life'.[136] According to this interpretation, Yehezkel Hefetz's prayer is an outburst of religiosity translated into the language of tradition. It is almost tempting to state that this is a conversion resembling the metamorphosis of Ivan Ilyich, the hero of Tolstoy's story, when he is close to death.

Only at his final moments does Ivan Ilyich locate himself outside the realm of self-deceit and common lies. Ilyich's despair about existence allows the voice of the soul to rise: the negation of a lifestyle focused on the finite enables a glimmer of truth to surface and Ilyich gradually finds, in Tolstoy's words, 'the real direction',[137] harmony and peace – he 'caught sight of the light'.[138] The end of the story is the end of the process: religious truth is revealed.

The prayer of Yehezkel Hefetz does not mark such a moment. Hefetz does not undergo an absolute metamorphosis, and he does not replace existence with a conversion move. Quite the contrary. Glimmers of self-acceptance flicker in his threatened, dark, and desperate existence. They do not correct the existential chaos; rather, they accompany it. Hefetz's prayer rises together with the understanding that terror lurks at the gate of existence – 'there were no guarantees, none at all'.[139]

In a mood antithetical to the conversion of Ivan Ilyich, the prayer of Yehezkel Hefetz soberly contemplates an existence with only few moments of harmony in a continuum of rift and struggle. Life is an ongoing voyage, which does not move progressively towards a redemption found 'out there'. His prayer is existential and does not address the familiar God, even if his language is that of religious tradition. The linguistic utterance is carved from the reservoir of Yehezkel Hefetz's memory, which bears the memory of prayer. The gist of the prayer, however, is the self taking a stand in the world as an entity that accepts and endorses this world in all its manifestations. The prayer expresses a fullness, an outpouring that breaks its own borders.

Brenner does not assume a possibility of liberation from the sorrow of despair and the terror of death. We might attain peace with these experiences without negating life, but we cannot make them disappear. The affirmation of life is also an affirmation of the tragic and insoluble dimensions of human existence. This is the nature of the Brennerian hero who struggles against existence with existence. He does not renounce existence and, therefore, does not blur life's contradictory and painful facets. Even if one chooses what is coerced and even if this choice fills one's being, the rift and finitude of life and the sense of futility remain. These experiences are part of existence; they express its tragic character.[140] Brenner often emphasised this feature of life. In a personal note, he attests: 'I… I'm shattered to pieces, not one whole bone in me.'[141] He was the voice of 'tragic man, the man who has nothing in his world but a horrid scream, the man of the abyss, the man of the dim cellar'.[142] Yet, the source of this tragedy is life's fundamental contradiction. We are unequivocally caught in it, even if unable to disengage from its absurdity.[143]

This duality – the affirmation of life and the persistent despair – is transparently formulated by a Brennerian character who also ties together the personal and the national:

> What's here for me? Everything is finished, finished. There's no point to my life, no point. I am a dead man from the world of chaos afraid to return to his grave who, in the end, when forced to return, will regret not having gone back before, in due time, and having chosen instead the trials and tribulations. It is only that at this moment I don't wish to die, nor at this moment, nor at this moment – it is only this unwillingness that holds me back from tightening the rope. It is only this that continues my halting breath, it is only this, as they say, that keeps me alive.[144]

This passage from the story *Mi-Kan u-mi-Khan* is important because it presents the dominance of the negation of life and the yearning for death. And yet, it is within this yearning that the coerced hold on life, which becomes an object of desire, is revealed anew. This desire is reflected in the absolute affirmation of the past: 'All my past is in front of me, all my recent past… and a past not bad at all, an important past, long live psychology! No, really, I accept it willingly, my past, I do not regret anything in it, I'm sure that if I wasn't twenty-nine but nineteen, and if it depended on my desire to start everything anew – what?'[145]

This passage resembles Nietzsche's statements on eternal repetition.[146] According to Nietzsche, the supreme human test, which is suggested by a 'demon',[147] is in one's readiness to reaffirm his life, that is, to adopt his past, to be ready to relive his life and experience it without changing it. Nietzsche's eternal repetition is thus an absolute affirmation of immanent life without the longing to transcend it. The negation of life is the negation of the past and a turn to an undefined future horizon, the affirmation of 'what is not yet' and its preference over 'what has been'.

Brenner's position is different: despite the cited passage, the affirmation of life is not the acceptance of the past as it had been. Indeed, the Brennerian rebellion is precisely a rebellion against what was, in the past. Contrary to Nietzsche and Camus, Brenner does not endorse the thesis of the love of fate, of saying yes to the past and to destiny,[148] even if his characters do at times affirm the past. The unconditional affirmation of life means affirming human existence *per se*, including all that is negative in it. The affirmation is an affirmation of life, of the clinging to it, despite all that we discover in it.[149] The affirmation of the past means an affirmation of givenness or thrownness: we are not born from nothingness or into nothingness, we come from the past. Affirming the past, however, does not mean exalting it; affirming the past implies a sober recognition that we are constituted by the past and do not create ourselves: 'Yes, my past is dark and miserable and disgraceful, because it is mine, the past of a man like me; but to some extent, I am I because I have such a past, a past of trivialities, a dark, miserable, and disgraceful past.'[150]

Brenner's stance is thus dialectical, and includes the range of contradictions inherent in a complex attitude to existence, without allowing this complexity to affect our very grip on it.

The hold on life is not momentary nor, as Ewen claimed, merely a 'sudden sense, at times momentary and transient, which occasionally takes hold of this shaken figure and allows it to return to itself and to life, in the knowledge that life is man's only asset'.[151] The hold on life is primary, pre-theoretical, and constant, even if at times the yearning for death awakens more powerfully. It is precisely at such moments that the unconditional hold on life is revealed:

> This spark of light never dims in the soul of the Brennerian hero; even when powerful forces of destruction and extinction gain strength and his life tends to negation and nothingness, even then, they cannot prevail. Even at hard and terrible moments of breakdown and bereavement, even then, a smoking ember will flicker, will spread some light in the dying soul, and turn it toward life.[152]

Life is thus a dialectical voyage between the affirmation and the negation of life, and the voice of affirmation prevails. This affirmation neither does nor can ignore the negation, which is a permanent foundation that threatens to destroy life and sometimes imprisons us within our despair and within the loss of meaning. But it does not triumph, since we fight against it endlessly, out of the life force within us.

Kurzweil pointed out this unconditional affirmation of life and the closeness between this position and that of Camus:

> In this regard, in the reduction of the essence of life to the negation of all religious solutions or metaphysical consolations, in the acceptance of the absurd in life while renouncing what is beyond it, in this regard Brenner resembles Camus. For Camus or Sartre, however, by virtue of will, his free will, by virtue of his freedom, man fills his life with new meaning. He can, for instance, plan and make history! The perception of Brenner's characters appears more passive.[153]

Kurzweil's analysis is inaccurate concerning both Camus and Brenner. As I showed at length,[154] Camus presents a complex view. The absurd hero in *The Myth of Sisyphus* strives for the transparence embodied in absurd consciousness. He is not active in history or in any practical domain. Only in a later work – *The Rebel* – does absurd consciousness reach realization through action.

Kurzweil refers to the passage cited above – 'life was good not only because it could be filled with good deeds ...but in and of itself' – and sees it as a 'reduction of life that brings human existence closer to animal vegetative existence'.[155] But if my analysis of Brenner's affirmation of life is correct then, in this passage, Brenner formulates a view similar to that suggested by Camus. Moreover, Brenner also draws a practical conclusion from the experience of the absurd. In a world without metaphysical or religious meaning, the meaning and value assigned to life rest on human activity, whether individual or collective, as the following chapters will show.

Brenner's heroes do express a yearning for conscious transparence: 'I only want to be a whole person. To know the world and life, man and the self – is all this indeed unattainable without knowledge of algebra? I will read the good books – and I will find it.'[156] This approach, however, is merely part of a process of self-searching, which culminates in a practical conclusion such as that reached by Camus in *The Rebel*. For instance, in *Mi-Saviv la-Nekudah* [Around the Point], Abramson says: 'You learn from this that man clings to that hidden riddle, and even in all that evil, his soul finds some mysterious sweetness. Hence? Hence, we should not stand around life merely as observers. We must fight, amend, magnify, and exalt.'[157]

Like the rebel, Camus' later character, Brenner too proclaims that, given our unconditional affirmation of life, the proper human stance is to amend it and control it. The human gaze, released from metaphysical deceit, illusions, and big ideas, and having discovered its loneliness, turns to the surrounding reality. Man does not seek justice, truth, and meaning in distant ideas, but searches for an idea that grows from life itself.[158] The purpose of this idea is to direct us to the repair of life, the cognitive life within which we are coerced to remain. Yehezkel Hefetz turns away from the big ideas to the 'ordinary' reality within which he lives:

> Not that he need be afraid of paradoxes. Let it be both ways instead of just one! Let it be that because of his luck he still retained a bit of simple love for the lives of others.... And this love of life was redoubled and intensified further for those who were closest to him, for their trials and tribulations, for everything that was most immediate and concrete. It was not for him to worry about the World, Humanity, the Nation – no, *his* thoughts were for the members of his household alone, among whom he had come to live by pure chance. And he wasn't doing them any 'favors,' either...: it was simply that he overflowed with it, overflowed and was alive in every vein. It was something tangible – and he had use for what was tangible only.[159]

Turning away from abstract ideas means directing one's gaze to reciprocity. One who experiences 'being with the other', one who recognizes that his 'every vein' is sustained by concrete existence, turns away from the yearning for the transcendent, from the problem of the riddle of life to the toil of shaping it.

The recognition that life is doomed to be imperfect and disharmonious releases us from the longing for a utopia that strives to change reality completely, to re-create it. Some attention to the concept of utopia will be helpful in the understanding of Brenner's position.

Martin Buber defines utopia as 'something not actually present but only represented. The utopian picture is a picture of what "should be". What is at work here is the longing for that rightness.'[160] Implicit in this definition is an element essential to utopian thought, which Karl Manheim discusses at length. Manheim emphasises that utopia involves two opposite and complementary directions: first, it transcends the reality that served as the cradle of utopia. It rejects this reality and replaces it with another model of existence. In Buber's terms, utopia sets up 'what should be', contrary to what is. Second, utopian thought strives to return to reality in order to rebuild it. Manheim rightfully emphasises that transcendence *per se* is not utopia; transcendence becomes a constitutive element of utopia only if accompanied by a passion to redesign reality in light of the idea.[161]

Utopian thought imagines a perfect, harmonious world, the best of all possible worlds, the opposite of the real world that, naturally, is neither perfect nor harmonious. Since the utopian world is the most perfect, no room is left for alternatives – affirming an alternative would mean that the ideal world is not truly perfect.[162] The conclusion warranted by this analysis is that utopia establishes a static word view, leaving no room for change and amendment, which would attest to incompleteness and disharmony. In a utopian world, then, there is no room for development or progress.

This definition of utopia is clearly unsuited to Brenner. He rejects these utopian 'paintings of the imagination' and the dream.[163] Instead, he poses the challenge of a 'normal national life, in the sense of the economic-political unity' in which 'the whole nation must... take part to repair its plight'.[164] Brenner opposes the revolutionary component of utopia: 'If it depended on us, we would perhaps hamper every revolution, although we do see the destruction in the unspoiled "order".'[165] This rejection of absolute change is based on a mistrust of any building inspired by this idea. In Brenner's terms: 'We will not believe in its constructive dimensions.'[166] Brenner appears extremely sceptical of amendments based on radical moves detached from reality, and he writes: 'But how can we expect pure from impure? How freedom from slavery? How kindness and generosity from violence and cruelty?'[167]

Brenner targets here the weakness of utopian thought. Believers in utopia are convinced that the mended world that they imagine is the only valuable and meaningful one. This belief inevitably leads them to activate direct or indirect mechanisms of coercion and violence so as to lead individuals or societies to the 'light' of the utopian world.[168] History indeed shows that big ideas of reform have more than once culminated in appalling bloodshed – what began as a struggle against evil through an idea of a perfect world resulted in a worse one.[169]

As a sober and unenthusiastic observer of the Communist revolution, Brenner fears that 'in the chaos of the revolution, all the right, holy principles could become a cover for the arrogance of reckless adventurers to do evil and release their basest instincts'.[170]

This rejection of utopia merges seamlessly with an existentialist-realistic perspective. We live a specific existence, at a specific time and place, and absolute transcendence from thrownness, from factual givenness, results in an abstract and alienated life.[171]

Yosef Gorny considers Brenner's attitude to utopia.[172] In his view, Brenner presents a position of utopian realism or realistic utopia. This kind of utopia does not intend to invent something new; it is not an absolute transcendence of current reality but the transcendence of a given state of affairs in favour of better alternatives, which are revealed in reality as trends or currents that have not yet matured. A realistic utopia is a reshaping of reality, not a new creation *ex-nihilo*. The very use of the term, however, does not necessarily denote an internalization of utopian thought, and Brenner directs individuals to their real, finite, and limited lives, which they should amend as best they can:

> The whole world? Not really. It was too much to ask of a man to change the whole world. At any rate, it was a task best left to those universal souls who were on familiar terms with the Whole of Life. He, who knew nothing about the whole, who was only a part himself sitting in his corner, would grope in that corner as best he could, would do what he could in it, wherever and however he could do it.[173]

> Logic teaches man to explain everything according to the laws of nature, you understand? To take care of improving this world, to change its conditions, the conditions of the society, on which everything depends.[174]

Life will remain imperfect, entrusted to people toiling in Sisyphean ways to repair it. In a deep tone of religiosity, Brenner writes: 'We must sacrifice our souls and diminish evil in the world. The evil of hunger, slavery, scorn, hypocrisy, and so forth. We must understand everything, understand and keep away from mysticism and from fantasies; we must expand reality and holiness in the world .... Is there repair?'[175]

Like non-utopian thinkers, Brenner does not begin with an idea of the good but with the reality of suffering and evil. Distress can impel action, and we do not need an idea of the perfect good in order to repair reality.[176] Brenner demands adherence to reality and to actual experience, together with a critical consciousness constantly keeping away from mysticism and from fantasies. We must focus our gaze ceaselessly on the surrounding reality and work at its improvement. We will thereby expand holiness. This is the nature of holiness – the constant transcendence of reality as is. This transcendence, however, is not concretized in the liberation from the yoke of reality but in its very rootedness in reality itself. The contradiction between the expansion of reality and the expansion of holiness shapes a fruitful tension in the Jewish notion of *tikkun olam*, repairing the world, which remains impervious to the seduction of utopia.[177]

But Brenner knows well that the Sisyphean task of repair may prove disheartening, and often lead to questions as to whether repair is indeed possible. Failure, despair, and disappointment are built into human existence. Given that we do not live in the 'best of all possible worlds' and given that a perfect world is unattainable, contending with existence and its improvement means entering a battlefield where every victory is necessarily uneven and fragmentary.

Does this turning to the individual's concrete life and to the individual's relations with the other involve religious dimensions? Appelfeld maintains that this experience includes manifestations of negative religiosity:

> Since I do not find God neither within me nor outside me, and since I cannot bear this anarchy known as chance and accept it with equanimity, I consider myself responsible and assume with love the virtues once ascribed to the Creator. I am compassionate, I love. For as long as I live, I will go on being compassionate. This raw formulation does not appear in Brenner. He might even find such a formulation outrageous, but to me it seems that every single letter in him speaks in this language.[178]

Appelfeld's formulation, as he notes, is indeed not found in Brenner. Yehezkel Hefetz, the hero of *Breakdown and Bereavement*, speaks in the language of compassion. But the fundamental question is whether this is a kind of negative religiosity, where the individual who despairs about God takes God's place? Camus in *The Rebel* offers an approach where repair assumes metaphysical significance. Striving for human justice replaces the principle of divine justice that failed. Camus therefore emphasises that the basis of rebellion is a 'disenchanted religious experience'.[179] No longer able to understand the justice of the world, and failing to find a god that acts to repair evil and iniquity, human beings understand that responsibility lies squarely on their shoulders. They understand that they must find 'a new god'.[180] The rebellion is therefore an attempt to change the foundations of creation and reality: 'Metaphysical rebellion is the movement by which man protests against his condition and against the whole of creation. It is metaphysical because it contests the ends of man and of creation.... The metaphysical rebel declares that he is frustrated by the universe.'[181]

Camus, however, also offered another, entirely different perception of interpersonal relations, particularly in *The Plague*. The plague, like illness in general, is an opportunity to show compassion.[182] Illness sets a test to the healthy person, who can turn to the sick, share in their pain and console them, but can also turn away and ignore them. This turning away covers a wide range of actions, from failing to extend help up to an attempt to justify their illness in theological terms.

Brenner identifies human distress and maintains that the theological solution is unthinkable as a response to it, but not because of expectations from a god that failed. God is already dead and irrelevant to existential questions. The Brennerian starting point is the immanence of human existence. We are not on the border of immanence, as one who lives within it and seeks the shadow of a transcendence that has vanished beyond the horizon. We live within it, in this 'existence of thorns',[183] because this is the total and only existence, even if our passion and our questions represent self-transcendence. Hence, we turn to what is within reality – people. Brennerian compassion is not an alternative to divine justice; it is a primary phenomenon of a human existence aware of its borders. Through this awareness, we become conscious that human repair is incomplete, it is human and therefore limited – 'would grope in that corner as best he could, would do what he could in it, wherever and however he could do it'.

Brenner understands that this ethics of repair is fragmentary and ongoing. The ethics of fragmentary action neither strives for nor is driven by the desire to realize some utopian or metaphysical idea. It seeks to cope with the distress that poses the basic demand, out of loyalty to it.

Much before Camus, Brenner presented an ethic that can be described as an ethic of compassion.[184] It does not replace God; its starting point is the human creature, not as an alternative but as an entity concerned with human existence in all its painful and joyful manifestations. This ethic does not replace ideologies or metaphysics that have collapsed. It reflects a kind of existence responsive to the finitude of human life, to the unconditional will to live, and to life's inherent pain and sorrow. This ethic compels the ceaseless Sisyphean action of repairing and improving reality.

With exquisite sensitivity, Brenner discerned the uniqueness of compassion, and the danger of arrogance that lurks in pseudo-compassionate attitudes. In *Misaviv la-Nekudah*, Abramson states: 'Since he had come to live in these poor quarters, Abramson began relating to everyone closely and tenderly, himself unaware of how much this closeness was compassion and identification with the sorrow of the heavy burden borne by these people, and how much – scorn and condescension for all their concerns and values.'[185] Compassion is indeed identification with the other's pain.[186] But this identification can overwhelm the other, fail to respect the honour and the world of the other. Compassion for the other can easily blur the other, when we find in others our own pain rather than theirs.[187] Brenner is sensitive to this matter, and his characters express this sensitivity precisely through the critical reflection that ensures the necessary distance between self and other. This distance, which reflects recognition of the other's otherness, is the very foundation of compassion and of the formulation of an ethic of compassion concerned with the repair of life.

Gorny, who pointed out the closeness between Camus and Brenner, also noted the differences between them:

> Paradoxically, the imperative of work and the imperative of work for the collective turn absurd existence into a foundation of Brenner's socialism. Like Albert Camus' characters, who fought death in *The Plague* without looking up to a godless heaven and despite knowing that the 'plague' could not be absolutely eradicated, Brenner fought the danger of extinction threatening his people although he knew that no absolute redemption would be available. But we must remember that the problem that troubled Camus was the individual's moral decision in a society under siege, whereas Brenner faced the question of the individual's moral choice in a nation that faced failure…
>
> Man's existence [in existentialist tradition] comes to the fore in action. Action – faced with death and despite its certainty – is what distinguishes man from other creatures and objects in the universe and what inspires his existence. In Brenner, however, the concept of action was replaced by the concept of work. Action could be interpreted as an unspecified act, subjective and spontaneous, whereas work is for him a term imbued with conceptual, constructive, and national-social meaning… The demand of work, then, is the reverse of despair or its dialectical development. Out of the dread of extinction, Brenner holds on to it as if to save his life.[188]

These interfaces between Brenner and Camus reaffirm the basic insights of the present book: Brenner begins from an existentialist starting point. The foundation of Brenner, of the man and of his work, is the existentialist voyage of the individual confronting the questions of real life, including the questions of his existence as a Jew, an issue that will be at the focus of the chapters that follow.

Notes

1   Søren Kierkegaard, *The Point of View for My Work as an Author*, trans. Walter Lowrie (New York: Harper and Row, 1962), 70–71.

2   *Søren Kierkegaard's Journals and Papers*, trans. and ed. Howard V. Hong and Edna H. Hong (Bloomington, IN: Indiana University Press, 1967), § 5383.

3   Søren Kierkegaard, *Repetition*, trans. and ed. Howard V. Hong and Edna H. Hong (Princeton: Princeton University Press, 1983), 200.

4   Jean-Paul Sartre, *Nausea*, trans. Lloyd Alexander (Norfolk, CT: New Directions, 1959), 171.

5   *Ibid.*, 174.

6   Albert Camus, *The Myth of Sisyphus*, trans. Justin O'Brien (Harmondsworth, England: Penguin Books, 1975), 26.

7   Albert Camus, *The First Man*, trans. David Hapgood (New York: Random House, 1996), 26–7.

8   Yitzhak Bakon, *Brenner in London: The Me'orer Period – 1905–1907* (in Hebrew) (Beer Sheva: Ben-Gurion University, 2000), 97–8.

9   *Writings*, vol.1, 605–98.

10 Note that Brenner mentions Kierkegaard once (*Writings*, vol.3, 583), but he obviously could not have been familiar with Kierkegaard's literary works, which had not been translated from Danish at the time. Brenner, therefore, knew of Kierkegaard by proxy (apparently through the works of Georg Brandes), making the similarity between them even more significant.

11 *Writings*, vol.3, 247.

12 Martin Heidegger, *Being and Time*, trans. John Macquarrie and Edward Robinson (New York: Harper and Row, 1962), 231.

13 R. D. Laing, *The Divided Self: An Existential Study in Sanity and Madness* (New York: Pantheon Books, 1960), 44–66.

14 Rollo May, *The Discovery of Being: Writings in Existential Psychology* (New York: Norton, 1983), 110.

15 Yosef Haim Brenner, *Breakdown and Bereavement*, trans. Hillel Halkin (Philadelphia: Jewish Publication Society of America, 1971), 16, 257.

16 *Writings*, vol.3, 165.

17 *Ibid.*, vol.2, 1233.

18 Heidegger, *Being and Time*, 321.

19 *Ibid.*, 173.

20 *Writings*, vol.2, 1353–4.

21 *Ibid.*, vol.1, 46.

22 Brenner, *Collected Writings*, vol.3, 210. See also 217.

23 *Writings*, vol.4, 1315–16.

24 On the connection between Hume and Nietzsche, see, for instance, Friedrich Nietzsche, *The Will to Power*, trans. Walter Kaufman (New York: Vintage, 1968), 63–4, 294–5.

25 Friedrich Nietzsche, *The Gay Science*, trans. Josefine Nauckoff (Cambridge: Cambridge University Press, 2001), 214 (emphasis in original).

26 See Aaron Ben-Or (Orinovsky), *The History of Modern Hebrew Literature* (in Hebrew), vol.2 (Tel Aviv: Izre'el: 1959), 416.

27 *Writings*, vol.3, 538.

28 On borderline situations in Jaspers, see Hanoch Tennen, *The Conception of an Existential Ethics in Karl Jaspers' Philosophy* (in Hebrew) (Ramat-Gan: Massada, 1977), 123–5; Ronny Miron, *Karl Jaspers: From Selfhood to Being* (Atlanta, GA: New York: Rodopi [in press]).

29   On the connection between Brenner and Zeitlin, see Jonatan Meir, 'Hasidism in
      the World to Come: Neo-Romanticism, Hasidism, and Messianic Longings in the
      Writings of Hillel Zeitlin' (in Hebrew), introduction to *Rabbi Nachman of Bratslav:
      His Life and Work*, by Hillel Zeitlin, *Yeri'ot: Essays and Papers in Jewish Studies Bearing
      on the Humanities and the Social Sciences*, 5 (2006), 17–18; Jonatan Meir, 'Longing
      of Souls for the *Shekhinah*: Relations between Rabbi Kook, Zeitlin, and Brenner'
      (in Hebrew), in *The Path of the Spirit: The Eliezer Schweid Jubilee Volume*, vol.2, ed.
      Yehoyada Amir (Jerusalem: Hebrew University of Jerusalem, 2005), 795–9; Yosef
      Haim Brenner, *The Yiddish Writings* (in Hebrew and Yiddish), ed. Yitzhak Bakon
      (Beer-Sheva: Ben-Gurion University, 1985), 277–84.

30   Brenner, *Collected Writings*, vol.3, 283.

31   *Writings*, vol.3, 95. The references are to works by his contemporaries: '*Ha-
      Mahshavah ve-ha-Kinor*' [The Thought and the Violin] by Y. L. Peretz; '*Me-ever
      la-Nahar*' [Across the River] by Micha Yosef Berdyczewski; '*Be-emek ha-bakhah*' [In
      the Vale of Tears] by Mendele Mocher Sefarim, and '*Masa Nemirov*' [The Journey
      to Nemirov] by Hayyim Nahman Bialik.

32   *Ibid.*, 145.

33   On this question, see Iris Parush, *National Ideology and Literary Canon* (in Hebrew)
      (Jerusalem: Bialik Institute, 1992), 141.

34   See S. Y Penueli, *Brenner and Gnessin in Early Twentieth Century Hebrew Fiction* (in
      Hebrew) (Tel Aviv: Students' Association at Tel Aviv University, 1965), 56.

35   *Writings*, vol.3, 220–1.

36   See Abraham Yitzhak Hacohen Kook, *Orot ha-Rehaya* (in Hebrew) (Jerusalem:
      Mosad Harav Kook, 1970), 69.

37   Zeitlin, *Rabbi Nachman of Bratslav*, 44.

38   *Ibid.*, 49.

39   For an analysis of this issue in Jaspers' thought, see Miron, *Karl Jaspers*, Part 3.

40   On this question, see also Alan M. Olson and Leroy S. Rouner, eds. *Transcendence
      and the Sacred* (Notre Dame, IN: University of Notre Dame Press, 1981), especially
      Part 3.

41   *Writings*, vol.3, 178–9.

42   *Ibid.*, 247.

43   For an analysis of the concept of wonder, see Ephraim Shmueli, *Wondering and
      Thinking in a Techno-Scientific World* (in Hebrew) (Jerusalem: Bialik Institute,
      1985), 15–33. See also Bernard Jacques Boelen, *Existential Thinking: A Philosophical
      Orientation* (New York: Herder and Herder, 1971), 37–70.

44   Shmueli, *Wondering and Thinking*, 17.

45   For further discussion of religiosity in Brenner's outlook, see Parush, *National
      Ideology and Literary Canon*, 323–6.

46   *Writings*, vol.4, 1164–5.

47   Brenner, *The Yiddish Writings*, 203–16.

48   *Ibid.*, 202–203.

49   *Ibid.*, 208.

50   *Ibid.*, 209.

51   *Ibid.*

52 *Ibid.*, 212–13.

53 *Ibid.*, 209–10.

54 Penueli, *Brenner and Gnessin*, 37.

55 *Writings*, vol.4, 1164–5.

56 *Ibid.*, 1548.

57 *Ibid.*, 1166.

58 *Writings*, vol.1, 155. See also Abraham Shinan, *Trends in Modern Hebrew Literature* (in Hebrew), vol.4 (Ramat-Gan: Massada, 1967), 208.

59 *Writings*, vol.3, 97. Brenner uses the term *pardes* [literally orchard, referring to paradise] in an allusion to the Talmudic passage: 'Four entered the *pardes*' (BT Hagigah 14b). This passage is a classic text in Jewish mystical tradition.

60 Aharon Appelfeld, *First Person Essays* (in Hebrew) (Jerusalem: WZO, 1979), 69–70.

61 *Writings*, vol.3, 178.

62 *Ibid.*, 375.

63 *Ibid.*, 371.

64 See, for instance, *ibid.* 401–402, 489, 491.

65 *Ibid.*, vol.2, 1514.

66 See, for instance, Paul Tillich, *Dynamics of Faith* (New York: Harper and Row, 1957), 1–12; *idem, What is Religion?* (New York: Harper, 1973), 75–8.

67 See, for instance, *Writings*, vol.3, 379, 491.

68 The letter is quoted in Nurit Govrin, *From Horizon to Horizon: The Life and Work of G. Shofman* (in Hebrew), vol.2 (Tel Aviv: Tel Aviv University and Yahdav, 1982), 517.

69 *Writings*, vol.2, 1362.

70 *Ibid.*

71 *Ibid.*, 1361

72 Note that Aharon Avraham Kabak also draws a distinction between religion as an institution and religiosity as an experience. Kabak's religiosity turns to the transcendent, but is not embodied in institutional religion. See, for instance, *Between the Sea and the Desert* (in Hebrew), vol.1 (Tel Aviv: Shtibel, 1933), 211.

73 David Aryeh Friedman, 'Bereaved' (in Hebrew), *Ha-Tekufah*, 10 (1921), 475.

74 For a detailed analysis of this question, see Boaz Arpali, *The Negative Principle: Ideology and Poetics in Two Stories by Y. H. Brenner* (in Hebrew) (Tel Aviv: Hakibbutz Hameuchad, 1992), 41–3.

75 *Writings*, vol.3, 534.

76 See Penueli, *Brenner and Gnessin*, 125–6._

77 Franz Rosenzweig, *The Star of Redemption*, trans. William W. Hallo (Boston: Beacon Press, 1964), 3.

78 Plato, *Great Dialogues*, trans. W. H. D. Rouse (New York: New American Library, 1956), p.435.

79 *Ibid.*, 445.

80 Heidegger, *Being and Time*, 289.

81 *Ibid.*, 290.

82 *Ibid.*, 308, and also 232–3.

83   *Ibid.*, 231.

84   *Writings*, vol.2, 1350.

85   *Writings*, vol.1, 155.

86   *Ibid.*, vol.3, 369.

87   *Ibid.*, 370.

88   Nietzsche, *The Gay Science*, 119.

89   Brenner, *Breakdown and Bereavement*, 251–2 (emphasis in the original).

90   *Writings*, vol.3, 370.

91   Brenner, *Collected Writings*, vol.3, 438.

92   Nietzsche, *The Gay Science*, 119–20.

93   *Writings*, vol.3, 371.

94   Frederich Nietzsche, *Twilight of the Idols and the Anti-Christ*, trans. R. J. Hollingdale (Harmondsworth, Middlesex: Penguin Books, 1968), 54.

95   Nietzsche, *The Gay Science*, 199.

96   *Writings*, vol.4, 1075.

97   See *Writings*, vol.1, 156.

98   Matti Megged, 'The Tragic "Self" as Reality and as Ideal' (in Hebrew), in *Yosef Haim Brenner: A Selection of Critical Essays on his Literary Prose*, ed. Yitzhak Bakon (Tel Aviv: Am Oved, 1972), 188.

99   Hamutal Bar-Yosef notes that this option became increasingly dominant in the works that Brenner wrote in Eretz Israel. See Hamutal Bar-Yosef, *Decadent Trends in Hebrew Literature: Bialik, Berdyczewski, Brenner* (in Hebrew) (Beer Sheva: Ben-Gurion University, 1997), 365–8.

100 *Writings*, vol.1, 182.

101 *Ibid.*, 262. See also Menachem Poznansky, 'Y. H. Brenner: An Exchange of Letters' (in Hebrew), *Mi-Bifnim*, 29, 1–2 (1967), 88; Yeshurun Keshet (Yaakov Koplewitz), 'On Y. H. Brenner: A Profile' (in Hebrew), *Anthology of Literature, Criticism, and Thought*, 3 (1963), 151.

102 Camus, *The Myth of Sisyphus*, 11.

103 Arpali, *The Negative Principle*, 46–50; *idem*, 'Asymmetrical Contrasts – Between the Truth of Death and a Life of Falsehood: Ideological, Existential, and Psychological Crossroads in Y. H. Brenner's *Misaviv la-Nekudah*' (in Hebrew), *Sadan: Studies in Hebrew Literature at the Outset of the Twentieth Century*, 4 (2000): 211–65.

104 *Writings*, vol.2, 1224–5.

105 See also Yitzhak Bakon, *The Lonely Young Man in Hebrew Literature 1899–1908* (in Hebrew) (Tel Aviv: Tel Aviv University, 1978), 78.

106 *Writings*, vol.1, 182.

107 *Ibid.*, 135.

108 *Ibid.*, vol.4, 1048. See also Samuel Schneider, *The Traditional Jewish World in the Writings of Joseph Haim Brenner* (in Hebrew) (Tel Aviv: Reshafim, 1994), 30–1, note 13.

109 *Writings*, vol.3, 140. See also *ibid.*, 595–6.

110 On the term 'mood', and on the mood of despair, see Avi Sagi, *Kierkegaard, Religion, and Existence: The Voyage to the Self*, trans. Batya Stein (Amsterdam-Atlanta, GA: Rodopi, 2000), 32–4.

111 *Writings*, vol.1, 450.

112 Megged, 'The Tragic "Self"', 191–2.

113 Josef Ewen, *Y. H. Brenner's Craft of Fiction* (in Hebrew) (Jerusalem: Bialik Institute, 1977), 21.

114 *Midrash Rabbah, Genesis*, IX:5 (London and New York: Soncino, 1983), 66.

115 Brenner, *Breakdown and Bereavement*, 146–7. Ewen notes that, in this story too, the character that commits suicide is Miriam, who is not a central figure. The central figure 'struggled throughout its life for a reason to exist and against the seduction of death' (Ewen, *Brenner's Craft of Fiction*, 21, note 89).

116 Heidegger, *Being and Time*, 233. See also Avi Sagi, *Albert Camus and the Philosophy of the Absurd*, trans. Batya Stein (Amsterdam-New York: Rodopi, 2002), ch.1.

117 Gila Ramraz-Rauch, *Y. H. Brenner and Modern Literature* (in Hebrew) (Tel Aviv: Aked, 1970), 53.

118 *Ibid.*

119 Matti Megged, 'Y. H. Brenner: Two Episodes' (in Hebrew), *Anaf: An Anthology of Young Writers* (Jerusalem: Schocken, 1964), 65.

120 *Writings*, vol.3, 158.

121 *Ibid.*

122 Megged, 'Two Episodes', 61–2.

123 Brenner, *Breakdown and Bereavement*, 147 (emphasis in original).

124 *Writings*, vol.2, 1234.

125 *Ibid.*, 1433.

126 Megged, 'Two Episodes', 71.

127 The use of this term by someone who claimed that Brenner is not part of existentialist tradition is worth noting.

128 Baruch Kurzweil, 'Breakdown and Bereavement: The Last Stop of an Absurd Jewish Existence' (in Hebrew), in Y. H. Brenner, *Breakdown and Bereavement, with an Essay by Baruch Kurzweil* (Tel Aviv: Am Oved, 1972), 266.

129 In my book on Camus, I show how groundless Kurzweil's assertions indeed are.

130 Camus, *The Myth of Sisyphus*, 111.

131 For further analysis, see Sagi, *Albert Camus*, 79–85.

132 Keshet, *A Profile*, 174. The term '*aher*' that Keshet uses alludes to Elisha ben Avuya, who is called '*aher*' in Talmudic sources and denotes the stranger, the different other.

133 But see, Ada Tzemah, *A Movement at the Spot: Y. H. Brenner and His Novels* (in Hebrew) (Tel Aviv: Hakibbutz Hameuchad, 1984), 109–22.

134 Brenner, *Breakdown and Bereavement*, 299.

135 *Ibid.*, 300.

136 See Moshe Yitzhaki, 'From Apostasy to Prayer: Religious Elements in *Breakdown and Bereavement* by Y. H. Brenner' (in Hebrew), *Alei Siah*, 55 (2006), 31. For further discussion of the prayer motif in Brenner, see Yariv Ben-Aharon, 'The Roots of Prayer in Y. H. Brenner' (in Hebrew), *Amudim*, 429 (September 1981): 336–40.

137 Leo Tolstoy, *The Death of Ivan Ilyich*, trans. Aylmer Maude, in *Classics of Modern Fiction*, ed. Irving Howe (New York: Harcourt, Brace, Jovanovich, 1980), 174.

138 *Ibid.*

139 Brenner, *Breakdown and Bereavement*, 300.

140   See also Matti Megged, 'The Tragic "Self"', 192–3, and Menachem Brinker, 'Epilogue', in *Breakdown and Bereavement* (in Hebrew) (Tel Aviv: Hakibbutz Hameuchad, 2006), 252.

141 Brenner, *Collected Writings*, vol.3, 221.

142 *Writings*, vol.3, 139.

143 See also Yeshurun Keshet (Yaakov Koplewitz), *In Brenner's Generation* (in Hebrew) (Jerusalem: Bialik Institute,. 1943), 268–9.

144 *Writings*, vol.2, 1318.

145 *Ibid.*, 1270–71.

146 See also Sagi, *Albert Camus*, 83–4.

147 See Nietzsche, *The Gay Science*, 195.

148 *Ibid.*, 157; Camus, *The Myth of Sisyphus*, 104.

149 Ramraz-Rauch, *Y. H. Brenner and Modern Literature*, 15–16.

150 *Writings*, vol.1, 155.

151 Ewen, *Craft of Fiction*, 22. His claim relates to the story *Ba-Horef* [In Winter].

152 Tzemah, *A Movement at the Spot*, 112.

153 Kurzweil, 'The Last Stop', 269–70.

154 Sagi, *Albert Camus*, 159–72.

155 Kurzweil, 'The Last Stop', 270.

156 *Writings*, vol.1, 165.

157 *Ibid.*, 450.

158 See *ibid.*, vol.4, 1493.

159 Brenner, *Breakdown and Bereavement*, 144–5 (emphasis in original).

160 Martin Buber, *Paths in Utopia*, trans. R. F. C. Hull (New York: Macmillan, 1958), 7.

161 Karl Mannheim, *Ideology and Utopia* (Routledge and Kegan Paul, 1979), 173–6.

162 See also Frances Theresa Russell, *Touring Utopia: The Realm of Constructive Humanism* (New York: Dial Press, 1932); Shyli Karin-Frank, *Utopia Reconsidered* (in Hebrew) (Tel Aviv: Hakibbutz Hameuchad, 1986), 40.

163 See *Writings*, vol.4, 1676–8.

164 *Ibid.*, 1676.

165 *Ibid.*, 1709.

166 *Ibid.*

167 *Ibid.*, 1710.

168 Karl R. Popper, *The Open Society and Its Enemies*, vol.1 (London: Routledge and Kegan Paul, 1974), 159–61.

169 Albert Camus analyses this issue at length in *The Rebel: An Essay on Man in Revolt*, trans. Anthony Bower (London: H. Hamilton, 1953). See also J. L. Talmon, *The Origins of Totalitarian Democracy* (London: Secker and Warburg, 1952).

170 *Writings*, vol.4, 1710.

171 Unsurprisingly, then, Brenner rejects Marxism, since basic questions of existence cannot be solved by a theory, and certainly not by Marxist theory. See *Writings*, vol.1, 778.

172 Yosef Gorny, 'There is no Messiah: To Work!' (in Hebrew), *Notebooks for the Study*

of the Work and Endeavor of Y. H. Brenner, vol. 2 (Tel Aviv: Tel Aviv University and Workers' Federation, 1977), 37–45; *idem*, 'Hope in Anguish: On the Zionist Views of Y. H. Brenner' (in Hebrew), *Assufoth: A Publication Devoted to the Study of the Jewish Labor Movement*, 2 (1971): 5–30.

173 Brenner, *Breakdown and Bereavement*, 256.

174 *Writings*, vol.1, 335.

175 *Writings*, vol.3, 222.

176 On this idea, see Avi Sagi, *Jewish Religion after Theology*, trans. Batya Stein (Boston: Academic Studies Press, 2009), ch.7. For an extensive development of this idea, see Adi Ophir, *The Order of Evils: Toward an Ontology of Morals*, trans. Rela Mazali and Havi Karel (New York: Zone Books, 2005).

177 For a different interpretation of the relationship between reality and holiness, see Matti Megged, 'Reality and Holiness' (in Hebrew), *On Poetry and Prose: Studies in Hebrew Literature*, ed. Zvi Malachi (Tel Aviv: Tel Aviv University, 1977), 111–32.

178 Appelfeld, *First Person Essays*, 71–2.

179 Camus, *The Rebel*, 101.

180 *Ibid.*

181 *Ibid.*, 23.

182 Albert Camus, *The Plague*, trans. Stuart Gilbert (Harmondsworth, Essex: Penguin Books, 1960), 6.

183 *Writings*, vol.2, 1440. The allusion is to Jesus' crown of thorns.

184 On this ethic, see Sagi, *Albert Camus*, 103–106, 159–72.

185 *Writings*, vol.1, 435–6, 488.

186 See Sagi, *Albert Camus*, 159–72.

187 A sensitive description of the dialectics of compassion appears in Stefan Zweig, *Beware of Pity*, trans. Phyllis and Trevor Blewitt (Harmondsworth, Middlesex: Penguin Books, 1982).

188 Gorny, 'There is no Messiah', 22–3. On Brenner's attitude towards work, see also Yosef Lichtenbaum, *Yosef Haim Brenner: His Life and Work* (Tel Aviv: Niv, 1967), 156.

FIVE

The Personal and the Jewish Dimensions

The existentialist perspective, which focuses on the personal voyage and on the personal stand of the individual in the world, is devoid of metaphysical meaning and significance. The individual as individual, however, is not an abstract figure but a concrete entity, living in specific circumstances and conditions – a Jew. Since existentialist ontology rests on the conception that people decide on the two constitutive poles of their existence – givenness and possibility – the decision can lead to the affirmation or negation of the givenness.

If an individual views Jewish existence as part of the existential thrownness that cannot be escaped, the existentialist voyage cannot ignore this facticity. Existentially, the decision to be a Jew is based on the adoption of givenness, on the recognition that negating Jewish givenness implies self-alienation. People are also, and perhaps above all, what they already are; they do not create themselves *ex-nihilo*. Jews are Jews not because Judaism is an abstract idea worth choosing, but because their Jewishness is a basic datum of their factual existence, similar to other factual data that is imposed on people. Yehuda Amichai expressed this insight in his poem 'All the Generations Before Me':

> All the generations that preceded me contributed me
> In small amounts, so that I would be erected here in Jerusalem
> All at once, like a house of prayer or a charity institution.
> That commits one. My name is the name of my contributors.
> That commits one.[1]

The self is 'all the generations before me'. These generations are not an addition to the nucleus of a self that exists without them. The self is cast and created from genealogical history, which creates the Jew's initial, involuntary commitment. Brenner formulates one expression of this mood, with all its implications:

> We feel ourselves Jews, children of Abraham, Isaac, and Jacob,
> children of Moses and the judges, children of the prophets
> and the Hasmoneans, children of the scribes and the tannaites,
> children of the *geonim* and of the Spanish poets, and so forth.
> We feel ourselves Jews, our existence and our personalities

inconceivable in any way without us being Jews until the last moment of our lives.[2]

And I say: I, at any rate, want to and must live as a Jew.[3]

Brenner outlines here the complex character of givenness: Jewish existence is coerced, and is the constitutive element of the concrete personality. Judaism is not an additional layer to the self, which can be shed. Judaism is an initial basic fact in existence. The horizons of this givenness, however, transcend the present wherein individuals find themselves, and include the association with the past.

The statement 'our existence and our personalities inconceivable… without us being Jews until the last moment of our lives' is an imposed fact, but the text does not suggest alienation from this fact. Rather, it is a celebratory declaration about the adoption of this givenness, concretized in a turn to the history of this givenness. The genealogy of past Jewish existence is located in the text not only as an imposed fact but also, and perhaps mainly, as a part of endorsing givenness. That is, since Jewish existence is endorsed, not only are its synchronic aspects affirmed but so are its diachronic depth aspects. The affirmation of Judaism is thus not only an affirmation of present Jewish existence but also of the past one. Brenner, then, fully exploits the existentialist insight whereby the adoption of givenness is not only the adoption of its top layer, the stratum of present life. An authentic existence implies adopting the historical horizons within which individuals find themselves, since a person's life is historical, not in the sense that people live and act in history but also in the sense that their very existence is constituted by history.[4]

The meaning of adopting the historical-diachronic aspect is not manifest in the affirmation of genealogy but in the affirmation of historical-cultural ideas.[5] Adopting the view that a Jew in the present is a descendant of the patriarchs, the judges, and the prophets is, above all, an acknowledgement of the facticity of these generations rather than of the validity of their ideas. Adopting this broad context leads to the affirmation of action and to the demand to restore Jewish existence in the Land of Israel. It is not the place – the Land of Israel – that will create the new Jewish person. It is the Jew who will create himself anew[6] and, through this creation, will re-create the place and attain liberation from personal existential exile. Brenner then proceeds to claim: 'We also know that as long as our Jewish nation is dispersed in exile, as long as our nation lacks a living flourishing settlement in the land of our forefathers – in the Land of Israel – there is no (hope that our lives will be complete) hope of rescue from all these.'[7] Zionism, then, is not an ideological position, and affirming it does not imply recognition of its general value.

Rather, Zionism derives from the actual fact of being Jewish; it is the deep expression of the individual's concrete identity rather than a theory or an ideology.[8] Bakon, who presented and analysed this text, summarized Brenner's view as follows: 'We are Jews, hence we are national-Zionists, hence we are Land of Israel Zionists.'[9]

This affirmation of Jewish givenness as part of thrownness is, nevertheless, not free of dialectics and contradiction, because one basic existentialist question is: what is the datum? The identification of the datum depends on the individual's decision. One might see Jewish facticity as part of an imposed datum, but a datum from which one can – and perhaps even should – be easily liberated. This is a fundamental existentialist paradox. This philosophy, which locates human existence between givenness and possibility, presumes to rescue givenness from its dependence on cognition. But although givenness purports to be transparent and unconditioned, this is not the case: the recognition of thrownness as a fundamental construct of human existence does not necessarily lead to a recognition of every situation in which human beings find themselves as part of thrownness. Determining that a particular fact is part of thrownness requires an initial judgment, which precedes the question of whether this facticity should be abandoned. Just as the subject is an active entity whose intentional act constitutes a world of objects, so does the subject's intentional activity constitute the 'facts' included in givenness. Hence, stating that the fact of Judaism is also part of givenness includes, at least implicitly, an act of judgment.

This phenomenon explains Brenner's fluctuations on this very point. Yirmiyahu Feuerman, the hero of the story '*Ba-Horef* [In Winter], conveys the fluidity of givenness. On the one hand, his Jewish world is the centre of his life and he is therefore tormented when contemplating the tragic Jewish reality that surrounds him: 'an ancient nation in agony for two thousand years... its outstanding children withering away in the cellar or leaving it, going to other worlds'.[10] On the other hand, questions awaken in his soul:

> What is the greatness I see in my people? Should I indeed worry about the survival of the nation? Am I indeed concerned about the survival of the forgotten tongue? Do Tolstoy students worry about such things? The main thing, after all, is individual advance and the rest – merely sophism.[11]

These thoughts highlight the dialectical relationship between Jewish existence and concrete personal existence. Jewish existence is perceived as a barrier to individual self-realization, as a kind of sophism that hinders concern with the main issue: finding the self. But separating existence from Jewish, concrete existence could result in detached creatures, whose freedom is an expression of their self-alienation.

In the story '*Misaviv la-Nekudah*' [Around the Point], Brenner draws a contrast between two characters, Abramson and Davidovsky. Abramson 'struggled to offload the suffering of old Judaism and to unclasp its handcuffs'.[12] By contrast, 'Davidovsky's soul, which had nothing to break loose from, is absolutely free'.[13] This tension between the two characters constitutes the existentialist field that the Jew contends with in the present: is his Judaism a factual datum with which he must establish a relationship, or can it be removed so that he may become a free soul, floating above existence and subsisting in the wide open spaces of philosophical thought?

Consequently, the following entanglement obtains: Jewish existence is a datum to be affirmed as part of the affirmation of the self but also a trap wherein individuals find themselves, a trap that precludes their existence as selves. The problem facing the Jew is whether to affirm givenness and how to affirm it, or perhaps to overcome it and live as a free individual. The latter option entails absolute detachment, not only from Jewish factual existence but also from concrete existence in general, since it includes a refusal of facticity and a location of the self in conceptual spaces unrelated to existence.

Jewish hesitations, then, are not an additional layer of human existence; they are part of this existence as a problem to be overcome, as a challenge to be faced or a datum to be affirmed a priori and unconditionally. Nor does the decision to affirm Jewish existence release the individual from doubt and tension, since the possibilities that were rejected still exist. They have not evaporated, since human existence by nature includes possibilities beyond givenness: individual freedom and creative imagination are not enchained to a datum, even after the person has chosen. The rejected options are present in human existence through their negation. As a choosing entity, the individual rejects options that could have been chosen. Their presence in human existence is in the ontological experience of guilt: individuals feel committed to human possibilities, including rejected ones, by the very fact that they are entities whose being is constituted by possibilities.[14]

The borders of givenness, as noted, are contingent on the person, both in the recognition of its contents and in its affirmation. This dialectical burden explicates why the question of Jewish existence and its meaning is a persistent existential question for Brenner, even though he adopted Jewish existence. The other, non-Jewish options, like the possibility of refusing to recognize Jewish existence as part of givenness, remain alive.

Brenner, however, decided to affirm Jewish existence, an affirmation that troubled him ceaselessly. Jewish existence is now a constitutive component of human existence: to be is to be a Jewish human being, not a human being and a Jew. As a result, the range of experiences that characterize existence characterize Jewish existence as well. The absurd, the meaninglessness of existence, and the recognition of the riddle of life are characteristics of Jewish existence as such. In 'Around the Point', Abramson feels as 'one whose loneliness too is the loneliness of the uprooted',[15] and goes through a dual experience: human and Jewish. His thought wonders between these two poles: 'A strange game, cruel, random, no beginning, no end; within it – an infinite number of worlds, without wisdom, without purpose, their beginning mist, their end devastation; within them – powerful lands, great nations, many peoples; between them – stray sheep, a panicked flock, sheep to the slaughter.'[16]

Sheep and flock are common metaphors for the Jewish people in prophetic literature. The existential state of this people is not perceived as unique, as part of a different metaphysical fate. Rather, it is a clear and sharp discovery of the absurd in human existence in general. It concretizes the lack of purpose and meaning in human existence. The existentialist riddle of life is also deeply connected to Jewish existence. In 'The Motto' ('From an Unpublished Manuscript'):

> Life is bad, but always mysterious… Death is bad.
> The world is strife-ridden, but also diverse, and at times beautiful.
> Man is wretched, but at times also outstanding.
> The people of Israel, logically, have no future.
> Nevertheless, we must labor.
> As long as you have a soul, there are sublime deeds
> And there are exalting moments.
> Long live human Hebrew labor.[17]

The life of the Jew bears the absurdity of human existence and its implications. Existence is not something diverse and self-evident that human beings, including Jews, cling to. They will cling to existence even if incomprehensible. This clinging to Jewish existence, then, need not lead the Jew to seek theological or metaphysical reasons for the fact of his Judaism, since Judaism is not a theological or metaphysical fact:

> If we are Jews, it is not because there is some Judaism entreating the interested parties to pray for its existence. Rather, it is because we and our children are necessarily in thousands of

special situations, physical and mental, economic and cultural,
that imprint us with a special stamp. The question to us is not
what will we do to Judaism but: We, the Jews, what will we do to
ourselves so that we may find a place of repose, so that we should
not be pushed out from the borders of human culture, from the
borders of creativity.[18]

The affirmation of the primacy of Jewish existence and its acceptance
as unconditional raises new questions, practical rather than theoretical:
'Our question-cry is: what do we do to ourselves, the Jews? How do we
live? How do we stop, in all senses, being parasites? How do we acquire
conditions for creating fair modes of life? How do we stop being children
of the ghetto?'[19]

The question that confronts the Jew is not – what is the correct idea?
Is Judaism the best idea? The affirmation of Jewish existence turns the
question of finding the personal, concrete truth – in Kierkegaard's terms,
'the truth for me, to find the idea for which I am willing to live and die'[20]
– into the crucial issue.

When the young Hebrew asks himself 'where to?,' this question
is not something outside him, just one more thought, but rather
one that weaves into all of them, threads its way into them and
entwines with them. He does not ask this because he suffers for
the sorrow of his people. He does suffer, but that is another
matter. The crux of his question is that, besides all the sorrows
of human life that one goes through just because one is human,
he is also hanging on burnt straw between two camps, between
different modes of life – something exiled, strange, remote,
something drowning in national-spiritual contrasts that stem
from the state of exile, something that makes his life so hard
because he is a Hebrew man, who gets nothing from Judaism…
in sum, something he cannot escape.[21]

The Jew must find a course to guide his concrete life as a Jew. 'Long live
human Hebrew labour' is not the extract of a metaphysical idea but a
practical course for the actual life of Jews in the world. Practice – Hebrew
labour – is an alternative to metaphysics. It reflects the consciousness
of Jewish individuals for the responsibility imposed on them in life to
improve and regulate this reality to the best of their ability.[22]

The personal is the Jewish, since Brenner does not separate the layers
of concrete existence: the fundamental questions of existence include
the fundamental questions of Jewish existence, 'which weaves into all

of them, threads its way into them and entwines with them'. Brenner identifies Jewish existence as absurd – 'exiled, strange, remote' – precisely like human existence. This identification is interesting because the basic questions of human existence are ontological. By contrast, the basic questions of Jewish existence are social-cultural-historical. Ontological questions are permanent; they are insoluble beyond the solutions that Brenner pointed out, but questions bound by a cultural-social context can be solved through an effort to change the reality that created them.

Brenner's equation of Jewish and general existential questions only implies that the human being is a concrete creature that lives in specific historical and social circumstances. From an existential perspective, removing historical Jewish questions is inconceivable because it implies removing factual givenness – the thrownness within which Jews find themselves. The basic question of existence – who am I and what is the meaning of my life – is: 'Who am I and what am I at this moment, in this place-no place, in this society that is entangled in the fetters of the past, suspended between ossified religiosity and hopeless detachment.'[23]

The specific facticity of being a Jew, then, is the link between the general ontological and the specific Jewish. This course explains the link that Brenner assumes between the experience of strangeness and alienation on the one hand, and Zionism and the search for a homeland on the other. Zionism and the search for a homeland appear as an option for solving the absurd, but also as an illusion that blurs it. In *Mi-Kan u-Mi-Kan* [From Here and from Here], the transition between them is smooth:

> The source of my despair about myself is my impatience, which actually intensified my despair. Things seem to have reached the point where I came to think of my stay in the country as sinful, as an act of deceit on my part, as a fraud and a swindle: I must not let this damned stay allow me to hold on to the terrible illusion of a renaissance dream! And I may even have added: sinful and forbidden – nonsense! But what do I have here? Everything is over, finished, there is no reason for my life, no reason. I am a dead man from the world of chaos, who fears returning to his grave... All I want is not to die only at this moment, nor at this moment, nor at this moment – it is only this unwillingness that curbs my hand and stops me from tightening the noose... And yet life, the whole of life, has become loathsome, since it has nothing of what could have meant something to me, I loathe even what I yearn for, and why, then, do I still hold on to the horns of the altar?[24]

According to biblical law, one guilty of premeditated murder cannot seek protection at the altar – 'thou shalt take him from my altar, that he may die' (Exodus 21:14). Yoav, King David's military commander whom the king had condemned to death, fled and 'caught hold of the horns of the altar' (I Kings 2:28), but this did not save him. Except for such a murderer, the altar protects one who holds on to it. But what is the Brennerian altar? It is no longer the original altar but the Land of Israel that is supposed to shield one from existential despair. The 'altar', however, is broken and fails to protect. This despair from the protective homeland is the complementary facet of one who had sought in the homeland escape for a tormented soul. The homeland is revealed as unable to dispel the terror of existence:

> To be precise, the abyss of fear will not be bridged with the oranges I will pick in the orchards of the Promised Land when I get there... but I still ran there... Quivering in the depths of my soul, sounds of longings for *Yefeh Nof*,[25] to use its literary name, may also have awakened me to the voyage... and perhaps also longings for the shadow of a homeland that, as a Jew, I have never known since my birth, all the days of my being.[26]

Longings for a homeland cannot heal the sorrow of existence, but the human-Jewish drama nevertheless takes place around it. It is within it that the endeavour of social reform, which is an endeavour of personal reform, will unfold, if at all. The value of the homeland is the existentialist horizon it enables, and the homeland therefore bears the intensity of the suffering and the difficulties of existence itself. The will to live is what remains clear as the solid foundation that drives life towards the Jewish chasm too. The Zionist experience, then, is the existentialist experience of one who is a Jew and chooses to remain one. It cannot confer upon existence anything that is not in existence itself.

Brenner's existentialist stance is further sharpened when compared with that of Jean Améry, who lost his German homeland and was thrown into Jewish fate in the terrors of the Holocaust. Améry experiences a deep sense of alienation, which ultimately leads him to suicide. For Améry, unlike for Brenner, a homeland has a deeper meaning. His stance is that our being and identity are shaped by our culture and our surroundings, by the streets and the alleys of the city of our childhood. These surroundings are the person's primary homeland (*Heimat*) the home that gives us security and trust.[27] This homeland is not the private environment of individuals but the political unit (*Vaterland*). Améry insists on rejecting the distinction between 'homeland', in the sense of the private home that gives a person security and meaning, and the national homeland:

> I dare to stand up for the value that homeland signifies, and I also reject the sharp-witted differentiation between homeland and fatherland, and in the end believe that a person of my generation can get along only poorly without both, which are one and the same. Whoever has no fatherland – that is to say, no shelter in an autonomous social body representing an independent governmental entity – has, so I believe, no homeland either.[28]

Through his searing life experience, Améry learned that a homeland is not a closed, sealed private unit, just as language, memory, culture, and history are not confined to an individual. A homeland is the personal and public space that gives people the networks of meaning within which they live and mould themselves. For Améry, pressing the homeland into the bounds of a *Heimat* means confining human beings to a realm that is not the one where real people live. Améry's approach is based on the view that human beings are cultural-social creatures, for whom the homeland is the basic datum of human existence.

Unlike him, Brenner is an existentialist. His starting point is the individual contending with the question of his factual existence: 'Individuals are the ones who ask questions, individuals. And because the individual carves the question from his heart, from the depths, from the depths of his own heart – then the answer, if he finds it, must necessarily be, and indeed is, his answer, found in his own heart, for himself.'[29]

The categories of existentialist thought, even if they take into account cultural-social aspects, view these aspects as merely a factual datum that should be addressed and on which one should take a stand. In this sense, the existentialist position acknowledges the existence of a 'self' as an entity that transcends the factual datum, since this self must decide and determine its position towards factual data, meaning it is not identical to them. Individuals stand at a persistent distance from their culture, their place, and their thrownness, a distance determined by the fact that their culture is an object of their choice. Ultimately, the self is free from its data, even if it affirms it in order to realize its historical-concrete being.[30] As Brenner phrases it: 'He does not ask this [where to?] because he suffers the sorrow of his people. He definitely suffers, but that is another matter.' Brenner's stance, then, is that of the individual seeking a way out of existential angst, which is woven from both human and Jewish existence. The individual is thus a free entity who transcends homeland and surroundings, even when affirming them.

For Améry, the homeland is a primary datum, part of the characterization of his existence as a member of a given culture. For Brenner, by contrast, the homeland is not primary in two senses. It is not part of the factual data, neither for him nor for his Jewish contemporaries. Furthermore, the homeland is the object of an individual decision – he must either endorse the homeland and the vision of a renaissance, or reject them. The relationship towards it remains complex and mediated rather than immediate, as it is for Améry. The loss of the homeland for Améry is the loss of human existence. The loss of the homeland for Brenner is a constant option that is conditioned by the individual's decision, by its place in the context of meaning it gives his life.[31]

Existential individuality is a fundamental anchor of Brennerian Zionism. In the play *Me-Ever la-Gevulin* [Beyond the Border], this is the stance of Naphtali, the Zionist: 'I too am an individualist, and despite your anger I say: Ibsen is my teacher and so forth. But from my individualism I go to Zionism.'[32] Naphtali insistently reiterates his individualist stance, which is also the anchor of his social connection: 'On all universal questions I am an individualist, on art and on thought I follow Ibsen, my "self" is for me the entire world. And yet, who can deny that the individual is highly dependent on the collective?'[33]

The Brennerian viewpoint, which begins from a concrete individual, is not committed to solipsism, since together with the affirmation of concrete and individual existence is also the necessary connection to the other. As concrete creatures, individuals depend on one another and each one's actions and omissions influence the other. The affirmation of Zionism in the sense that Brenner affirms it, then, rests on these existential foundations. Zionism is not a theoretical idea but an existential confrontation with the real existence of individuals: 'But we are after all individualists... we will put aside the question of the Jews, which is insoluble... we are busy with the question of our lives... just that... not for others... for ourselves.'[34]

This analysis clarifies that, according to Brenner, examining the meaning of Jewish existence must begin from an existentialist stance. Brenner's main contribution to the discourse on Jewish existence is to reject the theological or conceptual options and introduce a new perspective, concrete-real-existential. The tormented endorsement of the Jewish datum as a basic fact of givenness explicates the range of Brenner's references to Jewish existence. As an element in the givenness it is imposed, but as a real fact it is contingent and given to Jewish decision. The affirmation of existence cannot be based on what is beyond givenness, on an external truth that can be corroborated objectively. To be a Jew means to sustain the fact of givenness and to affirm it practically.

The question of Jewish existence for Brenner, as noted, is personal but not private. Its starting point is Brenner's factual givenness as a Jewish individual, but the existential voyage, like any personal philosophy, transcends the personal context.

Brenner does know that the Jewish existentialist question is located within the general existentialist question:

> The soul throes of the modern Jew are so much like those of the European… the individual outbursts, the universal concerns, the rebellions and the problems and the searches for the mysteries of creation – all this 'spirituality' that fills mainly the modern creations of European literature in the last fifty years is not only not alien to the Jewish 'individual,' but he may even be closer to it than the non-Jew.[35]

The Jew serves as a kind of seismograph of existential questions, which find increasing resonance in him. He is the one who strongly experiences the tension between imposed and worthless existence and the aspiration to freedom. He is the one who experiences the riddle of existence with special passion because this riddle touches on the foundations of his existence as a Jew, without leaving any comfortable and seductive space for evasion. The scepticism, the alienation, and the rift that are part of the modern experience resonate with special intensity in Jewish existence.

Brenner offers his reader a partnership in the Jewish existential voyage that he launches. According to the assumption he postulated about literature, writers serve as the organon of self-consciousness about the human realm in which they are planted. They have the ability to reveal to their readers the truth about human reality. Brenner's creativity is an invitation to a personal voyage that he conducts as a person and as a Jew. His detailed analysis of the existentialist voyage will be at the focus of the coming chapters, which will show how the Jewish existentialist voyage is the general existentialist voyage applied to Jewish existence.

Notes

1   Robert Friend, *Found in Translation: Modern Hebrew Poets – A Bilingual Edition* (New Milford, CT: The Toby Press, 2006), 147.

2   Cited in Yitzhak Bakon, *The Young Brenner* (in Hebrew), vol.1 (Tel Aviv: Hakibbutz Hameuchad, 1975), 204. For Bakon's analysis, see 204–206.

3   *Writings*, vol.2, 1434.

4   See Martin Heidegger, *Being and Time*, trans. John Macquarrie and Edward Robinson (New York: Harper and Row, 1962), 434–9.

5   *Ibid.*, 436.

6　S. Y Penueli, *Brenner and Gnessin in Early Twentieth-Century Hebrew Fiction* (in Hebrew) (Tel Aviv: Students' Association at Tel Aviv University, 1965), 113.

7　Bakon, *The Young Brenner*, 204–206. See also Dov Kimhi, *Brief Essays* (in Hebrew) (Jerusalem: Reuven Mass, 1984), 45.

8　See also Boaz Arpali, 'Asymmetrical Oppositions: Between the Truth of Death and a Life of Deceit' (in Hebrew), *Sadan*, 4 (2000), 258, and Ortsion Bartana, *Caution, Israeli Literature: Tendencies in Israel Fiction* (in Hebrew) (Tel Aviv: Papyrus, 1989), 11.

9　Bakon, *The Young Brenner*. Contrary to the analysis suggested in the text, see Yitzhak Bakon, *Brenner in London: The Me'orer Period – 1905–1907* (in Hebrew) (Beer Sheva: Ben-Gurion University, 2000), 15–16.

10　*Writings*, vol.1, 176.

11　*Ibid.*, 176–7.

12　*Ibid.*, 436.

13　*Ibid.*, 437.

14　Heidegger, *Being and Time*, 330–2. On ontological-existentialist guilt, see also Calvin O. Schrag, *Existence and Freedom: Towards an Ontology of Human Finitude* (Evanston, IL: Northwestern University Press, 1983), 163–9.

15　*Writings*, vol.1, 500.

16　*Ibid.*, 501.

17　*Ibid.*, vol.2, 1422.

18　*Ibid.*, vol.3, 218.

19　*Ibid.*, 215. On Brenner's attitude toward the Jewish ghetto and the modes of its description, see Shlomo Tzemah, 'Y. H. Brenner' (in Hebrew), *Ha-Shiloah*, 28 (1912), 465–6.

20　See Avi Sagi, *Kierkegaard, Religion, and Existence: The Voyage of the Self*, trans. Batya Stein (Amsterdam-Atlanta, GA: Rodopi, 2000), 7–8.

21　*Writings*, vol.3, 266–7.

22　On Brenner's attitude to labour, see also Aaron Ben-Or (Orinovsky), *The History of Modern Hebrew Literature* (in Hebrew), vol.2 (Tel Aviv: Yizre'el, 1968), 434–5.

23　Aaron Appelfeld, *First Person Essays* (in Hebrew) (Jerusalem: WZO, 1979), 70.

24　*Writings*, vol.2, 1318.

25　Jerusalem's name in a celebrated poem by Judah Halevi.

26　*Writings*, vol.2, 1234. See also Yeshurun Keshet (Yaakov Koplewitz), 'On Y. H. Brenner: A Profile' (in Hebrew), *Anthology of Literature, Criticism, and Thought*, 3 (1963), 159.

27　Jean Améry, *At the Mind's Limits: Contemplations by a Survivor of Auschwitz and Its Realities*, trans. Sidney Rosenfeld and Stella P. Rosenfeld (Bloomington, ID: Indiana University Press, 1980), 47.

28　*Ibid.*, 54.

29　*Writings*, vol.3, 267.

30　On the difference between existentialist philosophy and cultural thought, see Avi Sagi, *The Jewish-Israeli Voyage: Culture and Identity* (in Hebrew) (Jerusalem: Shalom Hartman Institute, 2006), 212–18.

31　From many perspectives, Brenner's is an essentially Jewish stance, since the contingent nature of the hold on the land is a deep element in traditional Jewish historical consciousness. See Hagai Dagan, 'Homeland and the Jewish Ethos: An Ongoing Dissonance' (in Hebrew), *Alpayim*, 18 (1999): 9–23. See also Asaf Sagiv, 'Zionism and the Myth of Motherland', *Azure*, 5 (Autumn 5759/1998): 98–112; Zali Gurevitch, *On Israeli and Jewish Place* (in Hebrew) (Tel Aviv: Am Oved, 2007), 22–80.

32 *Writings*, vol.1, 731.

33 *Ibid.*, 741.

34 *Ibid.*, vol.2, 1168.

35 *Ibid.*, vol.4, 1354.

SIX

Moulding Jewish Life

What determines that a Jew is a Jew? Is it religion or perhaps other necessary beliefs and ideologies? Does 'Judaism' make Jews, or does the actual existence of the Jew precede all ideas or essentialist features? What is 'Judaism'? These basic questions underlie Brenner's conception of Jewish existence. Brenner's significant innovation, which reflects his existentialist stance, is that Judaism, in any meaning ascribed to the term, depends on the existence of Jews as real people.[1] Indeed, only because there are Jews do they generate a culture that we call Judaism.

The Critique of Judaism

Brenner challenges the essentialist conception of Judaism, which he ascribes to Ahad Ha-Am. According to Ahad Ha-Am, 'Judaism' exists as such, independently of real Jews. Indeed, Jews are Jews only because there is an entity called Judaism; the essential feature – Judaism – is what determines that Jews are Jews. The removal of this feature, that is, the relinquishment of Judaism, negates their Jewish existence. Against this approach, Brenner claims:

> When Ahad Ha-Am is told: Judaism was created for the Jews and not the Jews for Judaism, that is, Jews create Judaism and not vice-versa… so that wherever Jews actually live they will create something that we will call Judaism – he quibbles and says: Aha! So you admit that Judaism was created for the Jews, and I add: Not only for the Jews, but by the Jews.[2]

Brenner's basic claim is that cultural creativity is secondary and contingent on the existence of actual people who create it. The existence of these people is not contingent on their creativity, just as the creator is not dependent on the creature. Brenner drew the conclusion warranted by this stance: if Judaism is not an autonomous entity but contingent on the activity of Jews, then Judaism has no essentialist features of its own. Judaism is Judaism because it is the Jews' cultural creation, and only its being such a product determines its being Judaism:

> All that the Jews do within their surroundings and for the purpose
> of their existence is Judaism. The crux is to look everywhere for
> the Jews first – Judaism is then bound to come. If Jews do their
> work and live their independent lives – there will be some kind
> of Judaism. Or whatever there will be – will be called Judaism.[3]

Brenner sets two conditions for determining that a culture is Jewish. The
first refers to what 'the Jews do within their surroundings' – practices of
Jews performed within the actual Jewish living space are Judaism. The
second condition – the purpose of these practices – is the continued
existence of the Jewish collective. These two conditions create the
distinction between Judaism and other cultures. The first condition
differentiates between kinds of practices, when Jewish practices are those
that are unique to the Jewish living space. A variety of practices prevails
within this space because all people, including Jews, share a broad range
of practices in the course of their lives. Only those practices unique to the
Jewish environment, that is, practices that create a network of meaning
and communication between Jews, are Judaism. Obviously, these practices
might also be widespread in other surroundings. Determining them as
Jewish follows from their being typical of the Jewish environment. A Jewish
environment is not necessarily closed off from all others and separated by
a barrier of unique practices. Brenner does not seek to create spaces that
marginalize the other. For him, the fact that these practices are typical of
the environment where Jews live is enough.

But Brenner did not confine himself to presenting the field of
Jewish culture through its Jewish players. He added that this network
of practices must satisfy a primary inner purpose – the preservation of
the existence of Jews as Jews. This condition, resonating with Darwinian
echoes, assumes that the creation of a culture is meant to serve life and,
therefore, Judaism too is meant for this purpose.

This characterization of Judaism defines Judaism as wholly immanent.
It cannot be 'Torah from Heaven', since it is the practice of a human
group whose purpose is internal. Moreover, this purpose points to its
changing and dynamic character, since Jews at different times and places
shape different practices that diversify according to their needs. Judaism
does not have a history independent from, and unconditioned by, the
concrete activities of Jews. The only element of continuity in Judaism is
formal and external – practices that Jews call Judaism and meet the two
noted conditions are Judaism, notwithstanding the differences between
its various manifestations. The history of Judaism is the history of the
Jews' cultural intent, directed to the preservation of their existence.
Brenner resolutely states: 'There is no Judaism outside us and outside

our lives. There are no fixed and permanent beliefs that compel us.[4] [...]
We ourselves are the Jewish atmosphere.'[5] This approach leads Brenner
to the following conclusion, which he again directs against Ahad Ha-
Am:

> If all Jews were to accept Tolstoy's teachings, an obviously
> inconceivable hypothesis, these teachings would become
> Judaism, and our Hebrew nationality would in no way be
> diminished, just as Tolstoy's Russian nationality would in no way
> be diminished... We do not denigrate any religion and we do not
> praise any religion. We say: a people does not live by opinions
> and beliefs.[6]

This non-essentialist conception of Judaism is an expression of the
basic Brennerian view whereby 'the Jew is not a Jew because he has
been infused with certain opinions and beliefs, from which he can be
liberated'.[7] Brenner rejects the idea that 'the Jew is what he thinks'.[8] That
is, 'the idea external' to the existence of the concrete person does not
'make the Jew a Jew'.[9]

With great sensitivity, Brenner discerns that ideas, opinions, or
ideological conceptions are by nature contingent. Adopting them
invariably conveys belief in their positive value. But this belief, like any
belief, can become invalid, and what had been considered worthy at
one time may be considered worthless at another. One can be liberated
from 'certain opinions and beliefs'. Brenner formulates this insight quite
blatantly: 'What is Judaism to me? What are tragedies to me? What are
beauty, courage, and the prophetic vision to me? What are to me things
that one can repudiate, or cast doubt upon, or negotiate?'[10] Brenner
searches for unconditioned certainty, for a primary unquestionable
truth; a truth that compels human beings. Judaism is not like that. Like
any idea, it is subject to review.

It was Wittgenstein who, in his later works, discerned the special status
of religious dispositions. In his view, every statement about the world is by
nature subject to review, but not religious beliefs: 'Those people who had
faith didn't apply the doubt to any historical propositions.'[11] Wittgenstein
therefore concluded that religion does not compete with metaphysics
or science, and offers something entirely different – faith. Faith is not
contingent on any outside factor; it is the primary basis that does not rest
on statements of truth through which the believer perceives the world.
In the terminology of post-Wittgensteinian philosophers, it is an absolute
disposition of the believer regarding the world; a disposition that shapes
an entire 'way of life'.[12]

Brenner strives for the stance that Wittgenstein ascribed to faith, that is, for unconditioned, primary certainty. He does not find it in the various ideas included in the 'Judaism' family, nor in Jewish religion as a normative framework. What Wittgenstein ascribed to faith, Brenner does not apply to Jewish religion, to which he does not ascribe any privileged status.

Ostensibly, this is the vulnerable point in Brenner's conception of 'Judaism' and Jewish religion. The primary certainty of faith is not a matter discerned 'from outside'. The disposition of faith is within the believers themselves.[13] Brenner's critique of Jewish religion, however, targets an ideology that views the validity of Jewish religion as an objective matter, independent of the believers' faith. His sociological acuity leads Brenner to reject the idea that Jewish religion has a special status as an autonomous and fundamental condition for the preservation of Jewish existence, and he cites religion's standing in recent generations as corroborating evidence. Religion lost its standing because it was no longer compatible with Jewish life but, as Brenner emphasises, the reason is not that religion failed the test of ideas but rather a more fundamental one:

> As the Jewish forms of life collapsed, so did religiosity, not because it was unable to stand up to some new philosophical ideas, but because of its inner weakness. Religion does not fall apart because of ideas nor is it built because of new ones. From the start, as Jewish life was pervaded by religion, so was Jewish religion founded and supported by defined forms of life, and 'when the helper stumbles, the one who is helped shall fall down.'[14]

Brenner draws a distinction between 'forms of life' and religion. Forms of life are the constructs and the social institutions of real people, into which they pour various practices and networks of meaning. Jewish religion used to be such a network of meaning within a particular way of life that characterized life in the ghetto, but 'there are no fixed and special forms of life'.[15] As historical circumstances change, so do social constructs. The standing of religion, like that of any cultural content, is contingent on these very constructs, on its ability to serve them and buttress their existence. The instrumental perception of religion, the view of religion as fulfilling a role in Jewish existence, implies a view of the concrete social context as primary. Religion's standing in real existence is contingent on its compatibility with 'Jewish forms of life' rather than on the measure of its truth or falsity.

As Jewish forms of life collapsed, religion fell apart from within. It no longer plays a role, and cannot help to restore obsolete forms. The contingent character of religion is twofold: first, like every idea, it lacks necessary standing and can be replaced by another. Second, it is contingent on the purpose it is purported to fulfil – the preservation of Jewish life. Since Jewish existence is built upon social constructs, changes in these constructs lead to changes in the standing of religion. Thus, if to be a Jew is contingent on Judaism, then this existence is as contingent as Judaism itself. But Brenner absolutely rejected this approach. In his view, as this book shows, to be a Jew is a kind of necessity, an unconditioned existence that is therefore unconditioned by Judaism.

Jewish Existence as Thrownness

After a meeting with Brenner, Micha Josef Berdyczewski wrote in his journal: 'This man [Brenner] is not a Jew as such in his soul, because he curses Judaism.'[16] Without delving too deeply into the relationship between Brenner and Berdyczewski, the analysis so far shows that Berdyczewski was wrong: the recognition that Judaism is a contingent cultural product of Jews is not meant to deny Jewish existence but to point out the gap between this contingent character and the unconditional affirmation of Jewish existence. Precisely because Brenner *is* 'a Jew in his soul', he could not assume that Jewish existence is contingent, as is Judaism. Even if his statements are at times unconventional, they come, as Yehezkel Kaufmann remarked, 'from a loving, hurting heart',[17] since 'he [Brenner] was very Jewish and very human'.[18]

Brenner seeks basic foundations in Jewish existence, as in all other realms. In a manifesto he wrote for 'Ha-Adamah' [The Land], he outlines this general trend: 'Striving for bedrock fundamentals in all aspects of life, for a vision of things as they are, for knowledge of the foundations of reality.'[19] As a set of ideas and beliefs, Judaism is not fit to play this role. Indeed, the gap between the experience of necessity in Jewish existence and the contingency of these ideas points out that Judaism lacks this feature: 'If their future living conditions do not tear Jews away from the needs of their people, they will be Jews by default, no worse than you, even if they are not taught [the Talmudic tractates of] Eruvin and Pesahim and even if they are not told time and again about the God of Israel.'[20] As ideology or idea, Judaism is not entwined in the web of real life; it is an abstraction of existence rather than its encompassment.[21] What, then, is the basic fact that determines one as being Jewish? In Brenner's view, being Jewish is a primary necessary datum rather than a concern with, or the choice of, any idea or ideology. The Judaism of a Jew is 'Judaism by default', that is, a Jew is one who is already a Jew. In existentialist terms, Jewish existence is part of thrownness.

The coercive nature of Jewish existence emerges in a self-consciousness that negates the possibility of abandoning it:

> We are Jews in the better and more sublime sense of the term, and we cannot but be such Jews, because we ourselves are Judaism, in everything, we ourselves are the Jewish atmosphere....[22]
> We, who stand today, who feel ourselves Jews and do not think at all about the possibility of not being Jews... There is a riddle in the course of our lives, not one but many, many riddles, life-riddles and life-questions.[23]

Jewish existence, like all forms of existence, is purposeless. The fact of existence is a primary datum that cannot be explained by a conceptual or metaphysical purpose. The riddle of Jewish life, as part of the general riddle of life, leaves the question of purpose unsolved. It turns individuals back onto themselves and onto the fact of their Jewish existence as a primary existence:

> Here we are, children of Israel, descendants of the same multitudes, alive. This is a fact! So alive are we – necessarily, without any premeditated intention – living a Jewish life with all our blood, so strongly do we bear the pain – the yoke of the voiding of our national life... that the air around us becomes absolutely stifling; there is no air; we want to open the windows.[24]

Brenner points to the primary nature of Jewish existence. It does not lead to any purpose. It is not founded on a voluntary intention. It is a fundamental fact:

> What will be further – we do not know and may also be impossible to know. What we do know: we are today tens of thousands of Jews in this land, tied by our feelings to tens of thousands of Jews in all parts of the world and we wish to live; to grow and to develop; to act and to live. Life and literature.[25]

Brenner discovers the facticity of unconditioned Jewish existence; a facticity that seeks to continue and survive even without any reason or purpose. This facticity is unconditioned by the compelling gaze of the other, who views the Jew through Sartre's well-known formulations: 'The Jew is one whom other men consider a Jew.[26] [...] [He is] himself as others see him.'[27] By contrast, Brenner held that the facticity is internal; it embodies primary Jewish thrownness because Jews find themselves to be Jews. This is a datum found in transparent self-consciousness, and its recognition as a primary existential datum is the first step of authentic Jewish existence.

Because Brenner knew the primary power of Jewish thrownness, he could not but sense the negative facet of Jewish existence – its sorrow. The basic experience of a primary tie is, indeed, what generates and enables a critical, negative stance. Contrary to Kurzweil's claim, the motivation for this stance is not an 'ocean of self-hatred and the hatred and destruction of Judaism'.[28] One who acknowledges the 'holiness' of the people, its 'great powers',[29] does not experience self-hatred but self-love. Indeed, what the criticism conveys is recognition of the Jewish individual as part of a Jewish genealogy, tied to historical Jewish facticity and hence confronted with it. Brenner expressed this dialectical relationship in the 'Correspondence' in '*Ha-Me'orer*',[30] where he draws a contrast between '*Ha-Me'orer*' and '*Ha-Shiloah*'. He destines '*Ha-Me'orer*'

> to a small group of us, Jews-of-the-crisis who, on the one hand, are filled with longing for all the generations of the unparalleled Jewish past and hence have a wholly Hebrew soul and a wholly Hebrew pen, and on the other, are free of all spiritual enslavement and party discipline and understand the crisis and its aftermath. They wished for and worked to build a platform that would give them the full possibility of being free with their pen and faithful to themselves, to their understanding-their sorrow, and to the spiritual within them.... And we, fickle and unsettled, will not struggle and toil to reach the glens and valleys... In our small pamphlets...we will realize our own selves...in them we will sing and pray, love and hate, preach and curse, rave and build, magnify and extol ourselves, warn and tell our sorrows, bless and cry out from pain, deny and formulate, doubt and search.[31]

Hesitations, doubts, and pains are modes of existence for those who find themselves connected to facticity and who suffer, not because of Jewish thrownness as such, but because of its cultural, historical, and specific manifestations. These manifestations, which are by nature contingent, become a burden and an obstacle to Jewish existence in the present. The burden is made heavier precisely because of the image ascribed to these manifestations as reflecting a basic and unconditioned element, necessary for the Jews' real existence. This reversal, which determines the conceptual rather than the real as necessary, is what intensifies Jewish suffering in the present. For the Jew, the original fact is being Jewish rather than some idea or ideology called 'Judaism'.

Brenner strives to draw a sharp distinction between a set of ideas and the basic facts of existence that entail something pre-conscious, earthly, instinctive.[32] He grants precedence to reality over theory.[33] For Brenner, therefore, relating to ideas as the foundation of existence is immoral: 'In an ideal...relationship with the world, in sensitive childish dreams that have no basis in the deepest human instincts, I believe there is some immorality, yes, immorality, in that they are in a way ephemeral, since they result from an improper absorption of all the bitterness of reality.'[34] A moral attitude is anchored in real existence, not only as a driving impulse but also as the object of it. Ideas or ideologies that do not follow from reality and never take reality into account are immoral. They deny the real person, who generates moral activity.

Boaz Arpali analyses the story '*Mi-Saviv la-Nekudah*' [Around the Point] and points to five main flaws of ideologies at its foundation. Four of them, in my view, underlie the Brennerian stance in general. The first is the ineptness of ideology to understand reality. Ideology analyses complex reality through a schematic conceptual framework incapable of capturing reality's fullness. Second, ideology replaces independent critical thought. Instead of independent thought, ideology offers stable and fixed formulas. Third,

> All ideologies, whether revolutionary or conservative are, in the final analysis, no more than rationalizations. A cover for and a justification of social action, power struggles, the prominence and the rule of the strong over the weak within ideological movements, the arrogance and contempt for anything you do not understand or do not wish to understand, and for every person you enjoy looking down upon.[35]

Fourth, ideologies are based on a false consciousness, they reflect deceit and concealment. Arpali sums this up as follows:

> By their very nature, ideologies are incapable of providing an answer to truly important existential questions derived, on the one hand, from the annihilating certainty of death, and on the other, from the irrational character of life in general (existence as such) and of the motives and decisions of living people in particular. The first starting point (the certainty of death) suggests that, although ideologies pretend to change human reality through rational analysis, they do not consider the ultimate implications

of the basic data of reality and tend to disregard them and even blur them. The second starting point suggests that the forces spurring life and potentially capable of changing it insofar as this is possible, are actually needs, instincts, and other irrational impulses. From this perspective, ideologies are denied precisely because of their true or apparent rationality.[36]

This critique of ideas and ideologies is at the basis of Brenner's criticism of Jewish existence. People whose main concern are Jewish ideas rather than Jewish life could end up directing their actions against concrete Jewish life. In the world of ideas

> there is no difference between, on the one hand, people who actually live the life of their people, whose existence is a basis for the continued existence of their people whatever their thoughts about poetry and philosophy and, on the other, Hellenistic publicans of antiquity whose way of life jeopardized the people's existence, or Reform 'reverends' in Western countries today, whose conditions of life when 'sitting, lying down, rising up, and walking by the way' negate the life of the people and their very existence as a separate Jewish congregation. Even if they, these flaccid limbs, were to swear daily to their loyalty to monotheistic faith…in this world, the philosophical idea is everything.[37]

Jewish existence is the existence of living people, whose Jewish being is not contingent on anything. Their existence is not part of a set of beliefs and viewpoints but a primary elementary fact that begins with a coerced fact – thrownness into Jewish existence and fate. One of Brenner's protagonists sharply formulates this notion in radical terms: 'There is no Hebrew nation, there are no Hebrew souls, no Hebrew values, no Hebrew language, but there are Jews.'[38]

Jewish existence, as a primary elementary fact drawing the individual and unconditioned by contingent contents, is Brenner's starting point. Brennerian existentialism thus comes to the fore also and perhaps above all, in the analysis of Jewish existence.

Endorsing Jewish Thrownness

According to the analysis conducted so far, thrownness into Jewish existence is a primary and unquestionable fact. It is, however, only the first step in the process of being a Jew. The recognition of Jewish thrownness is a rejection of arbitrary voluntarism; a person cannot 'leap' into Jewish existence: 'A person is not born in a day! How will he become a Jew, and he has forgotten to speak Jewish!'[39] Birth, perceived as a one-time event that occurred in the past is, existentially, a prolonged and complex process. Its beginning is the recognition of Jewish thrownness, which is itself the existentialist birth. Birth, as Heidegger described it, never ends. In his words: 'Understood existentially, birth is not and never is something past in the sense of something no longer present-at-hand.'[40] Existentialist birth is the ongoing recognition of Jewish thrownness, of what the person already is – a Jew.

The second and definitive stage is concretized in a decision to endorse this factual datum. Existentialist return to the basic datum is not a return to some Jewish ideology. Rather, return is the affirmation of thrownness, which is the recognition of the special ontological character of Jewish existence as an existence that does not create itself *ex nihilo*, an existence that begins in the past rather than in the present and in the future. Through the existential decision, the coerced past becomes part of an ongoing present. In line with this approach, Sartre writes that to be an authentic Jew means 'to live to the full his condition as a Jew; inauthenticity is to deny it or to attempt to escape from it.'[41] An authentic existence is one where basic patterns of existence are transparent and freely adopted.[42]

The authentic moment of decision is the *Augenblick*, wherein the person exposes the connection between present and past, the tie between what one could have been and what one already is. The moment of decision raises the question of the connection between the two poles that constitute the ontological being of the person in general and of the Jew in particular – past and future. Following is Brenner's formulation of this unheroic moment:

> If we are Jews, it is not because there is some Judaism begging to be asked to exist, but because we and our children necessarily find ourselves in thousands of special unique situations, physical and mental, economic and cultural, which stamp us with a special seal, and the question to us is not what will we do to Judaism but rather what we, the Jews, will do to ourselves.[43]

The moment of decision turns us from the world of ideas onto ourselves, onto our real existence, which creates the space wherein the relationships between past, present, and future will be shaped.

Brenner often confronted this point of decision, which always led to the affirmation of painful Jewish existence. Coerced thrownness becomes the content of the positive decision. Necessity and freedom mediate one another in the life of the Jew: 'We are alive, and it is not our religion that links us to our people, nor will another religion take us away from it, and we neither want to nor can go to another society, because we cannot go away from ourselves.'[44]

The endorsement of thrownness is not merely voluntary. The individual can, as it were, choose or not choose Jewish existence, and both options are equally valid. For Brenner, however, choosing thrownness is the only proper option existentially, since denying Jewish existence leads the Jew to self-alienation. Brenner holds that to deny Jewish existence is absolutely impossible, since 'we cannot go away from ourselves'. For a Jew, existing as a Jew is inherent and integral to one's real existence and denying it is self-denial, which is existentially impossible.

Choosing Jewish existence does not mean choosing Jewish ideas or the more ethical parts of this existence, but choosing the totality of real Jewish life:

> We, therefore, are the children of the Hebrew nation faithful to ourselves, who live within our people and, whether our people are good or bad, cannot conceive ourselves otherwise. We are the last in the camp, because for us there is no other, as there is no other sun for us, even if we were to be sick of it and find in it all the spots in the world.[45]

Choosing Jewish existence, then, expresses self-loyalty and the preservation of a concrete self-identity, which precedes any judgment of this identity's practical and cognitive contents. Jews are doomed to be Jews, and they confirm this fact through their choice. This affirmation, however, is concretized not only in the cognitive disposition but in the readiness to live a Jewish destiny, to work within it out of a sense of solidarity, and to correct it as far as possible: 'The truly cultured Jew does not want to adapt under duress to another society – his feeling of self is far too developed for that. He remains to work together with other members of the Jewish people, even without "Judaism" or anything else.'[46] Affirming Jewish fate has a clear practical meaning – shaping a lifestyle that enables the continuation of Jewish existence as such – and does not imply adopting the metaphysical or theological posture of 'Thou hast chosen us':

> I, with enormous and passionate pleasure, would erase from the prayer book of the contemporary Hebrew person any form of 'Thou hast chosen us'. I would do that even today, dismiss and erase the false national verses and leave no trace of them.

Because empty national pride and hollow Jewish brag will not heal the fracture and delusive national metaphors will prove useless.[47]

The endorsement of destiny is not concretized in the adoption of a theological or metaphysical outlook, or in the affirmation of any conceptual content. Its only manifestation is practical – participation in Jewish life, in the pain and suffering of this existence, not as a bystander but as one who enlists in the amendment of reality:[48]

> You say Judaism, and I say the Jewish people, the Jewish people as is, with all its flaws and shortcomings, with all its wounds and pains, unparalleled in any other nation, large or small – this is an act, a real act, rather than the subject of certain thoughts.[49]
> A true son of the people, a son of the people engaged in an inner reckoning with it, with its nature and fate, cannot possibly live-act without strong faith in this people, in the truth of this people, its holiness, its great powers.... After all, every man of true feeling comes into the world through his people, scrutinizes humanity through his people and relative to his people, and will be touched to his deepest core only by the destiny of his people, that is, his own destiny, as a son of his people.[50]
> A Jew is not a Jew because certain beliefs and opinions have been implanted in him, from which he can be liberated... A Jew is a Jew only because he has the sorrow of life and the will of life – or in another formulation: the will of life that is the sorrow of life – of his people, with whom he is in one place.
> Obviously, when he goes away from them, when he leaves his surroundings due to the condition of the nation, which has no place, or whatever the reason may be, the common will necessarily weakens... but the passive sorrow of the people, the original sorrow of life, founded on time rather than place, cannot possibly be destroyed.[51]

These passages clearly indicate that Brenner's Zionism is the realization of his basic existential stance. In clear lines, Brenner traces the transition from the adoption of thrownness to the Zionist act of building:

> We, then, children of the Hebrew nation true to ourselves...we must find the strength to amend, and change, and improve our lives; to create our culture, hold on to our language, build our present. We do not wish to live thanks to the Bible that our

ancestors gave the world… Our hand will save us, and our aim is
to toil and create a new present for ourselves and for all of us by
building villages where we, Jews, will settle and live.[52]

Concrete action in the present, then, as synonymous with Zionist action,
is the clear sign of adopting and affirming the thrownness of Jewish
existence. This action does not draw on religious ideas and viewpoints.
The Bible, therefore, holds no special status in the concrete programme.
A Jew is a Jew regardless of the Bible. His actions in the real world do
not derive from the Bible; they express his real association with Jewish
existence. Brenner does not refrain from viewing Zionist action as a
realization of the prophecy: 'and thy children shall come back again
to their own border' (Jeremiah 31:16). But the Jews' return to their
homeland is not a return to the Bible,[53] or to religion. It is a return to
Jewish genealogy,[54] which had unfolded in a particular place – the Land
of Israel. Brenner's Zionism, then, is not an expression of territorialism
or of a political vision:

> Not the Zionism of a piece of land for immigrants anywhere, not
> some dubious corner for some of the poor from the East, but …
> 'behold, days are coming' – and the Hebrew people live; and thy
> children shall come back again to their own border. Not a state…
> a settlement, we need a free settlement for the renaissance of the
> Jewish people and through the Jewish people.[55]

Brenner rejects political Zionism – 'not a state'. Surprisingly, Brenner
joins his rival here, Ahad Ha-Am: both reject the 'myth' of the state as
a solution to the distress of Jewish existence and as the purpose of the
Zionist endeavour. Political Zionism is not on the mark concerning
Zionism's fundamental aim – to find a solution to the individual's
existential problem. Individuals will find answers to their problems, if at
all, in a free society of people linked to one another by compassion, by a
connection that affirms their existence as Jews, and by action designed to
restore this existence. Zionism, then, is the last step in the affirmation of
Jewish existence, an affirmation that itself will bring about the renaissance
of the Jewish people.

The affirmation of Jewish existence rests on two moves; the first
is epistemological – recognizing Jewish givenness as part of existential
thrownness. This stage, as described above, is not based on the observer's
neutral identification of the Jewish datum but on an act of judgment that
identifies this givenness as an ontological component of existence. In
other words, the individual determines that being Jewish is a necessary

rather than a contingent component of his existence: the individual is already a Jewish individual. The second and complementary move changes the status of this givenness from one constituted by the past into one constituted by the present and the future, in a transformation that is not merely cognitive. Rather, it rests on concrete action in real life through the Jew's self-placement as a moral agent, as Brenner understands it, evident in the endorsement of the surrounding reality and in action designed to amend it.

Ahad Ha-Am and Brenner: Genealogy and Voluntarism

So far, I have used the terms 'thrownness', 'facticity', and 'givenness' according to prevalent existentialist terminology. But what makes up this thrownness? Menachem Brinker[56] and Gideon Shimoni assume that Brenner's stance rests on a family-ethnic model: 'For Brenner as for Berdyczewski, the basis of Jewish identity was thus ethnic kinship rather than the beliefs and observances of religion. Not prescriptive beliefs but the individual's innate feelings were the core of national identification.'[57] Brenner (and Berdyczewski) found this approach in Ahad Ha-Am. The family model *à la* Ahad Ha-Am, so they claimed, had enabled to determine the precedence of Jewish belongingness and the liberation from any dependence on ideas. Following are Ahad Ha-Am's key sentences in 'Slavery in Freedom':

> I at least have no need to exalt my people to Heaven, to trumpet its superiority above all other nations, in order to find a justification for its existence. I at least know 'why I remain a Jew' – rather, I can find no meaning in such a question, any more than if I were asked why I remain my father's son. I at least can speak my mind concerning the beliefs and opinions which I have inherited from my ancestors, without fearing to snap the bond that unites me to my people.[58]

Ostensibly, Ahad Ha-Am's response to the question about the meaning of being a Jew is the family model. Family membership is not contingent on ideas. To be a father's son is a primary datum that does not require justification. If this is Ahad Ha-Am's reading, he is continuing the halakhic tradition whereby the model of Jewish ascription is indeed genealogical. A person who is born a Jew remains so, whatever his beliefs – 'even if he sinned, he is still a Jew'.[59]

On closer scrutiny, however, we find that Ahad Ha-Am is not offering the traditional family-genealogical model as a basis of Jewish membership, and family relationships serve merely as an illustration of non-contingent relationships. Ahad Ha-Am does not resort to arguments to affirm Jewish existence because he 'can find no meaning in such a question'. As evidence of this question's meaninglessness, he cites the parenthood relationship – 'any more than if I were asked why I remain my father's son'. The phrase 'any more than' does not point to equivalence but to analogy.

Ahad Ha-Am, then, finds several modes of non-contingent existence – being a Jew and being a father. These being primary relationships, judgments about them do not affect their primary nature. As a Jew committed to halakhic tradition, Ahad Ha-Am could not have failed to notice that the Jewish genealogical model is matrilineal: the mother, not the father, determines the chain of Jewish existence. Hence, the centre of his concern was not genealogy but the determination of Jewish existence as unconditioned. On this point, and only on this point, he continues halakhic tradition.

Ahad Ha-Am and Brenner seem to support identical positions, but this is not the case. Their models are similar, but Brenner's is more complex. First, he explicitly states that the ethnic dimension – belonging to Jewish genealogy as such – does not turn the person into a Jew. Relating to several celebrated figures in literary and cultural circles, Brenner writes:

> Brandes was born a Jew, but he is not a Jew, even though he never converted. The reason he is not a Jew is not that his opinions, as he thinks, are Hellenistic; he, as he is, in all his work, in all his life, would not be a Jew even if he upheld Hermann Cohen's 'method'… and I and others like me, despite our hatred for the Talmud and our scorn for the historical role we have played throughout our lives, are Jews in the better and more sublime sense of the term, and we cannot but be such Jews.[60]

Not even Herzl escapes Brenner's criticism:

> Herzl was a handsome, talented, and virtuous man. He 'abandoned' his 'non-Zionist' past and came to work for the Jews. But what did actually change in him? Did he become a Jew in the sense in which we are Jews? No, he remained as he was, a member of another culture, a member of the culture that had been his until his Zionist work. How did it help him? What did it change in the vision of his soul? He started off by writing a German column in a German newspaper, and went on writing the same column in the same newspaper.[61]

On these grounds, Brenner holds that Herzl cannot lead the Zionist movement:

> He did not understand even the languages of the Jews. He could not speak to us in our languages, and we the Jews may be what we may be, but our redeemer, should he come, will come from among us, from our dark alleys, from our very core… And yet, if Herzl could neither be the leader of the movement because no such movement ever existed, nor a guide to the best Jews outside the movement because he himself was not Jewish enough, he was still a leader who captured hearts.[62]

These statements indicate that the genealogical dimension does not play a decisive role in determining that someone is indeed a Jew. The fact that people are born Jews does not determine their status as Jews. Hence, Brenner argues:

> Meet any Jew who reads newspapers and knows writers' names and he will proudly tell you that Brandes, the celebrated critic, is a Jew, and Fischer, the great publisher, is a Jew, and Henri Bergson, the new great philosopher – some say, is also a Jew… Obviously, all of them deny and hide their Judaism, reject it, have no connection to it.[63]

Furthermore, contrary to the dominant halakhic tradition claiming that a Jew who converts remains a Jew, Brenner held that an apostate is no longer a Jew in any way, but not due to religious reasons:

> Assimilation depends mainly on the adoption of other forms of life. Therefore, those who adopt another religion – that is, other forms of life – are for all intents and purposes assimilated, no less, and also no more, than all the 'French, Poles, etc. of Mosaic persuasion,' and generally, than all those who could convert to Christianity according to their education and their status in society, even if they never did (Lasalle, for instance, who did not convert, is in my view no more Jewish than Heine and Börne, who did).[64]

Being Jewish is not contingent on a religious credo or practice but on participation in a Jewish way of life. Jews are attached to a language, to Jewish social institutions, and, above all, perceive themselves as part of the Jewish people. Ultimately, what makes people Jews is their decision to live a total Jewish existence. Faith in any Jewish system, or in a Jewish political ideology, does not make a person a Jew. People are Jews because they are partners to a Jewish way of life, solidary in the sorrow and suffering of Jewish existence.

A faint echo of ultra-Orthodox views resonates in Brenner's stance. R. Moshe Schick (known as Maharam Schick) formulated an approach in the 19th century whereby the Jewish collective, to which Jews owe a duty of responsibility, is only confessional. Included within it are people who abide by the commandments 'by virtue of the oath on Mount Sinai, where we swore to observe all the commandments'.[65] As for people outside this collective, no duty of mutual responsibility applies and no obligation is incumbent in their regard, not even to save them on the Sabbath.[66] Brenner and R. Schick agree that Jewish genealogy is insufficient to make a person a Jew, and that Judaism is contingent on a real disposition of consciousness. They disagree concerning what a person should do to be considered a Jew. Schick holds that a person must believe in the Torah's divine command and observe it. By contrast, Brenner holds that people must express their Judaism in their attachment to Jewish existence and to Jewish modes of discourse, and in a disposition concretized in a practical decision to share a common destiny with their Jewish brethren.

Brenner, justifiably so from his perspective, does not define the borders of the real Jewish existence a Jew must live to be considered a Jew. He considers these borders self-evident. Against ideas and ideologies, he places the concept of 'culture'. Although he does not develop this concept sufficiently, his use of it is clear. To be a member of a Jewish culture means to belong in one's whole concrete being to the fullness of real Jewish life, which seeks to preserve the existence of the Jewish collective. Jewish culture creates the 'vision of the Jew's soul', because it is the Jew's complete way of life. This is not a contingent idea but real action with and within Jewish life. Specifically: it is not enough for people to act for the sake of their Jewish brethren, as Herzl did; they must live with them and share in the shaping of a total Jewish way of life. Herzl did not share this approach, since he marginalized Jewish identity from those realms of existence[67] that are Brenner's most burning concern.

This approach could lead to the conclusion that, according to Brenner, to be a Jew and a voluntary decision to live as a Jew are exactly the same. This voluntarism means that individuals, all by themselves, make themselves into Jews without Jewish existence preceding their decision. This, however, is not Brenner's stance at all. To be a Jew, as noted, is, above all, a coerced fact. Jews are identified as members of the Jewish people, children of a nation. This primary fundamental fact, however, becomes the object of the person's voluntary decision. I choose what I already am. This choice, for the choosing Jew, makes Jewish existence total.

The gap between Brenner and Ahad Ha-Am is now evident. Both view Jewish existence as a given primary fact, requiring no justification. For Brenner, however, Jewish origin goes through a process of existential reflection at two levels. First, the Jewish fact is such only if recognized as such. Jewish thrownness is identified and established through conscious action. Second, it is endorsed by the individual. Ahad Ha-Am, who emphasised Judaism, could have been satisfied with the fact of Jewish origin. Brenner, who saw no role for 'Judaism' in the creation of a Jewish life, could not confine himself to facts of origin that remain as raw matter. Jews must choose their existence as Jews, and the meaning of choice is not merely cognitive. To be a Jew means to endorse Jewish fate and to see it as the arena for action.

The Pragmatic Meaning of Hebrew Literature

For Brenner, as noted, literature expresses life as is; in his words, literature is 'the product of our life and the expression of our life'.[68] Literature embodies and reflects the dialectic movement of life. Brenner passionately criticizes Ahad Ha-Am for his failure to understand the meaning of literature and its tie to real life:

> Only a logical and rational scholar like Ahad Ha-Am, only a writer who often approaches life mechanically rather than organically, only a man to whom the deep and the mysterious, the ingrained and the instinctive in the human soul are almost alien – only such a man could have expressed joy and satisfaction at the absence of 'rude and uninspiring' poems 'full of the idle prattle' of Yiddish folk songs from our Hebrew literature that, God be praised, is all wisdom, holiness, scholarship, and eternity... We discern only a mechanic, graphomanic attitude in this 'aristocratic' disdain for the unmediated linguistic works of our people.[69]

This critique indicates that literary linguistic form assumes value only if it expresses an 'organic' attitude to existence. Linguistic form must be ontological, that is, it must be associated with the entity and must therefore express the complexity of existence itself. Consequently, the question of language becomes decisive. If the linguistic medium is a means for conveying ideas, the question of language is not important. If, however, the linguistic medium concretizes and reflects the dialectic of existence, the question of language becomes decisive. Jews, whose language is Hebrew, the roots of whose lives are embodied in this language, are committed to express the fullness of their existence in the Hebrew language. Their attitude to it is not 'mechanical', it is the very mode in which the Jews are revealed to themselves.

Brenner continues his critique and claims that, for Ahad Ha-Am,

> there is no difference in the language, as long as you can trade! Others still wish to see in it greatness, purposefulness. For us Jews, the goal is everything, as it were, and the means are not important: all the means are legitimate. The crux is the idea, and literature has a right to exist only when it comes to express 'ideas'. Only then will it be respected. Language is only a means, and do not wonder about his language, so clear that it leaves no echo. A clever man like him will certainly choose the most appropriate, the simplest means...[70]

Contrary to the approach that views linguistic expression as a means for transmitting ideas, Brenner argues that the role of language is to express and expose life:

> Language, the human tongue, is not only a means for an idea but a creation in and of itself, an expression of the life that is beyond the 'idea' as well as a partner and a necessary condition of thought. In the furnace of speech, in the report to a friend, thought will be refined and distilled. And generally, no differentiation is possible between language and thought, saying that one will serve the other, since the two are but one.[71]

Brenner thus views linguistic expression as a medium for the expression of life itself. The life wrapped in mystery, the life whose depth is not easily revealed, is exposed through linguistic expression. This expression does not conceal the blurred countenance of existence, but raises it and brings it to the fore. Language is elusive, carrying within it what cannot possibly be said; the painful fragmentary statement that bears existence itself. What is said is polysemic; it involves mysterious implications. Linguistic expression also enables the refinement and development of thought. Being a kind of dialogue with the other, linguistic expression allows thought to reach clarity and transparence. Concerning the ages-old philosophical question about the relationship between thought and speech, Brenner's view is unequivocal: speech is what enables the formulation of thought, which cannot exist without it. Thought itself is dialogical. Brenner, then, assigns linguistic expression a dual role, as the expression of life and the expression of thought. Obviously, these are not separate aspects, since thought is a part of life. In other words, hidden existence is ultimately an existence of 'being with the other', and is therefore revealed in the linguistic expression, which is the turn to the other.

This analysis points to the closeness between Heidegger's notion of linguistic expression and his view of art. Heidegger, like Brenner, calls for recognition of the dark and unexposed character of existence, and views art as one of the ways that bring beings out of hiding.[72] The work of art is not a copy: 'The work, therefore, is not the reproduction of some particular entity that happens to be present at any given time. It is, on the contrary, the reproduction of the thing's general essence.'[73] Art does not create a new, autonomous field of meaning. It deals with being: 'The art work opens up in its own way the Being of beings. This opening up, i.e., the truth of beings, happens in the work. In the art work, the truth of what is has set itself to work. Art is truth setting itself to work.'[74]

According to Heidegger, and also according to Brenner, art enables the exposure of being. This move is inherent in Heidegger's basic existentialist approach. Neither existentialist reflection nor the work of art create being; they create the realm where it will be present.

The association between the work of art and the concealed Being, or between art and existence, determines also what is beautiful:

> Truth is the unconcealedness[75] of that which is as something that is. Truth is the truth of Being. Beauty does not occur alongside and apart from this truth. When truth set itself into the work, it appears. Appearance – as this being of truth in the work and as work – is beauty. Thus the beautiful belongs to the advent of truth, truth's taking of its place.[76]

The category of the beautiful, then, is not a judging category, external to the artistic occurrence, but a concretization of the Being's presence in the work of art. When the Being is present, beauty will be found. It is not a subjective addition to the work of art but a realization of the artistic manifestation – the exposure of the Being, its release from restraints.

Brenner, before Heidegger, connected the Being, a life wrapped in mystery, and the literary-linguistic expression. The formula he coined was 'life and literature',[77] meaning 'there is no art outside actual reality and outside the concrete content, which this reality provides'.[78] Hence, literature is definitely not judged according to external aesthetic categories – clarity of expression, wealth of ideas, and so forth. The supreme test of a literary work is it closeness to life, since it reflects it.

Brenner located literature at the centre of the confrontation over existence and over ideas. Berdyczewski was for him the hero of a view that connected literature to life,[79] having 'rebelled' against the thought that 'the external idea makes the Jew a Jew; the Jew is what he thinks'.[80] This view detaches thought from actual real existence, and Brenner viewed Berdyczewski as offering an alternative:

> Thought, meaning his self-reckoning, is for him the entire content of his life, the essence, and in this sense he is altogether thought, thought-poetry. For him there is not just thought, mere ideas that roll down like irreversible stones; the difference between the various concepts touches his very core, the essence of his being. And not only because cerebral work implies consequences for his conduct and his actions but mainly because thought-poetry is life itself, his life, life itself for him… Concerning the being of people such as Berdyczewski…life and thought for them are one. None of that rift we find, to some extent, but rather an enriching, connecting element.[81]

Brenner knew well that such a close association between thought, creativity, and life is not free from the basic rift of human existence. Life cannot easily become reflective in the linguistic expression: quite the contrary, the linguistic expression, because of its universal character, appears antithetical to concrete life. Reflection is thus doomed to pursue life.[82] Heidegger, who viewed the existential voyage as a voyage to discover the Being of beings, was not troubled by the contradiction. In his view, the Being becomes present through humans. Brenner's voyage, like that of Kierkegaard, is meant to expose and discover the concrete units. Like Kierkegaard, Brenner emphasises the rift and the contradiction of reflective existence.[83] He shares with Kierkegaard the insight that this rift does not disrupt life; quite the contrary, it deepens it and exposes its rich profusion.

Once it is clear that language is not external to human existence, its place in life becomes a decisive matter. Hebrew is no longer a tool of communication 'but simply a necessity of life'.[84] The cessation or re-establishment of the Hebrew language becomes a key question, since Hebrew is the leitmotif in the connection between reflection and life. The happiness and misery of Jews are related to language: 'Happy is the man who reads the books of his great writers in his mother tongue, because I am a child of a people that does not have a language and a literature – the most miserable of all.'[85]

This special standing of Hebrew and its connection to the Jew's concrete existence leads Brenner to state:

We live. And life has many worlds and many hues and infinite
combinations of powers. And these worlds of ours and these
hues, some of these hues, we want to place in the vessel of our
literature written in the new Hebrew language. Even if Hebrew is
in many senses a dead language, even if it is not the language of
most of our people, even if it is not the language that expresses,
that can express, all the life of our inner world – we can do
nothing about it! We cannot change this! Hebrew is still one of
the languages with the deepest hold on our soul, a language we
cannot erase without erasing our own selves. Therefore, as long
as we are alive, the song of our life, the Hebrew language, the
song of the Hebrew individual, will not die.[86]

Brenner is aware of the problematic of Hebrew as a 'dead' language
that many do not speak and that may fail to reflect the inner world.
Nevertheless, this language is the language of the Hebrew individual, a
potential medium for the liberation of the self. The linguistic expression
cannot come to the self 'from the outside'. The homeland of the language
is internal, in the concrete being of the Jew.

Apparently in the wake of the Hegelian legacy, Brenner excelled
at understanding the importance of the external expression as a
realization of the internal one. The internal expresses and concretizes
itself in the external. Language is the path through which the inner self
attains realization and, therefore, it is attached to the self and cannot be
replaced.

Due to the standing of the Hebrew language, it now becomes the
realm for the development and materialization of the Hebrew individual.
The importance of Hebrew is not due to the contents it bears, or to its
being a holy language; its importance is existential. Its weakness is the
weakness of human beings – it bears the ailments and anguish of the
Hebrew individual and hence the urgent need to promote it.

Notes

1   Yaakov Koplewitz (Yeshurun Keshet), *In Bialik's Times: Essays* (in Hebrew) (Tel
     Aviv: Dvir, 1943), 254–6; *idem*, 'On Y. H. Brenner: A Profile' (in Hebrew), *Anthology
     of Literature, Criticism, and Thought*, 3 (1963), 152.
2   *Writings*, vol.4, 1220.
3   *Ibid.*, 1369.
4   *Ibid.*, vol.3, 505.
5   *Ibid.*, 751.
6   *Ibid.*, 501.
7   *Ibid.*, 831.

8   *Ibid.*, 826.

9   *Ibid.*

10 *Ibid.*, 91. Despite Brenner's disparaging view of the 'prophetic vision', in his critique 'he resorted to the very same expressions used by the ancient Jewish prophets'. David Aryeh Friedman, 'The Cellar Man or the Hebrew Apostate' (in Hebrew), in *Yosef Haim Brenner: A Selection of Critical Essays on his Literary Prose*, ed. Yitzhak Bakon (Tel Aviv: Am Oved, 1972), 207–208.

11 Ludwig Wittgenstein, *Lectures and Conversations on Aesthetics, Psychology and Religious Belief*, ed. Cyril Barrett (Oxford: Basil Blackwell, 1970), 57.

12 See the detailed discussion in D. Z. Philips, *Faith after Foundationalism* (London: Routledge and Kegan Paul, 1988).

13 See Ludwig Wittgenstein, *On Certainty*, trans. Dennis Paul and G. E. M. Anscombe (Oxford: Basil Blackwell, 1969), 42e.

14 *Writings*, vol.3, 760. The last sentence in this passage is quoted from Isaiah 31:3.

15 *Ibid.*

16 Mordechai Kushnir, ed. *Yosef Haim Brenner: Selected Memories* (in Hebrew) (Tel Aviv: Hakibbutz Hameuchad, 1944), 110. For a discussion of this passage, see Menachem Brinker, *Normative Art and Social Thought in Y. H. Brenner's Work* (in Hebrew) (Tel Aviv: Am Oved, 1990), 157ff.

17 Yehezkel Kaufmann, *Exile and Estrangement: A Socio-Historical Study on the Fate of the Nation of Israel from Antiquity until the Present* (in Hebrew), vol.2 (Tel Aviv: Dvir, 1961), 407.

18 Asher Barash, 'On Y. H. Brenner' (in Hebrew), *Notebooks on Literature, Philosophy and Criticism*, 30 (1954), 238.

19 *Writings*, vol.4, 1594.

20 *Writings*, vol.3, 665–6.

21 See also S. Y. Penueli, *Brenner and Gnessin in Early Twentieth-Century Hebrew Fiction* (in Hebrew) (Tel Aviv: Students' Association at Tel Aviv University, 1965), 46.

22 *Writings*, vol.3, 751.

23 *Ibid.*, 856.

24 *Ibid.*, 742.

25 *Ibid.*, vol.4, 1022.

26 Jean-Paul Sartre, *Anti-Semite and Jew*, trans. George J. Becker (New York: Schocken, 1970, 69.

27 *Ibid.*, 78.

28 Baruch Kurzweil, *Our New Literature: Continuity or Revolution* (in Hebrew) (Jerusalem: Schocken, 1962). See also Adir Cohen, *Brenner's Literary Oeuvre* (in Hebrew) (Tel Aviv: Gome, 1972), 230.

29 See *Writings*, vol.4, 1269.

30 *Ha-Me'orer*, 1 (1907), 45.

31 *Writings*, vol.3, 151. The ending of this passage refers to the *Kaddish* of the daily prayers and to the *U-Netaneh Tokef* prayer of the Day of Atonement.

32 See, for instance, *ibid.*, 730; *ibid.*, vol.4, 1090, 1170.

33 See also Hamutal Bar-Yosef, *Decadent Trends in Hebrew Literature: Bialik, Berdyczewski, Brenner* (in Hebrew) (Beer Sheva: Ben-Gurion University, 1997), 331–2.

34   *Writings*, vol.4, 1038.

35   Boaz Arpali, 'Ideology and Anti-Ideology in "Around the Point" by Y. H. Brenner' (in Hebrew), in *Literature and Society in Modern Hebrew Culture: Papers in Honor of Gershon Shaked*, ed. Judith Bar-El, Yigal Schwartz and Tamar S. Hess (Tel Aviv: Hakibbutz Hameuchad, 2005), 103.

36   *Ibid.*, 103–104.

37   *Writings*, vol.4, 1581.

38   *Ibid.*, vol.1, 780.

39   *Ibid.*, vol.3, 763.

40   Martin Heidegger, *Being and Time*, trans. John Macquarrie and Edward Robinson (New York: Harper and Row, 1962), 426.

41   Sartre, *Anti-Semite and Jew*, 91.

42   This is the basic meaning of the concept of authenticity for Heidegger, as he describes it in *Being and Time*. On the development of Heidegger's stance, see Michael E. Zimmerman, *Eclipse of the Self: The Development of Heidegger's Concept of Authenticity* (Athens, OH: Ohio University Press, 1982). See also Corey Anton, *Selfhood and Authenticity* (Albany, NY: SUNY Press, 2001).

43   *Writings*, vol.3, 218.

44   *Ibid.*, 493.

45   *Ibid.*

46   *Ibid.*, 761.

47   *Writings*, vol.2, 1280.

48   See also Boaz Arpali, *The Negative Principle: Ideology and Poetics in Two Stories by Y. H. Brenner* (in Hebrew) (Tel Aviv: Hakibbutz Hameuchad, 1992), 72.

49   *Writings*, vol.3, 848.

50   *Ibid.*, vol.4, 1269.

51   *Ibid.*, vol.3, 831.

52   *Ibid.*, 493–4.

53   On the attitude to the Bible among Brenner and his contemporaries, see Anita Shapira, *The Bible and Israeli Identity* (in Hebrew) (Jerusalem: Magnes Press, 2005).

54   See also Ariel Hirschfeld, 'On "Nerves" by Y. H. Brenner' (in Hebrew), in *Literature and Society in Modern Hebrew Culture: Papers in Honor of Gershon Shaked*, ed. Judith Bar-El, Yigal Schwartz and Tamar S. Hess (Tel Aviv: Hakibbutz Hameuchad, 2005), 76–7.

55   *Writings*, vol.3, 76.

56   See Brinker, *Normative Art*, 159–64.

57   Gideon Shimoni, *The Zionist Ideology* (Hanover and London: Brandeis University Press and University Press of New England, 1995), 299.

58   Ahad Ha-am, 'Slavery in Freedom', in *Contemporary Jewish Thought: A Reader*, ed. Simon Noveck (London: Vision Press Limited, 1964), 39.

59   TB Sanhedrin 44a. For an analysis of this saying and its further transmutation in halakhic literature, see Jacob Katz, 'Though He Sinned, He Remains an Israelite', in *Halakhah and Kabbalah: Studies in the History of Jewish Religion, its Various Faces and Social Relevance* (in Hebrew) (Jerusalem: Magnes Press, 1986), 255–69. On the

centrality of ethnic ascription in Halakhah, see Avi Sagi and Zvi Zohar, *Transforming Identity: The Ritual Transition from Gentile to Jew – Structure and Meaning* (London: Continuum, 2007); *idem, Circles of Jewish Identity, A Study in Halakhic Literature* (in Hebrew) (Jerusalem and Tel Aviv: Hakibbutz Hameuchad and Shalom Hartman Institute, 2000).

60 *Writings*, vol.3, 751.

61 *Ibid.*, 849.

62 *Ibid.*, vol.4, 1011.

63 *Ibid.*, vol.3, 716.

64 *Ibid.*, 488.

65 See Sagi and Zohar, *Circles of Identity*, 161–9.

66 *Ibid.*, 167.

67 For an extensive discussion of this issue, see Avi Sagi and Yedidia Stern, 'Exiling Identity: *Altneuland* and *Der Judenstaat*' (in Hebrew), *Alpayim*, 30 (2007): 46–70.

68 *Writings*, vol.3, 605.

69 *Ibid.*, vol.4, 1090.

70 *Ibid.*, 1090–91.

71 *Ibid.*, 1091.

72 See Martin Heidegger, 'The Origin of the Work of Art', in Martin Heidegger, *Poetry, Language, Thought*, trans. Albert Hofstadter (New York: Harper and Row, 1971), 34–7.

73 *Ibid.*, 37.

74 *Ibid.*, 39.

75 In this text, as well as in *Being and Time*, Heidegger interprets primordial truth as revelation and exposure or as unconcealedness. Hence, his formulation here equates truth with unconcealedness.

76 *Ibid.*, 80.

77 *Writings*, vol.4, 1022.

78 *Ibid.*, vol.3, 746.

79 See also Iris Parush, *National Ideology and Literary Canon* (in Hebrew) (Jerusalem: Bialik Institute, 1992), 144–56.

80 *Writings*, vol.3, 826.

81 *Ibid.*, 828–9.

82 On this issue, see at length, Avi Sagi, *Kierkegaard, Religion, and Existence: The Voyage of the Self*, trans. Batya Stein (Amsterdam-Atlanta, GA: Rodopi, 2000), 46–56.

83 See *Writings*, vol.1, 165.

84 Ada Tzemah, *A Movement at the Spot: Joseph Chaim Brenner and His Novels* (in Hebrew) (Tel Aviv: Hakibbutz Hameuchad, 1984), 40.

85 *Writings*, vol.1, 167. As Bakon showed, the commitment to Hebrew is part of the Brennerian '*af al pi khen*' [nevertheless]. See Yitzhak Bakon, *In the One Year* (in Hebrew) [Papyrus: Tel Aviv University, 1981), 84–5.

86 *Writings*, vol.3, 742–3.

The Diachronic Dimension

The analysis of Brenner's position so far leads to the conclusion that the crucial dimension shaping existence is the present. The present's existentialist primacy is twofold. First, the present epitomizes the primary mode of Jewish existence. It is here and now that Jews find themselves as Jews. They do not return to their past to become Jews, nor do they need to concretize some utopia or future ideal vision to enter the temple of Jewish existence. They are Jews now. The original givenness of Jewish existence is the present. Second, the decision to endorse Jewish givenness is also made now, in the present. The present is the primary dimension of time, from which one returns to the givenness that is itself revealed as a mode of existence in the present.

Ontologically, however, Brenner understands that the horizon of the present does not exhaust human and Jewish existence, and the present of givenness, as well as the present of the decision, are deeply entrenched in the past. Even if givenness is revealed in the present, then, the 'now' of the present is merely the top layer of an existence that begins in the past, the ending of the genealogical chain. The decision to endorse existence is rooted in the understanding that Jewish existence comes from the past to the present. The act of the decision takes place in the present, but draws on the past and returns to the past.

The association with the past, which starts from the present, is at the very core of Brenner's diachronic consciousness. Beyond an affirmation of genealogy, the affirmation of Jewish existence is also concretized in literature, since literature is impossible without a past:

> Indeed, there is no productive national literature in the full sense of the term without selected ancient traditions and deep roots in the soul of the nation and a spiritual national patrimony accumulated in previous generations...[1]

> Our Hebrew literature, although its branches are few, its roots are many. The roots of this literature – let us not forget this! – spread over three thousand years. Its beginnings are in early and later writings. It draws on many feeders and on generations of

a nation that was powerful and yearned for a martyr's death. In its course, it has accompanied the sages of the Mishnah and the Aggadah, the *amoraim* in Babylon and the *tannaim* in the Land of Israel, the sages, the *savoraim* and the *geonim*, the halakhists and the sophists, the kabbalists and the scholars, the rabbis and their followers, the anthologists and the first *maskilim*. All this is a trove of energy that lies at the foundation, all this is wealth, an enormous force that has struck deep roots in the soul of the nation and will not fade away – it cannot fade away.[2]

Hebrew literature in the present, therefore, does not emerge *ex nihilo* but builds on generations of literary creativity that begin with the Bible. Brenner obviously does not mean to disparage modern Hebrew literature through this description. He does not claim that Hebrew creativity must bear the yoke of the work of centuries as an 'ass bearing books'. Rather, he means to point to the depth of Hebrew literary creativity on the one hand, and to the need for a new beginning on the other. Since the connection to the past has been severed, literature cannot be its unbroken continuation:

> Literature in the sense of a building standing forever, each generation adding a layer…in that sense we do not have a literature, we did not have one and it is impossible for us to have one. In our situation and in the situation of our language, the flowers of our affirmation will for sure not bloom in their punctured flowerpot, and may our dried wellspring not be swamped in a mire, may it not be emptied altogether.[3]

Literature is supposed to weave the ties between past and present. Now, claims Brenner, there is no literature but there are 'isolated writers, talented Hebrew men bearing God's candle in their hearts'.[4] Individuals bear the burden of the problematic, crisis-ridden connection. But these individuals express the necessary foundation of life – the mediation between past and present. Connecting present and past through literature is not a surprising step because literature is closely related to life. Brenner thus views literature as mediating all eras: present, past, and future.

> And therefore, I say: Do you have a 'living literature'? There will be a living literature…but you should know that a casual, temporary, unoriginal literature, all of it vulgar, without a past, whose present is only apparent and that certainly has no

successors – such a 'literature' will necessarily be incapable of bearing fruit, such a 'literature' will necessarily remain frozen and dry.[5]

Despite the necessary connection with the past through both life and work, the past has no canonical coercive standing. It provides the 'material' foundation, from which the present will be shaped: 'For us Zionists, our hard and terrifying past was very dear and holy, not as something that we must or can return to, but as valuable material that exists and expects to be retrieved and used to create.'[6]

Brenner recognizes that the human being is created and not creator, and therefore connected to the past. But this past is 'given' as material elaborated by one's contemporaries, it is part of the basic givenness that has a past dimension but only assumes meaning, significance, and shape in the present. This is true for actual reality as well as for literature. Regarding actual reality, recognition of the genealogy of Jewish existence becomes fixated in the present. Becoming a Zionist implies the recognition of Jewish genealogy; Jews return to the land of their ancestors although they do not believe in what their ancestors had believed.

The literature of the past is only the 'material' of present literature, but its contents have no special status in the shaping of the present. Indeed, insofar as contents are concerned, the literature of the past and that of the present confront one another. In an essay in the inaugural issue of '*Ha-Me'orer*',[7] Brenner specifically refers to a broad range of the most celebrated rabbinic sources cited in the traditional literature, repeatedly stating that 'we have no shadow of faith in the God' invoked in them.[8]

The opposite view, which I will call the cultural-historical position, will help to clarify the existentialist meaning of Brenner's claim. According to this position, as explicitly formulated by Hans Georg Gadamer, the past is a constitutive foundation of the present. In his view, past and present are not separated by a gap or an abyss but marked by continuity:

Time is no longer primarily a gulf to be bridged, because it separates, but it is actually the supportive ground of process in which the present is rooted...In fact, the important thing is to recognize the distance in time as a positive and productive possibility of understanding. It is not a yawning abyss, but is filled with the continuity of custom and tradition, in the light of which all that is handed down presents itself to us.[9]

Gadamer, together with other theoreticians of culture, offers a historical-cultural view of human existence that rejects the Cartesian myth of the pure subject. People come from a real history, from a past that determines their identity. Tradition and culture play a dual role in the determination of identity. First, they provide the materials of personal identity, the conceptions, beliefs, norms, myths, and the ethos that substantiate what we already are, the basic language of our culture.[10] Second, tradition provides a precondition of human freedom by offering possibilities that endow the concept of choice with meaning.[11] Personal identity is an ongoing dialogue between present and past. Rather than based on an abstract origin, it is rooted in the past and returns freely to the present. Personal identity, in Gadamer's terms, is 'a fusion of horizons' between present and past.[12]

According to the cultural-historical stance, the personal decision neither denotes an unconditioned starting point nor does it reflect a detached, 'pure' self, cleansed of history and reality. Indeed, the decision on the quality of the dialogue with the past is already affected by the crucial presence of the past in the creation of the self. The movement of the decision, then, is not from the present to the past but from the past to the present, and from it, through the decision, to the past. The self neither is nor can be shaped without the past, since it does not exist without it.

This approach contrasts with the prevalent existentialist view, which is extremely close to the modernist stance that adopts the Cartesian myth. This stance assumes a pure self existing beyond givenness. The past, history, culture, and tradition are part of the ontological construct of thrownness, but their fixation as part of the self and the recognition of the past and of givenness are acts in the present. Their only source is the consciousness and decision of the pure self, which is separate from givenness: the unconditioned self is the one that identifies and affirms the givenness.[13]

Brenner's view is close to that of existentialism. He too holds that the starting point is the present – the self decides in the present to endorse or reject the past. He negates the view of Ahad Ha-Am, who postulates continuity between past and present and thus assigns the past a significant role in the creation of identity.[14] Brenner follows Berdyczewski, who affirmed the primacy of the present: 'People of every nation and tongue begin in the present and end in the past...the present is the broad foundation below and the past is the short head above.'[15] Like Berdyczewski, Brenner too holds that the past wields no compelling power in the shaping of identity, and granting decisive power to the past restrains the renaissance of the nation and the individual. Brenner understood the deception entailed by a presumption of continuity between the religious past and the present, since the religious past of Jewish culture is alien to the culture of the present, just as the culture of the present is alien to the culture of the past. The meaning ascribed to Jewish creativity in the past is exclusively religious, and postulating an uninterrupted flow between the present and the past ultimately implies suppressing the religious meaning of past creativity.

Conscious clarity, then, required Brenner to conclude the absence of cultural continuity. He clung to genealogical continuity instead, affirming the concrete, unbroken flow of Jewish existence without recourse to culture. More precisely, from an existentialist perspective, this affirmation emerges in the recognition that the individual is a member of the Jewish people. The Jewish people has largely undergone a cultural metamorphosis but remains unchanged because, as noted, a people and even individuals are a genealogical continuation of the same chain even if its cultural contents change dramatically. Real historical facts are unconditioned by a conceptual identity. Brenner, like Berdyczewski before him, did not want to blur these differences by tracing a shared cultural content between past and present.

From the perspective of the present, the Hebrew language is the only cultural connection between the cultural creations of the past and those of the present. But Brenner did not assign to Hebrew the role of cultural mediator. He did not see language as the bearer of cultural contents. The Hebrew language he affirms does not assume its value because the basic works of Jewish tradition were written in Hebrew but because of its hold on the existence of the Hebrew person that Brenner, as noted, assumes as a given: 'We write in Hebrew because we cannot but write in Hebrew, because the divine spark within us comes forth only in this flame, because this flicker never dies and never fully materializes anywhere except in this language and in no other.'[16]

A surprisingly thin link joins the present and the cultural past. Brenner does acknowledge that the past is 'valuable material that exists and expects to be retrieved and used to create' and that a 'literature…without a past…will necessarily be incapable of bearing fruit'. But how does the past function as material, if the constant process of adopting past givenness is confined to such thin aspects? What is the depth of the past in literature? Statements of this kind about the past reflect, above all, the anguish of those for whom the cultural-historical past is not part of their present identity, although they still acknowledge the past as part of the givenness.

The border between affirming the genealogical past and negating the cultural one is hard to trace. Real people are not abstract entities, and culture is inseparable from their existence. Indeed, they are not human creatures without it. Culture determines human identity, practices, language, the entire range of human associations. Culture supplies the materials of memory as well as their conscious representation, and itself organizes the horizon of hopes and the expected future.[17] The historical-cultural conception outlined briefly above is extremely accurate when tracing the character of human existence. As human creatures, we are not merely links in a genealogical continuum; indeed, the continuum is cultural from beginning to end, since human beings are cultural creatures and do not exist outside the cultural manifestation. Clifford Geertz formulates this approach as follows:

> Whatever else modern anthropology asserts…it is firm in the conviction that men unmodified by the customs of particular places do not in fact exist, have never existed and, most important, could not in the very nature of the case exist. There is, there can be, no backstage where we can go to catch a glimpse of Mascou's actors as 'real persons' lounging about in street clothes… to draw such a line is to falsify the human situation or, at least, to misrender it seriously.[18]

In line with existentialism, Brenner rejected this stringent characterization of human existence and, by default, of Jewish existence as well. But precisely against the background of his basic affirmation of Jewish givenness, he was unable to point to a demarcation line between what he affirms and what he denies. His approach leaves open the question: how to affirm Jewish givenness without also affirming, in some way, the cultural givenness of the past? Rather than a merely theoretical issue, this is the most existential of questions for Brenner.

In his novel *The Empty Space*, Aharon Avraham Kabak engages in a hidden dialogue with Brenner. Actually assuming a Brennerian starting point, Kabak too seeks to affirm Jewish culture, and even Jewish religion, as part of his affirmation of Jewish existence and Jewish fate. Yosel, the book's protagonist, shifts his support from *Haskalah* to traditional Judaism and criticizes the *maskilim* who seek to renounce the Jewish past:

> In vain do you try to escape the Jewish world, throw off the yoke of Jewish life, in vain…Either you are Jews, and you must then carry the Jewish rucksack on your back with all the poverty, the penury, the sorrows, the edicts, and the insults packed within it, together with faith in the living God, and with the tradition and the Jewish commandments, or you exclude yourself from the Jewish collective. There is no middle! None![19]

Brenner, contrary to Kabak, posed the question about the horizon of Jewish givenness but failed to find an answer, and I return to this issue in Chapter 8 below. In these circumstances, his unswerving affirmation of the Hebrew language heightens the tension following from the affirmation of Jewish givenness. In the essay in '*Ha-Me'orer*' cited above, Brenner raises the opposite aspect of the centrality of Hebrew:

> What shall we do that if we totally erase this dead language from the book of our lives, we become responsible for the loss of all that our spirit has acquired through the generations? What shall we do, that this dead language has a strange quality and speakers of Arabic and Spanish like R. Solomon Ibn Gabirol and R. Judah Halevi and speakers of Polish and Russian...write and create in it, and at times only in it?[20]

In the previous passage from this essay, which was cited above, Brenner rejected the contents and Hebrew, perceived as the embodiment of the Hebrew self, remained the main issue.[21] In this passage, the picture is reversed: the centrality of Hebrew rests on its character as the bearer of 'all that our spirit has acquired through the generations'. Hebrew is not an end in itself but a means for transferring the historical culture, which is its actual purpose. This approach reflects, at least implicitly, awareness of the cultural-historical character of human existence. 'Our spirit' is not replenished automatically and from the present, but emerges and evolves from the baggage of generations.

The Brennerian text, then, conveys a basic tension that develops around the meaning of affirming the horizon of Jewish givenness. Brenner does not pretend to offer a final position on this question. Although his main line of thought is clear, he does leave room for the alternative, historical-cultural option. The contradiction between the two approaches, even concerning the meaning of the Hebrew language, did not frighten him because, like Nietzsche or Kierkegaard, he did not view consistency as a mark of spiritual greatness. Relating to Nietzsche, Brenner writes:

> The crux is not the doctrine but the way, the ways of the abysses of madness, the doubts, and the straining of the soul...For who indeed among the great thinkers of history was free of contradictions? Who among the great luminaries, whose ideas are a product of their exceptional course, could have been free of contradictions?... Indeed, wherever you find their big, necessary contradictions, the contradictions in their theories,

there you find their distinction, the greatness of the path they covered...[22]

Brenner's contradictions concerning modes of Jewish affirmation and the resulting tension are a definite expression of spiritual greatness, which he himself so admired.

Brenner, then, proposes a tense mesh between the synchronic affirmation of actual Jewish existence and the dialectic affirmation of its diachronic dimension, a dimension that includes both Jewish genealogy and the cultural heritage. Ahad Ha-Am sought to restore Jewish tradition in the Gadamerian sense, that is, as an ongoing cultural dialogue that fuses the horizons of past and present.[23] Ahad Ha-Am held that this ongoing dialogue is what determines Jewish existence. By contrast, Brenner considered such a dialogue impossible, since an abyss separates the old and new Jewish cultures. Nevertheless, he could not entirely renounce this dialogue, which follows from his very affirmation of actual Jewish existence.

This tension led to the shaping of a dialectical and dynamic position, which dooms the question about the affirmation of Jewish existence to remain unanswered. Indeed, the aporia underlying Jewish affirmation turns it into a currently relevant question that cannot be avoided. We can no longer rely on ideas, or on texts, or on a firm, sealed tradition that will lead this question to vanish. Affirming Jewish existence means constantly affirming the question about its meaning and its horizon. To be a Jew, then, implies the ceaseless experiencing of 'the ways of the abysses of madness, the doubts, and the straining of the soul'. Any other position is self-deceptive, an attempt to found Jewish existence on something contingent, and thus replaceable.

How to Build a New Jewish Life

Awareness of the gap between the affirmation of Jewish existence and the dialectical attitude towards historical Jewish culture leads Brenner to recognize the need for cultural-social change. This change, however, cannot occur outside the contexts wherein Jews actually live their lives. Culture cannot be created artificially. In order for a new social-cultural style of life to evolve, one must begin by shaping the actual self of the Jews, the very self that will restructure Jewish existence:

Forms of life are not created and destroyed deliberately, but by life. Our social character, however, is gradually strengthened by what we learned from others. New forms of Jewish sociability

are emerging, but have yet to assume concrete shape…The way
ahead, then, is to develop the Jewish personality and to expand
social education through the creation of modes of action for the
national collective. The means are open to discussion, but the
way is one: to strengthen the national body.[24]

Brenner's central claim is that the development and fostering of a
new Jewish life will not come about through exclusion and closure
and through borders on one side of which will be the Jews and on the
other, those excluded from Jewish existence. Instead, we must work for
a deep social-cultural change within 'sick' Jewish existence.[25] The first
and decisive stage in this change is the fostering of a new Jewish self.
Repeatedly, Brenner calls for a change in Jewish life that will lead to the
shaping of a new cultural character, not in art or in specific ideas or
metaphysical conceptions but in life itself. The change in life will lead
to cultural change, given that culture is a product of life: 'Do you not
yet know that culture is not in professors but in a cultural life? In a
productive, creative Europe, life is cultural by default, and Europe would
now have a cultured "appearance" even without the Scriptures, just as we,
the great Jewish people, have no culture in our lives even with the Torah
and the Prophets.'[26]

Following Berdyczewski,[27] Brenner holds that culture emerges in
the course of life, not as the result of an active and deliberate conscious
stance. Brenner believes in the power of life to create culture and new
social frameworks. He does not identify life with culture. Apparently
following Nietzsche, he recognizes the creative power of life and therefore
concludes:

Culture is only one of the things that fill life with contents – it
is not life itself. Hence, it is impossible to come to a group of
people who necessarily have no life, who necessarily lack any
national-cultural values, and say to them: 'Your main problem
is that your old culture (the product of the old national life!)
has been emptied of content and now, if you create a new
national culture – that is good, and if not – this is the end of
you.' 'Gentlemen!' – say the sensitive people in this group – 'just
leave us alone with your culture question! That is not what we
are dealing with here…what we seek above all is – the possibility
of life, life in the simplest sense of the term, to live and not to
die, to live by our own efforts…to live like any other human
being and not in a ghetto (because life in a ghetto is not in the
category of human life). This is our main problem! If we still

have power to lead such a life – then, "House of Jacob, let us rise and go!" [Isaiah 2:5] Let us go! And then in due time, by default, our independent life will be filled with cultural content.'[28]

In this programmatic passage, Brenner clarifies the nature of the connection between culture and life. Culture, in the sense of practices and beliefs, myths, and ethos, is not identical to life. Brenner acknowledges the existence of a primeval life power that, in its regular mode of action, creates culture as well. Culture is a by-product of the fullness of life. But what is the core of human life? Brenner's answer: a life of freedom and liberty.

> 'An answer to Judaism'? No! Human work! Agricultural work, educational work, artistic work. For now, let it all be even minute – but let it be! To us, the freedom of the individual is more priceless than anything, and freedom – is in work. The working man does not depend on the opinion of others – and he is free. The Hebrew man who begins to work in earnest, not as his parents and his ancestors had – by that he is already free. The Hebrew man who lives in a Hebrew village and engages in Hebrew work is not thereby released of all human suffering, but he is no longer in exile.[29]

Freedom is the very foundation of life. There is no life without it. Freedom does not release the individual from life's sorrows and the free individual continues to bear the burden of absurdity. Freedom does not provide metaphysical answers to the question about the meaning of life either. The value of freedom is unconditioned by the purposes it achieves, it is a primary value 'more priceless than anything'. The primary meaning of freedom is negative in the sense coined by Isaiah Berlin, that is, 'I am free to the degree to which no man or body of men interferes with my activity.'[30] But Brenner does not confine himself to this negative aspect of freedom. He holds that human existence must, in Berlin's terminology, realize positive freedom, implying that individuals must be active subjects who determine and shape themselves out of themselves. In Berlin's formulation:

> The 'positive' sense of the word 'liberty' derives from the wish on the part of the individual to be his own master. I wish my life and decisions to depend on myself, not on external forces of whatever kind. I wish to be the instrument of my own, not of other men's, acts of will. I wish to be a subject, not an object, to

be moved by reasons, by conscious purposes, which are my own, not by causes which affect me, as it were, from outside. I wish to be somebody, not nobody; a doer – deciding, self-directed and not acted upon by external nature or by other men as if I were a thing, or an animal, or a slave incapable of playing a human role.[31]

Negative liberty, which is the concern of liberal philosophy, focuses on ensuring the various liberties preventing the other from interfering in the life of any person. This is the object of Berlin's interest. By contrast, positive liberty is the core of existentialist thought. It was Nietzsche who clarified that negative liberty is not *per se* a value. We are tested by our ability to realize our personal freedom. Zarathustra, Nietzsche's hero, objects to negative liberty as an independent value and argues:

Are you such a man as *ought* to escape a yoke? There are many who threw off their final worth when they threw off their bondage.

Free from what? Zarathustra does not care about that! But your eye should clearly tell me: free *for* what?

Can you furnish yourself with your own good and evil and hang up your own will above yourself as a law?...

It is terrible to be alone with the judge and avenger of one's own law. It is to be like a star thrown forth into empty space and into the icy breath of solitude.[32]

The essence of existentialist liberty is concretized in people realizing their possibilities of being: these possibilities are not drawn from the outside but follow from one's existence, one's consciousness and self-interpretation. In this freedom, the person is revealed, in Sartre's terms, as 'being-for-itself', meaning as an existence that can examine, interpret, and set itself ends.

For Brenner too, existentialist freedom is a constitutive element of human existence. Self-evaluation and self-criticism, release from others' control and the ability to shape an autonomous world depend on liberty. Culture has no independent value, and is certainly not primary. Human existence and Jewish existence depend on an atmosphere of freedom wherein, after attaining liberation from the domination of strangers, Jews will be able to develop the various possibilities of their independent existence.

As we know, literature is crucial in shaping the possibilities of life – it is 'our illuminating beacon, the pillar of fire and the pillar of a cloud';[33] it is 'the concretization of the open and hidden forces of the nation'.[34]

Literature is not a description of real Jewish life as it is; rather, it is the critical reflection that extracts from Jewish life its possibilities, examines, and tests the worthy ones. Literature thus expresses the transcendence of the self, in the sense that it is anchored in life but transcends it. Its closeness to life together with its distance from the immediacy of life ensures that the possibilities it will offer will indeed be the pillar of fire and the pillar of a cloud, of which we are told in the Bible that they go before the camp. 'And the Lord went before them by day in a pillar of a cloud, to lead them the way; and by night in a pillar of fire, to give them light; that they might go by day and night' (Exodus 13:21). Literature goes with the camp, but before it. Literature becomes the leading medium for developing a new Hebrew self, and Brenner does not hesitate to call Hebrew literature 'the great treasure for the nation's soul'.[35] The self does not need 'culture' or a value system to be imposed on it from outside. Literary self-reflection can shape life. A culture will thus be built in the course of Jewish existence, loaded with its suffering and riddles.

The shaping of the self, however, is contingent on freedom. According to Brenner, Zionism is not only a political movement but the context for the growth of the free self, and its deeper concern, is individual self-redemption. It is practical in the sense of creating the economic and social context for the growth of personal freedom, which is the key for the structuring of culture as part of the shaping of life itself.

Parallel to the expansion of freedom, whose horizon is the future, Brenner repeatedly stresses the challenge of cultural structuring. In the deep sense, freedom as the foundation of self-transcendence conveys a dialectical attitude to the cultural project, because culture is an inter-generational endeavour within which individuals find themselves. By contrast, freedom distinguishes individuals from their location within the culture. Brenner, who emphasised freedom, emphasised no less the meaning of cultural structuring, built brick by brick[36] as a 'long-term creative project shared by the people and the intellectuals'.[37] This tension creates the crisis typical of a new culture that Brenner, however, views as a driving force of renewal and creativity. Literature and culture 'feed only on the crisis, on the longings for the impossible, on this very lack – not to say: on the emptiness'.[38]

In sum, the question of cultural structuring is the question of the relationship between present and past. This question, rather than its answer, feeds the process of shaping the new culture, which therefore bears all the signs of the tension arising from the complex relationship between present and past.

Nationalism and Zion

Brenner's Jewish existentialism, as outlined so far, also explains his attitude to nationalism and to the Land of Israel. He does not find nationalism intrinsically valuable. Like all ideas, the national idea is contingent and, therefore, does not express the primary foundations of human existence.[39] On these grounds, it cannot be an idea that directs the life of the individual or that of the Jewish people:

> My friend! Do not frighten me with nationalism. Our ancestors frighten us with the word 'Judaism,' and please do not scare me with the word 'nationalism.' I know the meaning of this word and know its value. For me, it has no absolute value. The idea expressed in this word is dear and important to me only insofar as it is contrasted with assimilation, the assimilation that diminishes individual creativity, degrades the soul, and debases the self. For me, therefore, the concept of nationalism is not the litmus test for everything…For better or worse, I have only one litmus test: all that enriches life, that makes existence agreeable, all that makes the human soul courageous, beautiful, rich, all that strengthens our body and makes it upright and beautiful, all that inspires creativity – is good; all that opposes this – is bad. The idea of nationalism…is for me fundamentally important only insofar as it makes us free, proud, resolute in our views, rich in spirit, creative.[40]

His starting point for nationalism is existentialism, paying special attention to the Nietzschean stance. Nietzsche replaces the theological-moral questions related to 'good' and 'bad' with an existentialist test: bad is what impoverishes life, good is what enriches life.[41] In his application of the Nietzschean distinction to the question of nationalism, Brenner diverts the significance of national approaches from the political to the personal-existential realm:

> The land, nature, the national language, the national literature, the national assets, the national in general – all are the atmosphere of individual activity, the open expression of the self's creative soul. What is the foundation of individual happiness? What does the self-aware personality aspire to? To feel it has attained the possibility of making its life richer and more beautiful by moving from the simple to the multi-layered. The free, natural nationalism of noble distinguished men serves them to strengthen and broaden their individualist habits and aspirations.[42]

Nationalism is an important idea, not because it has absolute value but because it can help to shape free individuals that realize their powers, people who are not forced to live the life of 'no one'.[43]

In this perception of the national project and of Zionism, Brenner gives voice to a trend widespread among members of the Second Aliyah. In his autobiography, Shlomo Lavi describes his Zionism in Brennerian terms:

> One could not say that Shalom felt in himself a calling or a pioneering command. The most accurate definition will be that he sought and found a path to self-redemption; he found a way of bringing change into his life, of which he was weary. All he did was just for himself. This was not the ordinary egoism of a young man who feels the ground slipping under him and seeks, for better or worse, a way out, but rather the one and only way out he could find.[44]

Brenner repeatedly uses variations on Ibsen's term 'no one'[45] for describing Jews: 'Types of no ones whose name is Jews.'[46] The Jew lives a life of alienation, in which the self is corrupted. The expression that Brenner uses – 'debases the self'[47] – is a rabbinic phrase denoting a defilement of the divine image in human beings.[48] For Brenner, self-alienation and the loss of creative power are an essential violation of the human self. The remedy to this injury is nationalism, which provides the space for the person to prosper and for the realization of human freedom and creativity. The Jewish individual and the concrete Jewish collective are repeatedly at the centre of Brenner's concern. He is not interested in big theories but in real people and in the conditions that enable them to realize their existence.

The attachment to the Land of Israel is interpreted in similar terms, and rooted in the desire to normalize life. This is the backdrop for his unique dialectical relationship with the land – if the underlying aspiration is merely to normalize life, to attain conditions suited to freedom and creativity, what difference could place make?

Indeed, a 'normalizing' view of the Zionist project leads Brenner to minimize the significance of the Land of Israel. The main concern is the renewal of life. This is the nature of the yearned 'redemption' that, rather than a metaphysical metamorphosis, is the repair of individual existence. The Zionist 'redemption' liberates us from metaphysical or theological-conceptual redemption.

For Brenner, the Land of Israel in the Zionist context is not its role as a 'spiritual centre' *à la* Ahad Ha-Am, or 'the place', the '*axis mundi*' where all the children of Israel will gather. Its standing depends on its ability to serve as a space for action and creativity that will lead to the repair of life. This standing is contingent, as noted, meaning it is not 'the place' but another Jewish place.

Indeed, as a normal place, the Land of Israel is measured by what it allows the individual to do and by what actually takes place in it. Nurit Govrin notes that Brenner 'did not admit to the existence of a new reality in the Land of Israel, and emphasized in his writing that the state of exile continues within it, the sole difference being that the place has changed'.[49] Nevertheless, amending this place, as amending any other, is only possible through liberation from the metaphysical yearning for the land and the understanding of its relative position. S. Y. Agnon understood that Brenner lowers the land's metaphysical height and that, indeed, the land *per se* promises nothing: 'Brenner wrote that, since a Jew has no other place in the world I shall go and try, perhaps there is a place for a person in the Land of Israel.'[50] The place – the Land of Israel – ensures nothing and does not rescue the individual from exile but it may enable something new, not because it contains something but because it may allow self-realization. This insight could shape a correct attitude to restoration and building:

> For one awaiting the 'Zionist realization' – there is nothing to do here. Only one who thinks – in Russia is exile, in Poland is exile, in America is exile, in the Land of Israel is exile, and there is no escape from exile, so let one live within his people and devote all his powers to the creation of some basis within exile, only one with such 'thought' will be able to live here too, and improve and perfect his life and the life of his brethren around him. A false 'center' that will tie all the exiles to it is not what we need, but rather Jewish communities that will become established, each in its way and influencing one another.[51]

But unlike nationalism, which is an idea like any other, the connection to the land is more complex.[52] Brenner discerns in it a romantic element, and does not find it easy to integrate it with the desire to normalize life. What he had been able to do concerning nationalism, he could not do concerning the attachment to the Land of Israel:

> A settlement anywhere will definitely not negate exile, that is, will not satisfy all our aspirations, all the vision of the nation's heart ever since. Until recently, I had never thought of our hopes and longings for Zion as mystical issues beyond time and

transcending simple causes and this 'romantic' appeal had, for me, been only the simple concretization of the desire for freedom and for a normal life...And yet, our exilic wandering will definitely be eradicated only in the Land of Israel; satisfying the feeling of love for the motherland – only in the place for which the heart of the Levite yearns...[53]

The existentialist perspective indeed explains the gap between nationalism and the romantic association to the land. Nationalism, as noted, is an idea. But the Jews' connection to their motherland is a primary element of their being, and they yearn for it as Jews and as human beings. True, this yearning is also a longing for freedom, but human beings are not merely unencumbered rootless entities shaping their lives *ex-nihilo*. Above all, they are creatures whose historical facticity, their vessels of memory and myth, pull them with chains of longing to the Land of Israel. One can disregard an idea, since its contingent nature creates distance from it for an actual person. By contrast, a primary connection cannot be ignored, since it grows from the person's concrete experience. Jews long for their motherland with the same intensity with which they purportedly long for their freedom, and these two cravings of the soul find a response in the real attachment to the Land. Zionism is now an existentialist matter, the deep expression of the unconditioned affirmation of Jewish existence.

But neither the connection to the land nor Zionism will redeem us from the tortured and painful existential voyage. Brenner's Zionist stance has been called 'minimalist',[54] since it does not seek to achieve what cannot be achieved in real life. Zionism will not compensate for the despair and the absurd of human and Jewish existence. Indeed, the Zionist protagonists of Brenner's novels, and Brenner himself, continue to be troubled by the fundamental questions of Jewish existence; they have not reached a 'utopia', they are shackled by the human predicament. Now, however, despite the despair, 'the yearning for life within us says: everything is possible. The yearning for life within us whispers to us hope: workers' settlements, workers' settlements. Workers' settlements – this is our revolution. The one and only.'[55]

The unconditional affirmation of life and the longing for a changed and amended life lead to minor deeds – building workers' settlements;[56] moulding a new society that would turn the Jew from 'no one' into a 'man' – but no more than that. Jews will thus continue to experience the complex modes of human existence but, at least, will be able to live as human beings.[57] Zionism as a life struggle is not derived from logic but from the 'yearning for life' that, for Brenner, is 'beyond logic'.[58] Brenner is wary of big ideas but has no doubts concerning concrete action nurtured by a non-utopian hope to amend reality.[59] This non-utopian hope is the very essence of Brennerian Zionism, which does not strive beyond human existence; indeed, it strives to realize it fully, aware of its limitations and its fragility.

The Individual and the People

Affirming real Jewish existence is an act of individuals. Only individuals stand at a crossroads where they must contend with the possibility of self-alienation and with the implications of affirming Jewish thrownness. This existentialist approach is the basic perspective through which Brenner considers the big questions of the Jewish people. The starting point is the individual, not the people; in Yehezkel Kaufman's terms: 'The beginning of Jewish nationalism is the feeling of the Jewish individual.'[60] Following is Brenner's formulation of the national theory of the individual:

> By now it is clear to all that, despite all the various definitions of a people, there is no Jewish people in the world but only isolated and separate Jews in all corners of the universe; that despite all the learned articles about Jewish art, there are only artists in Germany, in Russia, in France, and in England whose names are Jewish; that notwithstanding all the essays and the translations of Hebrew literature, there are only a few individual Hebrew writers...[61]

A rash reading of this passage out of context could lead to the conclusion that Brenner does not recognize the existence of a Jewish people; no such entity exists in the world, as it were, and there are only individual Jews. This was indeed the understanding of Kaufman, who unhesitatingly noted that Brenner and his followers had embarked on a radical reformulation,

> basing the national entity on the feeling of the 'self,' on the character of the personality. The connection to some lasting set of ideas, values, assets, is denied. There is no national partnership, no unity resting on a cultural community of values. There is national similarity: a group of people, resembling one another in some sense, insofar as their character is determined by their birth.[62]

According to Kaufman, Brenner expresses a radical existentialist stance, which leaves the individual in absolute isolation. The nation, according to this interpretation, is merely an artificial construction based on a certain similarity between individuals. Kaufman implicitly assumes that the primacy of the nation can only be established through 'cultural values' and, since these values have been denied, Brenner and his followers are thrown into a radical individualism.

I do not accept this analysis. My view is that such a position never occurred to Brenner. Rather, the cited passage reflects consciousness of a certain social reality, that is: the Jewish people is vanishing and, instead, there are Jewish individuals. This individuality, however, is not an ontological starting point but an undesirable consequence of the Jewish social reality. Hence, Brenner describes this individuality as oppressive:

> The words 'the Hebrew individual' do not sound as a pugnacious cry, as a demand for a privilege, as a call for liberation. The individuality of the new Hebrew poetry is cold and not at all light-hearted. There is nothing to be released from; there is no collective and its yoke. It is cold and empty around. Our individuality is not a transition from self to non-self. Needless to say, it is very far removed from the egotistic individuality of Max Stirner and Nietzsche. In some sense, it has a kind of submissive, tragic loneliness...[63]

Existentially, the perception of the individual as lonely is an implicit recognition of the connection to the other. As Heidegger notes, the person can experience loneliness only because it is a being-with-the-other rather than an autarchic, self-created entity.[64] With great sensitivity, Brenner discerns that the experience of individual sovereignty is not coextensive with loneliness. Individuals as individuals do not sense loneliness. They are self-fulfilled and self-sufficient. By contrast, the experience of loneliness is precisely a challenge to this fullness, 'it is very far removed from the egotistic individuality'; it is a tormented call for release from this oppressive plight.[65] The loneliness of Jewish existence, then, even if only by implication, is an affirmation of the connection to the Jewish people and, by default, an affirmation of its existence.

Yet, Brenner draws a distinction between two basic definitions of the existence of a people: one biological and one sociological.[66] The Jewish people, so Brenner claims, exists as a biological fact, but is crumbling and vanishing as a social fact:

> Our people exists, but there is a sociological existence and a biological existence...Yes, we exist, we live, but what is our life?

We have no heritage. Generations do not add to one another. And as for what they have bequeathed – rabbinic literature – we would have been better off without this legacy. And in any event, it is now fading away… All the visions of our life tell us that there are only Jewish masses, life is biological, antlike, but if the Jew exists in the sociological sense, a people where each generation adds a layer to the preceding ones and every single part of it is united with every other – such a Jewish people is almost no longer found in the world…If we do not become different now, if now, with the changing surroundings, we do not become a chosen people, that is, a people like all others, who are all chosen for themselves, we will quickly be lost – that is: we will be lost as a people, lost in the sociological sense…in the biological sense, we will be able to live for many days and years, as we have lived so far, even if we do not change anything and nothing changes…[67]

How does the Jewish people survive in a sociological sense? In this passage, Brenner does not answer this question but describes the negative facet, that is, when the Jewish people ceases to exist in the sociological sense. An analysis of Brenner's answer to this question leads to a surprising conclusion: the Jewish people ceases to exist in a sociological sense when the tradition – 'heritage' in Brenner's formulation – is truncated. The Jewish people is no longer adding a 'layer to the preceding ones' and, therefore, it is crumbling. If this reading is correct, then Brenner in this passage is granting weight to the tradition he had rejected. Whereas his emphasis had so far been on the importance he assigns to the synchronic dimension in the shaping of life, in this text Brenner returns to the historical-cultural stance against which he had struggled.

Is Brenner returning here to Ahad Ha-Am's position and acknowledging the importance of the Jewish cultural past? A close reading of this passage suggests this is not so. Brenner's claim is that a people cannot survive without cultural creativity. The collapse of the Jewish people is not due to having lost touch with the past, but to the failure to create its own culture. Brenner's argument is that the past can no longer supply the Jewish people with the necessary and relevant culture.[68] Hence, it must build up its culture anew, without being able to resort to the legacy of the generations: 'We now live in non-surroundings, entirely in non-surroundings, and we must begin everything anew, lay the cornerstone. Who will do that? We? With our character? That is the question.'[69]

The fundamental task facing isolated individuals who affirm their Judaism is how to build the people. A people is not a conceptual-metaphysical entity but a real one, which will survive sociologically only through the actions performed by individuals. The Jewish people has no guarantee of its existence as a separate sociological unit, and will become one only through real action in the world:

> One does not become a Jew through a belief in certain ideals and views, but only by having a living connection with the masses of the Jewish people, by speaking its language, and by taking part in the fulfillment of its vital needs.[70]
>
> The Jewish people is not a people. If we wish to be a people, we must find the first opportunity to acquire assets and share them as a people, to extend the national light over all human needs, to weave a unique historical thread through all our acts and all our needs. Not a 'spiritual center' for the Diaspora. That will not save us. What we needed is to concentrate masses of Jews, who will be part of the *Yishuv*. What we need are workers. What we need are actions and the fulfillment of needs at a popular and national level – actions and work. A person will render account to the God of life for the failure to live and to work. And a people who does not have a piece of land on which to live and to work is a spider web, a web that stretches, flourishes, and ends up in the air.[71]

The existence of a people as a separate sociological unit is thus contingent on several factors. First, recognition of its uniqueness and importance – its being a chosen people. Contrary to the tradition holding that Jewish chosenness holds *vis-à-vis* others, however, Brenner turns his gaze inward: the individuals making up the people must recognize the importance of the Jewish people for themselves. A sense of value is not dependent on the other's gaze, but on one's own consciousness. But consciousness alone is not enough. The second factor is the change in the individual's basic disposition – a readiness to share in all aspects of Jewish destiny. Solidarity with the Jewish other is what determines for the Jewish people the limits of existence.[72] This partnership must be concretized in action in the world, that is, in the building of a real society whose value, in its own perception, is intrinsic and internal, and is not a means for something else – some Jewish idea of the Ahad Ha-Am's 'spiritual centre' brand.[73]

This detailed description clarifies the current loneliness of the Jew. He affirms his existence as a Jew but, in the present conditions, the object of this affirmation is the Jewish people in a biological sense. In the sociological sense, the Jewish people in the present and the Jewish people in the past are at two unbridgeable ends.

The Hebrew writer plays a crucial role in the reshaping of the Jewish people. As a Hebrew writer, then, he affirms the existence of the people, bearing both the deep reflection on the meaning of Jewish existence and the first bricks for building the new cultural network of communication. Hence, more acutely than anyone else, he feels the existentialist loneliness of affirming Jewish existence:

> The Hebrew writer stands like a juniper in the wilderness, without any bountifulness from outside, without any source of nurturance, torn from the people or, more truly and accurately – without a people. He has no Jewish people, no Jewish surroundings depending on their own view and on their independent means of existence. And yet, necessarily – he is a Jew with all his might and all other gates are locked to him, so that his loneliness is so hard as to be unbearable...[74]

The Hebrew writer is a paradigm of every Jew living in the new Jewish reality, who affirms Jewish existence without thereby affirming the tradition and the entire historical-cultural context. He is alone in his life, and his deep loneliness is evidence of his link to Jewish existence, of his being 'with the Jewish other'. This mode of existence is the condition for the rebuilding of the people. But precisely because the people (in the sociological sense) does not yet exist and may always be a future task, the fear for Jewish existence is deep. It intensifies given the mystery of our long existence as a people in the biological sense. This mystery is part of the dark side of existence in general, but this does not hide the need for contending with the question about the 'value of our existence' for us, as a unique sociological unit.[75] Ultimately, if the Jewish people is rebuilt, Jewish individuals will affirm, out of freedom, the facticity of their existence as Jews. Out of this freedom, they will assume the yoke of building the people as a task that should be realized in a given Jewish reality and in a specific geographic space – the Land of Israel.

Relating to Berdyczewski's literary *oeuvre*, Brenner states: 'Unquestionably, his merit is that he differentiated the "spiritual attachment to the Jewish people" from any "fixed and defined *Weltanschauung*". He thereby provided a metaphysical option to all thinkers and free spirits to remain...'[76]

Brenner embraced this distinction unreservedly, developed it, and perfected it, intensifying feeling and mutual commitment at the expense of ideas. The stronger his reference to the 'question of Judaism' as a dead issue,[77] the stronger his emphasis on the primeval link to Jewish existence and to the real Jewish people. Contrary to the position of Kaufman presented at the beginning of this section, Brenner stresses the primary nature of the link to the Jewish people, which he views as a relationship of attachment unmediated by 'cultural values'. Hence, he points to personal, experiential dispositions as the motivation for action rather than to theoretical approaches.

Since everything depends on the individual, who would purportedly become the cornerstone of Jewish revival, the experience of doubt and rift typical of individuals charged with an endless task intensifies. Rift, hesitation, and existential despair are modes of expression for one seeking ties to what is beyond the borders of individual existence.

Affirming Jewish Destiny: Brenner and Soloveitchik

Underlying Brenner's brand of Jewish existentialism is the affirmation of Jewish destiny. What is imposed on the Jew turns into the Jew's realm of action. Jews are those who affirm their thrownness, their destiny, and act to amend it and improve it. The recognition of the centrality of destiny as an expression of thrownness and as the domain of human action is also found in the writings of Joseph B. Soloveitchik, who devoted a special essay – 'Kol Dodi Dofek: Listen – My Beloved Knocks' – to the elucidation of the existentialist aspect of destiny, both in the life of the individual and in the life of the people. The comparison between them will help to shed light on the depth of Brenner's position.

Following Heidegger,[78] Soloveitchik distinguishes between two modes of existence: an existence of fate and an existence of destiny.

> What is an Existence of Fate? It is an existence of duress...It is a factual existence, simply one line in a [long] chain of mechanical causality, devoid of significance, direction, and purpose...The 'I' of fate emerges as an object. As an object, man appears as acted upon and not as actor...Man's existence is hollow, lacking inner content, substance, and independence.[79]
>
> What is an Existence of Destiny? It is an active existence, when man confronts the environment into which he has been cast with an understanding of his uniqueness and value, freedom and capacity; without compromising his integrity and independence in his struggle with the outside world...Man is born as an object, dies as an object, but it is within his capability to live as a 'subject' – as a creator and innovator who impresses his individual imprimatur on his life and breaks out of a life of instinctive automatic behavior into one of creative activity.[80]

This Heideggerian distinction, in Soloveitchik's formulation, fits Brenner's position. Jews find themselves as objects of Jewish existence, as creatures rather than creators. The immanent opposition to this kind of existence rests on the ability of human beings to shape their lives; as creatures, they are not prisoners of their past and can transcend it to the horizon of the future. Indeed, Soloveitchik goes on to write: 'According to Judaism, man's mission in this world is to turn fate into destiny – an existence that is passive and influenced into an existence that is active and influential.'[81]

How are these existentialist categories translated into Jewish existence? Soloveitchik points to four aspects in the awareness of a shared Jewish fate:

> First, the awareness of shared fate appears as that of shared experience. We are all in the realm of a shared fate that binds together the different *strata* of the nation and does not discriminate between classes and individuals...Second, the awareness of shared historical experience leads to the experience of shared suffering. A feeling of empathy is a basic fact in the consciousness of shared Jewish fate...Third, shared suffering is expressed in a feeling of shared obligation and responsibility...Fourth, shared experience is expressed by cooperation...[82]

The awareness of shared fate is concretized in three subjective realms: consciousness – the awareness of sharing; experience – sharing in the suffering; and a sense of obligation and responsibility in practical action. Shared fate is not found 'out there' in the world or imposed on the person from outside but established by the active subject. This characterization points to the large gap between the characterization of the general existence of fate as objectified existence, and the Jewish existence of fate, which transcends the objectified course and crushes it.

Soloveitchik holds that a shared fate indeed establishes the nation as a unique collective.[83] The nation is neither a primary organic entity nor an artificial construct, as proposed by modern theories of nationalism. The nation is a human community established through shared fate in all its dimensions. Soloveitchik holds that the human association called nation serves to amend the oppressive experience of fate: 'The oppressive experience of fate finds its correction in the coalescing of individual personal experiences into the new entity called a nation.'[84]

So far, Soloveitchik's analysis of Jewish existence is superbly existentialist; he does not convert actual existentialist categories into metaphysical-theological ones. But this is only a partial representation of his position. The metaphysical aspect is already evident in Soloveitchik's analysis of the Jewish existence of fate, at two levels. At the first level – the analysis of the historical fate-laden separateness of the Jewish people through metaphysical categories – Soloveitchik rejects the thought that separateness can be described 'rationally'. In his view, this separateness expresses God's deliberate action: 'He is the Almighty who does not wait for the supplications of man and his voluntary summons. He imposes His sovereignty upon him against his will. A Jew cannot banish the God of the Jews from his world.'[85]

Soloveitchik does not accept the classic Zionist thesis whereby the separateness of the Jewish people follows from sociological reasons. Furthermore, he is not ready to stop at the recognition of the 'riddle of Jewish existence', in Brenner's terms. He therefore rejects immanent approaches to real Jewish history, which lack phenomenological justification. In his view, Jewish fate is obvious evidence of God's activity; the real history of the Jewish people transcends history, it is meta-historical, in the terms coined by Yitzhak Breuer, in the sense that a metaphysical system of laws applies to it.[86] Contrary to the personal fate that expressed facticity, Jewish fate is not another factual occurrence in the world but a 'covenant of fate'. His stance is thus obviously circular: as a believer, he assumes that Jewish history has a transcendent meaning open to human understanding: the 'whence' and the 'whither',[87] doomed to remain hidden in Heidegger's thought, are clear and open to Soloveitchik.

The second level touches on the place of shared fate, in all its aspects, within the fate-laden existential realm. Even if Soloveitchik acknowledges, at least implicitly, that the fate-laden realm includes more than the given facticity, the existence of destiny is not, from his perspective, exhausted at this level but at another, new level that is detached from Jewish fate. Jewish existence, therefore, will not find its repair and its meaning in a re-entry into Jewish fate but through its transcendence into destiny.

In Soloveitchik's analysis, the phenomenon noted above at the existential level of fate recurs at the existential level of destiny: between the analysis of a life of destiny at the personal level and its application to the life of the people, he introduces metaphysics or, more precisely, theology. Notwithstanding existentialist intimations in the language that Soloveitchik uses to describe destiny in the life of the people, his explanation is entirely metaphysical. As was true of fate, so concerning destiny: it expresses a covenant with God. That is, the self-transcendence typical of a meaningful existence does not rely merely on human creative activity, be it the individual's or the people's. It is transcendence towards the purpose set by God. The individual or the nation are only saved by turning to God:

What is the content of the Covenant of Sinai? It is a special way
of life that directs the individual to the fulfillment of an end
beyond the reach of the man of fate – the striving of man to
resemble his Creator via self-transcendence....Acts of lovingkindness and fraternity, which are integrated into the framework
of the Covenant of Sinai, are motivated not by the strange sense
of loneliness of the Jew, but by the sense of unity experienced
by a nation forever betrothed to the one God....At Sinai, God
elevated the Covenant of Fate, which He had concluded with a
collective that was forced to be alone...to a Covenant of Destiny
with a collective of people of free will and volition that directs
and sanctifies itself to confront the Almighty.[88]

Soloveitchik's existentialist stance is refracted through the prism of
classical metaphysics. The shaping of the self is not the work of the
individual; it requires divine grace: 'lovingkindness' in Soloveitchik's
language.[89] Ultimately, self-transcendence is contingent on a transcendent
entity. True, this is not a condition for the very act of self-transcendence,
but can only be realized through association with it.

Clearly, Brenner neither does nor can endorse this containment of
the existentialist perspective within theological language. The affirmation
of Jewish fate is the affirmation of thrownness and the readiness to act
for its amendment and elevation. Brenner, like Heidegger, assumes that
self-transcendence takes place out of, and within, fate. Transcendence
is a refusal of Jewish life as is, yet an affirmation of Jewish existence *per
se*. This tension creates room for human action, which is not meant to
attain liberation from Jewish fate but only to act within it. Brenner seeks
to repair Jewish existence within existence itself, not by describing it but
through actions that will change the factual existence of Jews in the world,
turning a detached, feeble, and alienated existence into a meaningful
one. Hence, he reiterates:

Our questions...are more day-to-day questions than merely
descriptive ones...The time has come for all national Jews, those
closest to the life of the people, to give up abstraction, to join
and unite in action, concretely, in order to strengthen the forces
of our people as far as possible so as to enable it to face the
enemy.[90]

Notes

1   *Writings*, vol.4, 40.
2   *Ibid.*, 191.
3   *Ibid.*, 237.
4   *Ibid.*
5   *Ibid.*, 48. See also *ibid.*, 91.
6   *Ibid.*, 79.
7   '*Ha-Me'orer*', 1 (January 1906), 12–14.
8   *Writings*, vol.3, 107.
9   Hans Georg Gadamer, *Truth and Method*, trans. Joel Weinsheimer and Donald G. Marshall (New York: Crossroad, 1989), 264–5.
10 See also John Thompson, 'Tradition and Self in a Mediated World', in *Detraditionalization: Critical Reflections on Authority and Identity*, ed. Paul Heelas, Scott Lash, and Paul Morris (Cambridge, MA: Blackwell, 1996), 89–108.
11 See Charles Taylor, *Hegel and Modern Society* (Cambridge: Cambridge University Press, 1996), 157–9; Will Kymlicka, *Liberalism, Community and Culture* (Oxford: Clarendon Press, 1991), 47–52.
12 On this concept, see Gadamer, *Truth and Method*, 273, 337–41. See also Avi Sagi, *Tradition vs. Traditionalism: Contemporary Perspectives in Jewish Thought*, trans. Batya Stein (Amsterdam and New York: Rodopi, 2008), 10–12.
13 See also Avi Sagi, *The Jewish-Israeli Voyage: Culture and Identity* (in Hebrew) (Jerusalem: Shalom Hartman Institute, 2006), 212–18.
14 For an analysis of Ahad Ha-Am's position, see Rina Hevlin, *Coping with Jewish Identity: A Study of Ahad Ha-Am's Thought* (in Hebrew) (Tel Aviv: Hakibbutz Hameuchad, 2001).
15 Micha Josef Berdyczewski, *Collected Works* (in Hebrew), edited by Avner Holtzman and Yitzhak Kafkafi, vol.6 (Tel Aviv: Hakibbutz Hameuchad, 1996–2009), 71.
16 *Writings*, vol.3, 107–108.
17 For further analysis of this issue, see Sagi, *The Jewish-Israeli Voyage*, 185–7, and references therein.
18 Clifford Geertz, *The Interpretation of Cultures: Selected Essays* (New York: Basic Books, 1973), 35–6. On Mascou's view, see *ibid.*, 34. For further sources and their discussion, see Sagi, *The Jewish-Israeli Voyage*, 65–9.
19 Aharon Avraham Kabak, *The Empty Space* (in Hebrew) (Tel Aviv: Am Oved, 1953), 600–601. This book is the second volume of a trilogy entitled *History of One Family*. In the third volume, entitled *Story without Heroes*, Yosel reiterates this view, which is directly intended against Peretz Smolenskin. See *Story without Heroes* (in Hebrew) (Tel Aviv: Am Oved, 1953), 285.
20 *Writings*, vol.3, 104.
21 See Berdyzcevsky, *Collected Works*, vol.6, 71.
22 *Writings*, vol.3, 657–8.
23 On this perception of tradition, see Sagi, *Tradition vs. Traditionalism*, ch.1; Sagi, *The Jewish-Israeli Voyage*, ch.4.
24 *Writings*, vol.3, 760–61.

25   *Ibid.*, 761.

26   *Ibid.*, 800

27   See Berdyczewski, *Collected Works*, vol.6, 38–40. Brenner also refers to Berdyczewski. See *Writings*, vol.3, 838–9.

28   *Writings*, vol.3, 399.

29   *Ibid.*, 401.

30   Isaiah Berlin, *Four Essays on Liberty* (Oxford-New York: Oxford University Press, 1969), 122.

31   *Ibid.*, 131.

32   Friedrich Nietzsche, *Thus Spoke Zarathustra: A Book for Everyone and No One*, trans. R. J. Hollingdale (Harmondsworth, Middlesex: Penguin Books, 1961), 89.

33   *Writings*, vol.3, 108.

34   *Ibid.*, 606.

35   *Ibid.*

36   *Ibid.*, 237.

37   *Ibid.*, 523. See also *ibid.*, 605.

38   *Ibid.*, 413.

39   See also David Aryeh Friedman, *Prose Studies: Essays and Articles on Narrators and Literature* (in Hebrew) (Tel Aviv: Mahbarot le-Sifrut, 1966), 99–100.

40   *Writings*, vol.3, 233–4.

41   See, for instance, Friedrich Nietzsche, *The Genealogy of Morals* (New York: Dover Thrift Editions, 2003), 3.

42   Y. H. Brenner, *The Yiddish Writings* (in Yiddish and Hebrew), ed. Yitzhak Bakon (Beer-Sheva: Ben-Gurion University, 1985), 224.

43   See also Muki Tzur, *Doing It the Hard Way* [*Le-lo Kutonet Passim*] (Tel Aviv: Am Oved, 1978), 50-53. Muki Tzur described Brenner as a 'post-Zionist living within a very personal world and, at the same time, bearing a sense of a shared fate with many others' (53). See also David Aryeh Friedman, *Y. H. Brenner: The Man and his Work* (in Hebrew) (Berlin: Judischer Verlag, 1923), 41–4.

44   Shlomo Lavi, *The Aliyah of Shalom Layish* (in Hebrew) (Tel Aviv: Ayanot, 1957), 68.

45   Peer Gynt, who goes through an existential voyage, recognizes himself at the end of the play as 'no one', and asks that on his grave be written 'here lies No One' (Henrik Ibsen, *Peer Gynt: A Dramatic Poem*, trans. Christopher Fry and Johan Fillinger [Oxford: Oxford University Press, 1989], 166).

46   *Writings*, vol.3, 124; see also pp.104, 467, and others.

47   See above, p.148.

48   See, for instance, *Genesis Rabbah*, 17, *s. v. 'lo tov'*; ibid., 34, *s. v. 'shofekh dam'*, and others.

49   Nurit Govrin, *Roots and Tops: The Imprint of the First Aliyah on Hebrew Literature* (in Hebrew) (Tel Aviv: Papyrus, 1981), 167.

50   S. Y. Agnon, *Only Yesterday*, trans. Barbara Harshav (Princeton: Princeton University Press, 2000), 169.

51   *Writings*, vol.2, 1433.

52   See also Boaz Arpali, *The Negative Principle: Ideology and Poetics in Two Stories by Y. H. Brenner* (in Hebrew) (Tel Aviv: Hakibbutz Hameuchad, 1992), 60–73, 190–96.

53 *Writings*, vol.3, 86. See also Hamutal Bar-Yosef, *Decadent Trends in Hebrew Literature: Bialik, Berdyczewski, Brenner* (in Hebrew) (Beer Sheva: Ben-Gurion University, 1997), 344–60; Gershon Shaked, *Dead End: Studies in J. H. Brenner, M. J. Berdyczewski, G. Schoffman and U. N. Gnessin* (in Hebrew) (Tel Aviv: Hakibbutz Hameuchad, 1973), 61–3; Nathan Schechter, 'Truth from the Land of Israel: Post-Zionism and "Mi-Kan U-Mi-Kan"'(in Hebrew), *Keshet ha-Hadashah*, 9 (2004): 160–78.

54 See Avner Holtzman, *Literature and Life: Essays on M. J. Berdyczewsky* (in Hebrew) (Jerusalem: Carmel, 2003), 267, and references therein.

55 *Writings*, vol.4, 1296.

56 On Brenner's call for the establishment of workers' settlements, see Menachem Brinker 'Brenner and the Workers' Movement: A Critic from Within' (in Hebrew), in *Hebrew Literature and the Labour Movement*, ed. Pinhas Ginossar (Beer-Sheva: University of Ben-Gurion, 1989), 50–51.

57 Holtzman, *Literature and Life*, 265–75.

58 See *Writings*, vol.4, 1296.

59 See also Brinker, 'Brenner as an Inside Critic', 48–9.

60 Yehezkel Kaufmann, *Exile and Estrangement: A Socio-Historical Study on the Fate of the Nation of Israel from Antiquity until the Present* (in Hebrew), vol.2 (Tel Aviv: Dvir, 1961), 409.

61 *Writings*, vol.3, 744.

62 Kaufman, *Exile and Estrangement*, vol.2, 409.

63 *Writings*, vol.3, 744.

64 Martin Heidegger, *Being and Time*, trans. John Macquarrie and Edward Robinson (New York: Harper and Row, 1962), 157.

65 For further discussion of the distinction between loneliness and self-affirming individualism, see Eliezer Schweid, *Judaism and the Solitary Jew* (in Hebrew) (Tel Aviv: Am Oved, 1974), 16–18.

66 *Writings*, vol.4, 1284.

67 *Ibid.*, 1283–4

68 See *ibid.*, 1288–96.

69 *Ibid.*, 1295.

70 *Writings*, vol. 3, 750–51. See also Daniel Ben-Nahum, 'Y. H. Brenner through a Contemporary Perspective' (in Hebrew), *Orlogin*, 4 (1951), 46.

71 *Writings*, vol. 3, 848. See also Ben Nahum, 'Brenner through a Contemporary Perspective', 47.

72 This approach, pointing to a link between solidarity and the definition of the 'we', reached extensive theoretical development in the thought of Richard Rorty. See Richard Rorty, *Contingency, Irony, and Solidarity* (Cambridge: Cambridge University Press, 1989), 177–92. Brenner's approach differs from Rorty's on several counts, and a discussion of these issues exceeds the scope of this book. One fundamental difference, however, is important for my discussion here. For Rorty, the 'we' depends on social processes, so that what had been defined in the past as 'they' can become part of the 'we' in their course. In his view, moral development is partly tied to increasing expansion in defining the borders

of the 'we' (see *ibid.*, 192). Brenner does not accept this stance. He speaks of solidarity with the Jewish people as is, that is, with the people in the biological sense.

73   See also Iris Parush, *National Ideology and Literary Canon* (in Hebrew) (Jerusalem: Bialik Institute, 1992), 142–3.

74   *Writings*, vol.3, 744.

75   *Ibid.*, vol.4, 1283.

76   *Ibid.*, vol.3, 845.

77   Y. H. Brenner, *Collected Writings* (in Hebrew), vol.3 (Tel Aviv: Hakibbutz Hameuchad, 1967), 327.

78   See, in particular, Heidegger, *Being and Time*, 439–49.

79   Joseph B. Soloveitchik, *Kol Dodi Dofek: Listen – My Beloved Knocks*, trans. David Z. Gordon (New York: Yeshiva University, 2006), 2–3.

80   *Ibid.*, 5–6

81   *Ibid.*, 6.

82   *Ibid.*, 55–61.

83   *Ibid.*, 63.

84   *Ibid.*, 63.

85   *Ibid.*, 54.

86   See Yitzhak Breuer, *Moriyah* (in Hebrew) (Jerusalem: Mosad Harav Kook, 1982), 53–7.

87   Heidegger, *Being and Time*, 173.

88   Soloveitchik, *Kol Dodi Dofek*, 66–7.

89   *Ibid.*, 66.

90   *Writings*, vol.3, 703.

EIGHT

Brenner's Manifesto: 'On the "Vision" of Apostasy'

'On the "Vision" of Apostasy' is unique within Brenner's journalistic output.[1] Published in *Hapo'el ha-Tsa'ir* in November 1910, it became an event in Zionist cultural life within and outside Eretz Israel. The storm it provoked came to be known as the 'Brenner Affair',[2] and was extensively covered.

Hillel Zeitlin, who was Brenner's friend, saw this article as the testimony of a man seeking truth who has lost his way, a tormented soul led to destruction by a crippling anguish: 'This is the tragedy of a person who, despite his ceaseless searching, has not yet found his true "self"... This is the tragedy of a person seeking truth to the point of madness – and truth is beyond him, like the shadow that, no matter how much you chase it, will run away from you.'[3] Zeitlin did not rest until he had characterized Brenner as 'fallen' – a term he drew from Hasidism referring to a great soul that has fallen into the world of chaos.[4] He then went on: 'Brenner falls now – and one who falls, may be trusted to rise one day.'[5] If 'On the "Vision" of Apostasy' is indeed a document that chronicles a great spirit in its torments and hesitations, an analysis of its arguments is pointless since they are merely the external garb of a unique soul's convoluted voyage.

As shown below, however, Ahad Ha-Am and his followers[6] understood that Brenner was offering a significant alternative to Jewish existence, one that does not rest on a connection with historical Jewish culture. Because of Brenner's radical style, however, they too refrained from entering into a serious argument with his claims and presented him instead as one seeking the destruction of the historical Jewish people. They identified the deep negative dimension in Brenner's claims and, therefore, ridiculed his view and rejected it outright. Thus, for instance, Joseph Klausner wrote:

> It is clear: the war we have fought for centuries to refrain from 'transgressing our religion' has been just one long mistake. Even if all Jews were to convert to Christianity in spirit, for as long as they lived in the Land of Israel, stood on its ground, and spoke Hebrew, we would lose nothing since, for Mr. Brenner, 'all this [Jewish beliefs and opinions]' has no more than a tenuous connection to what for him is the core, that is, to his free national

consciousness in the present, which is entirely secular, atheistic, a-theological.[7]

This view focuses on Brenner's extreme formulations and on his linguistic hyperbole, without relating seriously to Brenner's systematic argument, one that not only negates but also, and perhaps mainly, affirms.

Samuel Schneider offers a deeper and more balanced perspective. In his view, Brenner is not merely formulating a critique of Ahad Ha-Am, who had placed 'the question of Judaism' – the issue of culture – at the centre. Schneider views Brenner's article as an attempt to define a fundamental position on the question of Jewish belongingness. He sees this text as an anticipation of the '"who is a Jew" problem',[8] and finds similarities between Brenner's views and the controversy that surrounded the 'Brother Daniel' case:

> An actual case that concretely illustrates Brenner's view is that of Brother Daniel, a friar in the Carmelites Order who petitioned the Supreme Court in its capacity as High Court of Justice to recognize him as a Jew according to the Law of Return, and to issue him an immigrant document and an Israeli ID after the Ministry of Interior had refused to do so. Brother Daniel points out in his petition that he views himself as a Jew for all intents, although his religion is Catholic...In his petition, Brother Daniel articulates the same assumption that underlies Brenner's claim, whereby a person can be a 'good Jew' by nationality, even thought his religion is not Jewish. This petition was indeed rejected by the Supreme Court but, as is well-known, the problem has recurrently emerged in Israeli courts. The argument of those demanding separation [between Jewish religion and Jewish nationality] is often formulated in light of the same ideas expressed by Brenner.[9]

Schneider placed Brenner's position in a broad context. In his view, the concern of Brenner's article is the separation between Jewish nationality and Jewish religion. Brenner, says Schneider, holds that Jewish nationality is not contingent on Jewish religion, which was the claim in Daniel Rufeisen's petition.

The Existentialist Manifesto

A more detailed comparison between the 'who is a Jew' issue and Brenner's position will enable a better understanding of Brenner's argument. Several prominent differences separate the matter that concerns Brenner and the 'who is a Jew' question. Brenner is interested in what is a Jew, whereas the petition deals with the question of who is a Jew. The difference between them is not merely semantic. Brenner is interested in an identity discourse, whereas the 'who is a Jew' question focuses on an identification discourse. The act of identification, and thus the identification discourse, is performed by identifying terms such as names, descriptions, characteristics, and so forth. The identification discourse enables individuation and differentiation of one object from others. Through identification, the object being discussed is perceived as the same thing by all: a fixed, specific entity separate from others, which can be talked about and whose social status can be determined. The Jewish identification discourse enables the various speakers to distinguish those 'outside' from those 'inside'.

The act of identification is not an answer to the question of identity, since it is mainly a means of communication in a discourse between various speakers about a certain object, without the object itself playing an active role in its identification. Identification is imposed on the object from 'outside' by those talking about it, be it individuals or social institutions. The factor that serves to identify the object may function as a component of its self-identity, but this is not a necessary condition for the act of identification. The act of identification may determine the identity of the object that is at the focus of the discourse, but this is merely someone's identity as perceived by others.[10]

The legal discourse on the 'who is a Jew' question deals with identification, not with identity. Its concern is how others – the State of Israel and Israeli society – identify the person, an identification that used to be recorded as an ID annotation. Brother Daniel and all the other petitioners on the matter of 'who is a Jew' demand to be identified as Jews and registered as such in their IDs. The decision of whether to identify them as Jews deals with questions of identity, since the judges will determine identification based on their notion of Jewish identity, either as perceived by the public or as formulated in the letter of the law. The Jewish identity considered by the judges, however, is an identity imposed from outside and therefore related to identification, not part of an identity discourse.

In 'On the "Vision" of Apostasy', Brenner does not deal at all with identification and his concern is Jewish identity. Brenner is not concerned with the epistemological question of a person's identification as a Jew by society. Instead, he raises a fundamental question: what features are constitutive of a person as a Jew? His article is a voyage in the footsteps of Jewish identity, an attempt to decode it from the inside, that is, to submit the account of a Jew living as a Jew about his Judaism.

His analysis points to a further difference between these two issues. The 'who is a Jew' question deals with entry into and exit from the Jewish collective. Its main interest is with borders: when does a person cross the border and enter or leave the circle of Jewish identity? By contrast, Brenner's interest is not the border but the constitutive content of the identity circle as such.

Finally, one important difference between the Brother Daniel case and Brenner's concern in the article is that, in Brother Daniel's case, the issue hinged on his belongingness to the Jewish nation after his conversion to Christianity. Nationality was contrasted with religion, and the petitioner wanted to determine his Judaism according to his nationality, despite his religious affiliation. Brenner does not present this position. He never even considers the possibility of someone converting and remaining part of the national Jewish collective. His claim is the exact antithesis: if a person is not connected to the Jewish collective, then this collective need not be bothered by this person's religious conversion.

> I just do not understand: Who do these pitiable Adolfs and Bernhards trouble, people who from their childhood had been strangers to Jewish society and religion and who, in order to gain entry into Christian society, accepted its 'faith' as well? What had they given us previously, when they did or did not go to the Jewish temple, and what have we lost by their being sprinkled with holy water?[11]

Brenner holds that conversion poses no threat to the national existence of the Jewish people,[12] and he therefore wishes to remove the issue from the agenda of the discourse. It does not thereby follow that he is granting legitimation to a combination of Jewish nationality and Christianity. Indeed, the article is pervaded by a sense of alienation from Christianity, particularly evident when Brenner relates positively to Christian ideas. When Brenner hypothesizes that a person might think that 'the daughter's power is greater than the mother's', he resolutely states his distance from 'current forms of life among the masses of the Christian faithful'.[13] Brenner acknowledges that Jewish religion is 'part of the forms of life that people have created voluntarily-by force'.[14] It has now lost its power, however, and the Jewish way of life has become concretized in other modes, though none of them includes Christianity as an option. Clearly, then, a vast distance separates the public discourse on who is a Jew, as conducted in Israel, and the question posed by Brenner.

'On the "Vision" of Apostasy' is Brenner's basic existentialist manifesto, where he thoroughly explores his stance on Jewish existence as presented in the previous chapters. It is a conscious attempt to reach the 'origin', the unequivocal foundation of the existentialist problem:

what is the nature of being a Jew? How does a Jew become one? Brenner examines two fundamental approaches – the religious and the cultural – that have tried to answer this question. He conducts this examination as a process of self-reflection: he recurrently writes about himself in the first person and repeatedly formulates his personal positions and his reactions. Self-reflection functions in the text as a Jewish existential experiment. If Brenner the man, who affirms his Jewish existence, can reach certain positions in the course of his self-reflection, the implications will transcend his personal report. Self-reflection is the tool for explication and development meant to distinguish between possible and impossible, between possible and necessary, a distinction gradually leading to the discovery of the element necessary for Jewish existence. Even if the discovery is personal, it is not private – it is valid for other Jews who affirm their existence as Jews. Brenner moves cautiously between personal reflections on the one hand and general claims on the other, a course that will purportedly lead him to reach clear answers in his quest for the constitutive components of Jewish existence.

To explicate Brenner's move, I will compare it to one adopted by Freud. In the special introduction that Freud wrote to the Hebrew version of *Totem and Taboo*, he deals with the meaning of his existence as a Jew:

> No reader [of the Hebrew version] of this book will find it easy to put himself in the emotional position of an author who is ignorant of the language of Holy Writ, who is completely estranged from the religion of the fathers – as well as from every other religion – and who cannot take a share in nationalist ideals, but who has yet never repudiated his people, who feels that he is in his essential nature a Jew and who has no desire to alter that nature. If the question were put to him: 'Since you have abandoned all these common characteristics of your compatriots, what is left to you that is Jewish?' he would reply: 'A very great deal, and probably its very essence.' He could not now express this essence in words, but some day, no doubt, it will become accessible to the scientific mind.[15]

Freud is not in Brenner's position. From Brenner's perspective, Freud is not actually a Jew. And yet, the Freudian self-reflection does move within the web of the Brennerian one. Yosef Hayim Yerushalmi held that in this text, as in others, Freud conveys a 'stubborn insistence on defining himself *via negationis*, by a series of reductions. He is not a Jew by religion, or in national terms, or though language…yet in some profound sense he remains a Jew.'[16]

I do not accept this analysis, since the text points out that the negation is only a means for exposing the positive and essential 'remnant'. The reflection that has shed religion, national ideas, and even the language, confronts the person with a foundation hard to decode and express in language – the primordiality of Jewish existence or, in Freud's terms, the 'Jewish self'. This self is concealed under the weight of cognitive perception sets: ideas and language. But their removal actually allows the basic discovery of primordial Jewishness, unconditioned by changing signs.[17]

Obviously, we cannot conclude from the analysis that Freud's position is close to that of Brenner. Indeed, their reflections lead them to different conclusions: Freud finds his Judaism in the subjective-individual realm, and possibly the ethnic one, whereas Brenner, as shown in this book, finds his in the realm of solidary action with other Jews. But both adopt the reflection that leads to the removal of whatever is unnecessary, a removal that sheds new light on what remains – the affirmation of Jewish existence.

Brenner appears to open with a discussion of apostasy, but apostasy will emerge for him as the litmus test of Jewish religion. Apostasy, in the sense of conversion to Christianity, is part of the religious conceptual framework. It becomes a problem only if we assume that Jewish religion plays a constitutive role in Jewish existence. Brenner's basic argument involves two claims: the first, real-historical, states that Jewish religion no longer plays this constitutive role. The second, theoretical-analytical, reduces religion to the 'form of life' that creates it.

Brenner's real-historical claim is: 'I do not see that the question of religion and faith is of such great concern to my people.'[18] He considers this claim to be true about all strata of Jewish society. The 'Jewish bourgeoisie' does preserve the ritual tradition, but does so 'through habit, through an inertia that will certainly persist for a very long time'.[19] Observant Jews, then, are not driven by the validity of religious faith but by psychological factors. Brenner engages here in a psychological reduction of religious practice, which fits his view about the dubious power of ideas or of cognitive knowledge. The analysis of reality should not rest on the validity of ideas but on the deep penetration of the person's 'psycho-physiological feature'.[20]

This reduction is problematic, however, not only because of the flaws inherent in psychological reduction that were discussed in Chapter 3 above but also, and mainly, because Brenner declares in this article that 'not study but practice is the essential thing'.[21] If what is essential is practice, and if the bourgeoisie complies with religious practice, it is ostensibly unjustified to reduce religious practice to another context.

One could argue in Brenner's defence that his claim seeks to point out the gap between the public discourse, which ascribes great significance to the problem of apostasy, and the lack of religious 'warmth' and 'enthusiasm'[22] in a religious practice unaccompanied by faith. If apostasy is the mirror image of religion, the public concern with apostasy warrants the assumption that religious existence encompasses the Jew's entire life, which is precisely the claim that Brenner attacks. Religion does not touch on the Jews' existence, it is external to them.

Brenner also points out that the young generation has already stepped beyond the routine of religious practice and has shifted its focus:

> Again I meet…Hebrew youths, the children of those bourgeois, and I hear them talking about relations between people, between man and woman, between nations, between classes; talking and concerned with the riddle of life and of existence in general, with the realms of matter and spirit, with various trends in poetry, with different movements in world literature… they would not dream of sitting down to discuss theological trifles.[23]

The young generation is bothered by typical concrete and existentialist issues described in previous chapters, and untroubled by issues of Jewish religion.

Brenner, as noted, draws a sharp distinction between religiosity and established religion. Religiosity is a perennial question in human existence. Members of the young generation 'know the…hardship of a life without God'.[24] Recognition of the problem of existence as a problem of religiosity, in the sense analysed in Chapter 4 above, does not contradict the negation of religion. Brenner actually states that deep religiosity may be compatible with anti-theology and anti-theism.[25] The young generation, then, though deeply imbued with religiosity, feels no attachment to Jewish religion and culture.[26]

Jewish existence in the present, then, proves that the claim 'there are no Jews without Jewish religion' is mistaken, because 'a Jew and phylacteries are not the same thing'.[27] This is a factual claim reflecting a specific Jewish reality, but Brenner is formulating a principle here, whereby Jewish religion as such is a secondary life phenomenon, contingent rather than basic. Religion is a product of circumstances that Brenner, as noted, calls forms of life:

> The main forms of life for the individual and the nation do not draw on religion for their survival. Religion *per se*, with all its

ceremonies and absurdities, is merely a part of the form of life that people have created voluntarily-by force, impelled by the economic-spiritual and human-national circumstances of their lives. Religion wears different garbs, is born, and will die.[28]

Forms of life that people adopt are a combination of freedom and necessity. They contain an element of initiative and autonomy, but also an element of necessity. Necessity, as noted, denotes the thrownness within which individuals or societies find themselves. This complex texture of forms of life creates, out of freedom and necessity, the religious way of life. Religion, then, does not have a metaphysical validity unconditioned by circumstances; indeed, because it is dependent on life circumstances it can be removed from existence.

The removal of Jewish religion from existence is expressed, above all, in the Jews' attitude to Jewish religion. The contingent character of religion creates the potential for its dismissal from life, as Brenner claimed had indeed been the case. The concrete historical claim is thus intertwined with the analytical once. The actual fact – the Jews' attitude to religion – is evidence of its being a secondary and contingent phenomenon that is in the process of vanishing from Jewish existence.

Surprisingly, Brenner finds an overlap between ultra-Orthodox and assimilated Jews. Both 'imagine that Judaism and the *mezuzah* are one and the same',[29] which is why the former cleave to religion and the latter abandon it. Neither one acknowledges an alternative to Jewish existence without any basis on religion. Brenner persists in his attempt to discover an alternative to religion, more primeval and fundamental.

The removal of Jewish religion as a constitutive foundation raises the possibility that another element, primordial and unconditioned, may exist in Jewish life, namely, Jewish culture as embodied in Jewish literature throughout history. Brenner devotes a considerable section of 'On the "Vision" of Apostasy' to the status of texts as constitutive elements of existence, and utterly rejects the cultural approach typical of Ahad Ha-Am and his school.

The basic question that Brenner poses in this article is: how do people relate to texts? Do they perceive texts as primordial, as unconditioned, as modules of existence from which liberation is impossible? His answer is unequivocal: texts, even the most important ones, have no primary status in life. The attitude to texts is by nature contingent and amenable to change. People can be released even from texts that have sustained them from the cradle and as they were growing up. As usual with him, Brenner opts for a polemical formulation of this basic insight:

> As for me, even the Old Testament does not have the value that all scream about – 'Scripture,' 'The Book of Books,' 'The Holy Writ,' and so forth. I have been liberated from the hypnosis of the twenty-four books of the Bible for a long, long time...Many secular books of recent times are much closer to me, far greater and deeper in my eyes.[30]

The move of liberation from the weight of biblical literature is not meant to annoy or provoke. It is a product of self-reflection that learns to differentiate the necessary from the unnecessary. Scriptures are not part of the necessary unconditioned foundation. If Brenner the man is free from them, then Jews living among Jews and affirming their Judaism can be free from them. The desire to assign special weight to these texts as constitutive of existence is a fraud. Existentially, they are not so.

Brenner's use of the term 'hypnosis' is particularly interesting. Ostensibly, it entails a grave accusation against Jewish texts, above all the Bible: these texts influence people without their knowledge and deny them their consciousness and freedom. On closer reading, however, Brenner uses this term in another sense. He is responding to Ahad Ha-Am who argues that, through society, culture affects individuals without their knowledge: 'The social environment produces the hypnotic sleep in him [the individual] from his earliest years. In the form of education, it imposes on him a load of various commands, which from the outset limit his movements, and give a definite character to his intelligence, his feelings, his impulses, and his desires.'[31] Contrary to this view, which perceives the individual as a socially-culturally conditioned creature, Brenner claims that individuals can be free from this conditioning. The achievement of Brenner the man is a paradigm of or a testimony to the ability of individuals to be free and to adopt a judging stance on the culture and society of their birth. Texts, including those sanctified for generations, cannot deny us our freedom. Brenner does contend with the question of what had been the attitude to these texts in the past, but judges this to be entirely irrelevant, since it is impossible to extrapolate from the standing of texts in the past to their standing in the present. In the current Jewish reality, Scriptures have no constitutive standing.

Brenner also deals with the possibility that, even though texts may have no religious standing, their necessary and constitutive stance in Jewish existence follows from other, cultural reasons. He discusses two approaches widespread in contemporary Zionism and in the *Haskalah* movement. One claimed that the standing of Scriptures reflected their status as bearers of Jewish historical memory, and the other argued that they embody the best of moral values. He rejects both.

Brenner accepts that Scriptures bear Jewish national memory but, precisely because of it, he questions their exclusivity in this regard:

> The significance I recognize and find in the Bible as the remnant of distant memories and as the embodiment of our people's spirit and of the human spirit within us through many generations and eras, this same significance I find and recognize in the books of the New Testament…The 'New Testament' is our book too, bone of our bones and flesh of our flesh. And my making of the 'New Testament' part of our spiritual heritage (and I know not all my friends will agree with me) is, for me, not at all a sign of some revolution in my spirit…I do not see any fundamental difference between the ascetic submissiveness before God of the prophet from Anatot and the prophet from Nazareth.[32]

If the value of Scriptures rests on their status as bearers of the national memory, they are in no way preferable to the New Testament. Again, Brenner makes this claim in the course of his self-explication and emphasises that, 'for myself', that is, for Brenner, there is no difference. This emphasis is extremely important because it shows that what is ultimately constitutive of Jewish existence is not the text of Scriptures, since Brenner is a Jew and he can detach himself from them. Their standing is conditioned, not conditioning. The Jews' judgment determines the standing of the text, and they relate positively to the Old Testament and negatively to the New Testament although both bear the Jewish national memory. Both, according to Brenner, express a spectrum of possibly similar individual views, close to the similarity he discerns between Jeremiah and Jesus. Brenner, who repeatedly emphasises the centrality of the sovereign subject as the judge and evaluator of literary texts, leads this stance to its logical culmination in his saying about the 'Christian legend about the son of God who was sent to humans'. When he discusses his attitude to this issue, Brenner states: 'On this too, I will say: As I wish…according to my mood…and in any event, no national danger is involved, no matter how you relate to this…One can be a good Jew, devoted to one's people heart and soul, without fearing this legend as if it were some kind of "impurity".'[33] Self-reflection shows that the text does not control us but is rather controlled by us, by our judgments and our feelings. The hierarchical status of this text as a judged object leads to the following conclusion: Jewish national existence does not depend on the text or on the attitude to the text. A more primordial foundation must be found.

Similarly, Brenner also rejects the claim that Scriptures embody the perfect value idea. Brenner's critique on this issue reflects his general approach, whereby ideas are a matter of choice and criticism. A person, therefore, can think and believe that 'Christianity is more ideal, that the Christian rung is higher than the Jewish one in the scale of human development, that the daughter's power is greater than the mother's and has made great strides in the progress of the spirit'.[34] The attitude to ideas is not an element constitutive of life as a whole. Even if we recognize Christian ideas are preferable, it does not follow that we must change our lives: 'So what? Should I, a free Hebrew, therefore change something? I ask you: Should I therefore be Christian? ... That is, adopt the forms of life current among the masses of the Christian faithful who have no connection whatsoever with that good thing [Christian ideas]?'[35]

Brenner holds that a decisive difference prevails between ideas, texts, and cognitive culture on the one hand, and real life on the other. The latter is not constituted by the former. The fact is, claims Brenner, that people who studied the same texts act and react in different ways. And again, in the course of self-reflection, he writes:

> Not study but practice is the essential thing...There are many verses in biblical Judaism and many sayings in Talmudic Judaism...And I and my contemporaries were educated in accordance with all these mutually contradictory verses and sayings, and eventually they grew up and became what they are and I became what I am...'Study' thus played a very insignificant role here. And if someone is an extreme altruist or an extreme egoist...do not these attitudes depend on the depth of his psycho-physiological qualities rather than on the many proofs he has heard from teachers of Judaism or Christianity and on his allegiance to Jewish or Christian morality?[36]

The constitutive foundation of people's existence is not cognitive but pre-cognitive – their psycho-physiology. Brenner thus identifies existentialist necessary thrownness as the basic element of human existence. Into this thrownness, he introduces the psychological and physiological component and omits the cultural and sociological elements as if they were not constitutive of human thrownness. This omission allows him to deny any constitutive status to ideas and texts in human existence. Brenner's conclusion is that human existence is a synthesis of necessity and will. In his self-reflection, he determines: 'I do not think and do because the Talmudic Judaism in which I was brought up has taught me to think or do, but because I want to or because I must.'[37]

What is the implication of this analysis for the question of Jewish existence? Brenner's complex discussion is meant to dismiss the equivalence between Judaism and being a Jew, whether the term

'Judaism' denotes a religion or a culture. Being a Jew is a more primal phenomenon, pre-cultural and pre-religious, based on the combination of necessity and will. Even if Brenner did offer these two elements as alternatives to human existence, the analysis in previous chapters shows that these are not alternatives but rather a continuum: necessity *and* will. Hence, being a Jew derives both from necessity – thrownness into Jewish existence – and from will – the choice of Jewish existence. This contradicts the approach of Nurit Govrin, who bases Jewish existence solely on choice and writes that, according to Brenner in this text and elsewhere, 'a Jew is anyone who chooses to be a Jew'.[38] Choice is important, but this is a choice of Jewish existence by people who already find themselves Jews.

Since the affirmation of Jewish existence is based neither on religion nor on the idea of cultural Judaism, what is it based on? Brenner's answer is: on the concrete activity of Jews: 'There is no Messiah for Israel – let us brace ourselves for life without a Messiah.'[39] Brenner's non-utopian, existentialist realism reaches a pinnacle at this point. A Jew is already a Jew, and those affirming their existence as Jews can only rely on concrete action. This action is not designed to strengthen Judaism or Jewish religion, but actual Jewish existence:

> We the few, the children of the living Jewish people, will be stronger than flint, working and productive as far as possible, strengthening the work of our people and its material and spiritual assets. We, the living Jews, whether on Yom Kippur day we afflict our souls or eat meat with milk…we do not cease to feel ourselves to be Jews, to live our lives as Jews, to work and to create as Jews, to speak our Jewish language, to receive our spiritual nourishment from our literature, to toil for our free national culture, to protect our national honor, and to wage our war for survival in any form it might take.[40]

From Brenner's perspective, Jewish life will be built on an 'active identification with Jewish existence'[41] and not on ideologies of any kind. Nationalism is a foundation built on the present, and its test is the individuals' actual affirmation of their belongingness to Jewish existence. Rather than an extension of the family, as Menachem Brinker claimed,[42] nationalism is the shared field of action of individuals who affirm their existence as Jews. Nationalism, then, will survive for as long as people are willing to play an active role in this active partnership, which assumes various – all necessary – modes: practical work, a Hebrew literature functioning as a communication network, and a caring disposition towards Jewish existence up to, and including, a readiness to enlist in the struggle for the national honour.

Brenner does not offer yet another alternative in the discourse on Judaism. He seeks to change the field of discourse, to divert the question of Jewish existence to the existentialist-practical level. A Jew who is born a Jew, who lives within Jewish existence, cannot rely on cognitive-conceptual modes of concretizing Jewish existence. In order to invest Jewish existence with meaning he must act, take part in the shaping of Jewish life.

Brenner, as we know, does not define the contents of Jewish life but the frame within which this life will be built: a Jewish life is one intended to preserve the existence of Jews as Jews, as a unique human community. This uniqueness rests neither on ideas nor on metaphysical foundations common to all Jews. The uniqueness of national Jewish life is built on the Jews' concrete mutual associations. Jews who find that they are Jews and consequently affirm their Jewish existence, express this affirmation in concrete action, in the shaping of an actual cultural field shared by all partners. It is this partnership, rather than some essential, pre-historical, or pre-concrete element, that creates the meaning of Jewish existence. The Zionism that Brenner offers his readers differs from classic Zionist views. In David Canaanani's formulation:

> He loathed Zionist hyperbole, socialist phraseology...religious functionaries rolling their eyes upward. He found them all empty, they and their spokesmen. He did not place his trust in 'the people,' 'the class,' 'the masses,' 'the chosen people,' 'the processes,' the wheeler-dealers and the leaders. After a few brief ideological transfigurations (Bund, territorialism) he returned from faith in big Zionism, *à la* Herzl, to small, dubious, fragile Zionism – but still Eretz Israel and Zionism.[43]

One problematic point in the Brennerian approach merits attention here. Brenner counts literature and the Hebrew language among the concrete components that will shape life. In his conclusion, he reiterates his main points and again emphasises that the Judaism of Jews is not determined by faith or by religion. Among the elements he considers constitutive of Jewish existence, he includes language as well as literature: 'We do not cease to feel ourselves Jews, to live our Jewish lives...to speak in our Jewish language, to receive our spiritual nourishment from our literature...'[44] But such a deep and primal relationship with the language and the literature is not easy to reconcile with the Brennerian move of preferring the present. Acknowledging the centrality of the Hebrew

language and of Hebrew literature as vital to a new Jewish life immediately
implies a recognition of historical layers, both in the language and in
the literature. The linguistic-literary manifestation, however, is not
only synchronic but distinctly diachronic. Language and literature are
suffused with the tracings of the past. And yet, if Hebrew creativity and
language are so central, how can one begin life in the present without
commitment to a connection to the past?

Iris Parush deals directly with this question:

> Brenner holds that contemporary writers cannot negate
> childhood teachings, which had been based on traditional
> Hebrew literature. These teachings have become an integral part
> of their personality, even though their views and their feelings
> call for liberation from them. Regardless of their attitude to
> traditional Hebrew literature, therefore, the language of this
> literature will go on being a reservoir of meanings, associations,
> and allusions entwined with their soul and with the soul of the
> nation…Furthermore, the artist's reckoning with his people, his
> character, his history, can only be conducted in a language that
> also reflects the form of his life in the past. The Jewish artist, who
> wishes to express the full scope of his spiritual world, must resort
> to his national language. Nevertheless, because of the imperative
> of liberation from rigid thought patterns and from contents no
> longer related to the life of the contemporary Jewish artist, he
> cannot choose the familiar road and use the language 'in the
> spirit of the sources.' A new experience and new thought demand,
> according to Brenner, a free and independent language.[45]

Brenner, who is well aware of thrownness as a fixed feature of human
life, understands that people cannot begin their lives *ex-nihilo*. They
are forced into a historical context that stamps them with its seal and
determines their real existence, and it is against this background that
they must bring about change. Change and transformation do not
imply a rejection of thrownness and absolute deliverance from it, but
its reshaping. The Hebrew language imprinted in a person's existence
as part of factual givenness is not a matter of choice. As shown in the
previous chapter, Brenner claims that Jews are forced to adopt Hebrew.
They must therefore wage their struggle with the past, with tradition, and
must realize their freedom within this language. Hebrew language and
literature are vital tools in the shaping of a new culture. Hence, within the
onerous historical continuum of traditional literature, a new language
and a new literature will emerge. Although the language will not be

fully liberated from traditional idioms – and who more than Brenner is shackled by them – it will definitely be able to turn to the present and to life by placing them above the authority of tradition and of the past.

A comparison with Bialik will help to clarify Brenner's stance concerning Hebrew language and literature. Brenner's position appears to resemble that of Bialik, who assigns a unique place to Hebrew regardless of its contents and assumes that the expression '*umah ve-lashon* [nation and language]' is 'a kind of tautology, a repetition in different words'.[46] He explains this statement as follows:

> Language is what differentiates one nation from another.... Everything flows and changes, everything is taken, stolen, grabbed, even land – everything except the language. Contents (religion, commandments and actions, thoughts, opinions and beliefs, practices), all change and pass, but the form (the language) remains: language is the eternal, the perennial. No asset has eternal content. Fixed outlooks seemingly steadfast pass too, but they leave behind a handful of words, and through this small handful, the outlook passes from generation to generation, passes and lives on...The word was not only at the beginning, but also at the end, language is the only immortality of beliefs and opinions...Should you say: 'And religion and literature?' Both rest on language and, through it, have been preserved from extinction.[47]

The phrase that Bialik uses paraphrases the 'in the beginning was the Word', which opens the Gospel of St John. This verse expresses the exalted status of Jesus, who 'was with God, and the Word was God',[48] that is, he is as primal as God and precedes Creation.[49] Bialik's use of the Christian text, then, is meant to determine the ontological status of language as primordial and preceding any cultural creation. Language also transcends the course of cultural history as such, since it is the 'end' – the permanent element in all cultural transmutations.

Although similar to Brenner's approach, Bialik's can easily be seen to differ on several counts. Bialik seeks the permanent national element, which is not subject to change. He understands that this element cannot be identified with specific contents or practices, since these are not permanent in the national existence. Nor is literature such an element, but it does allow us to recognize it: language is the fixed foundation of existence, and since it is primal for national life, it resurrects literature and preserves contents and practices from extinction, even when obsolete. Language for Bialik is the foundation of life that enables the 'immortality' of 'beliefs and opinions'. Through language, then, the past in its entire range of forms and contents becomes alive again, even if not in the same terms it had represented in its original place and time. The affirmation of the Hebrew language, then, is not a result of our thrownness into it; it is not a destiny imposed on the Jew but the life channel of this existence, through which the past joins the present.

The crucial difference between the two approaches now becomes clear. Bialik's concern is to preserve the connection between past and present, even if he acknowledges the transient nature of the past. Language, then, is for him a cultural organon. Brenner's concern, by contrast, is the present. Language for him, therefore, has a different meaning, existentialist rather than cultural. It reflects the Jew's thrownness. Jews who affirm their existence as Jews and still reject their past will only be able to do this through the Hebrew language, which enables to negate the past while reaffirming the present.

The proper relationship between present and past is indeed what marks the split between Brenner and Ahad Ha-Am. This split is particularly significant because it exposes additional and, at times, particularly problematic aspects of Brenner's stance.

Idea vs. Existence

The 'Brenner Affair', which unfolded after the publication of 'On the "Vision" of Apostasy', took the discussion far beyond any specific concern with Brenner's theses. Ahad Ha-Am's essay 'Torah from Zion'[50] offers the deepest critique of Brenner's article, although this dimension has not been given due attention because of the focus on Ahad Ha-Am's political role in this affair – his attempt to block financial support for *Ha-Po'el ha-Tsa'ir* as a sanction for the publication of Brenner's article.

The confrontation between Brenner and Ahad Ha-Am moves along three main interrelated axes. The first is the relationship between the individual and the Jewish people; the second, the relationship between ideas and the concrete Jewish people; the third, the relationship between the present and the past and the meaning of the past. As noted in the previous chapter, Brenner assumes that the existence of the individual is primary and the people's secondary – a people is built through the actions of individuals who shape a concrete network of communication between them. Ahad Ha-Am, by contrast, assumes that the primal element is the people, and individuals find themselves within a people that provides them with the initial network of meanings.

The basic difference in the relationship between the individual and the people touches also on the second axis of confrontation:

given that Brenner takes the individual as his starting point, there is no room for speaking about pre-existent ideas that condition individuals and determine their lives. Sovereign individuals are in a position to judge the world of ideas and, therefore, are not conditioned by them. Indeed, they generate these ideas in the course of weaving a network of interrelationships. Ahad Ha-Am, by contrast, assumes the primacy of the people and also postulates the spectrum of Jewish ideas providing the life context to Jewish individuals. This conflict between Brenner and Ahad Ha-Am culminates in the question of the relationship between past and present. Brenner emphasises the present, from which the past assumes its standing, whereas Ahad Ha-Am posits a more complex relationship between present and past. The past, no less than the present, is constitutive of individual and national existence. Since the past plays such a decisive role in Ahad Ha-Am's thought, its interpretation is also more complex. It no longer represents a single pattern but a range of aspects.

Before entering into a detailed discussion of Ahad Ha-Am's critique, something should be said about Brenner's (as well as Berdyczewski's) disappointment with Ahad Ha-Am, which he articulates directly in '*Mi-Kan u-mi-Khan*' [From Here and Here]:

> When a Hebrew writer ages, he begins to speak about tradition and about national assets. Of course! The same writer who broke broken tablets in his youth, as he wearies of literary days and begins to feel that...that...that he himself is a bit of tradition, will call forth: 'Culture, youngsters! Respect for the tradition of an old and great people such as ours!'[51]

This story, which was published in 1911, is marked by the polemic between Brenner and Ahad Ha-Am. Brenner conveys his great disappointment with the rebel 'who broke broken tablets in his youth' and is now shackled by the fetters of tradition, having lost the power of denial. Repeatedly Berdyczewski,[52] and Brenner in his wake, refer to Ahad Ha-Am and point to the turn in the latter's position, claiming that they uphold his original stance while he has deviated from it.

This issue, as well as what I consider the misunderstanding of Ahad Ha-Am by both Brenner and Berdyczewski, will be the starting point of my discussion. This misunderstanding, or their talking at cross purposes, reflects the fundamental differences at the root of the confrontation between them. Ahad Ha-Am writes:

> I at least know 'why I remain a Jew' – or rather, I can find no meaning in such a question, any more than if I were asked why I

remain my father's son. I at least can speak my mind concerning
the beliefs and opinions which I have inherited from my ancestors,
without fearing to snap the bond that unites me to my people…
In a word, I am my own, and my opinions and feelings are my
own…And this spiritual freedom – scoff who will! – I would not
exchange or barter for all the emancipation in the world.[53]

A close examination of this basic text shows that his starting point is not
that of the reflective 'observer' detached from his heritage. Quite the
contrary, the text assumes that individuals are not born in a vacuum,
nor are they an Archimedean point in the shaping of their world. They
are born into a tradition bequeathed by their ancestors, a concept that
obviously does not refer only to direct ancestors, since parents do not
bear a private tradition of their own. Rather, it points to the previous
generations of one's people, who impart the tradition. Individual lives,
then, acquire meaning through the people.

Ahad Ha-Am articulates this primal connection of the individual to
the people and to its contents in a style reminiscent of Brenner. The
similarity, however, highlights the difference. In 'Three Steps', a later
article dated 1898, Ahad Ha-Am states that the arguments 'that Jews in
the West usually rely upon to "apologize" for upholding their Judaism
and wishing its continuity are definitely unsound'. Their reason for being
Jews is more primary: 'They are Jews because the Jewish national feeling
is still alive in their hearts and acts upon their will involuntarily.'[54] Ahad
Ha-Am quotes at length a 'Western rabbi', who he finds echoes his view:

> Why are we Jews? How strange the very question! Ask the fire why
> it burns! Ask the sun why it shines! Ask the tree why it grows!…
> Thus, ask the Jew why he is a Jew. We cannot but be what we are.
> It is inside us, not for our benefit, a law of the laws of nature…
> No! Not Jewish philosophy, not the Jewish Torah, not Jewish
> faith – not this is the original reason, the initial drive, but rather
> Jewish feeling, an instinctive feeling that cannot be defined in
> words. Call it whatever you wish, call it a blood relationship, the
> feeling of the race or the spirit of the nation, but more than any
> of them, it would be best to call it: the Hebrew heart![55]

This passage appears to lead to the conclusion that Ahad Ha-Am, like
Brenner or Berdyczewski, waives the conceptual dimension altogether
and renounces the Judaism that was added only later. But this claim fails
to distinguish between the individual's subjective connection and its
object – Jewish nationality. Although the connection is indeed primal and

unmediated by ideas, Jewish nationality *à la* Ahad Ha-Am bears within it a web of historical ideas, some fixed and some changing. The reflective recognition of this existential reality, which assumes a primal connection to Jewish nationality as a historical-cultural manifestation containing ideas, leads individuals to a point of decision requiring them to reconcile the primordiality of their connection with the ideas contained in its object – Jewish nationality. In this reflective conscious voyage, individuals discover that their primal connection is to a people and a cultural legacy. They are thus expected to account for the combination between the primary unconditioned connection and its objects – a cultural tradition whose contents are contingent. The solution that Ahad Ha-Am suggests for this tension is an unconditioned affirmation of tradition together with the admittance that its contents are contingent. Thus, he is proposing an unconditional affirmation of the frame, the 'cask' in Ahad Ha-Am's metaphor, but not of the 'wine' poured into it, which may change and vary.

A primal unconditional connection to the tradition actually enables a critical stance. Critics are not alienated strangers but heirs of the tradition and aware of their debt to it, and the critique is itself a profound sign of the connection.[56]

Contrary to Brenner, who assumes the stance of a sovereign subject able to detach from a tradition that is not primal in his existence, Ahad Ha-Am is already aware at an early stage of his thought that individuals establish their existence on the culture and the society within which they find themselves. Ahad Ha-Am also acknowledges a fact known to scholars of culture, namely, that the power of culture and society does not vanish; quite the contrary, the power of culture lies in its undetected influence on the individual. Culture is not analytical reflection but a style of life, uncharacterized by reflection and enlightenment and shaped instead by internalized social habits, Pierre Bourdieu's 'habitus'. Ahad Ha-Am formulated this notion as early as 1894, in his essay 'Two Domains':

> Every civilized man who is born and bred in an orderly state of society lives all his life in the condition of the hypnotic subject, unconsciously subservient to the will of others. The social environment produces the hypnotic sleep in him from his earliest years. In the form of education, it imposes on him a load of various commands, which from the outset limit his movements, and give a definite character to his intelligence, his feelings, his impulses, and his desires. In later life, this activity of the social environment is ceaselessly continued in various ways. Language and literature, religion and morality, laws and

customs – all these and their like are the media through which society puts the individual to sleep and constantly repeats to him its commandments, until he can no longer help rendering them obedience.[57]

Brenner's starting point is existentialist, so that his ability to judge thrownness, which also includes the cultural component he has inherited, is examined through this perspective. Individuals are sovereign – they are the ones who identify thrownness and endow it with meaning in their existence. Brenner does not ascribe decisive weight to culture, to tradition, and to the people as the one bearing them. Unlike Brenner, Ahad Ha-Am takes culture as his point of departure.[58] Individuals are not sovereign – they are part of a culture, a tradition, and a society that, without any awareness on their part, fixate their lives. The individual's critical reflection begins from the cultural datum; reflection identifies the datum but cannot confront it as a sovereign judge and evaluator. Any notion of such a sovereign stand is self-deceptive.

Within this cultural stance, thrownness is easily explained. Not only are we thrown into physical and psychological conditions, but into a society and a culture as well. Paraphrasing Sartre, one could argue that Ahad Ha-Am views individuals as doomed to belong to a culture and a society. A society has historical depth, and is decisively shaped by the diachronic aspect. In Ahad Ha-Am's formulation:

Society does not create its spiritual stock-in-trade and its way of life afresh in every generation. These things come to birth in the earliest stages of society, being a product of the conditions of life, then proceed through a long course of development till they attain a form that suits that particular society, and then, finally, are handed down from generation to generation without any fundamental change. Thus society in any given generation is nothing but the instrument of the will of earlier generations.[59]

According to this approach, tradition is shaped and consequently sealed 'without any fundamental change'. Tradition, then, does not emerge through a constant dialogue between past and present, contrary to the dynamic perception of it.[60] In an article from the same period, however, Ahad Ha-Am presents a more complex view. Concerning Scripture, a distinction is required between the 'cask' – the written word, or the normative act, and the contents – 'abstract beliefs'. In 'Sacred and Profane', Ahad Ha-Am states:

It is just the ancient cask with its ancient form that is holy, and sanctifies all that is in it, though it may be emptied and filled with new wine from time to time; whereas, if once the cask is broken or remoulded, the wine will lose its taste, though it be never so old.[61]

In this article, contrary to his view in 'Two Domains', Ahad Ha-Am did identify the changing and dynamic character of the tradition. He understood that the ability of a tradition to contain every truth is an essential part of its holiness. The meaning of Scripture is determined through the encounter between 'my truth' and the text. Hence, the history of Scriptural exegesis enabled believers in the holiness of these texts to find in them the views of Darwin and Copernicus as well. Believers 'sought in Scripture only the truth – each one his own truth – and all found that which they sought. They found it because they had to find it: because if they had not found it, then truth would not have been truth, or the Scriptures would not have been holy.'[62]

This dynamic view of the tradition later developed by Gadamer and his followers[63] was originally articulated by Ahad Ha-Am,[64] who saw no contradiction between autonomy and tradition and did not share in the dichotomy between past and present postulated by Berdyczewski[65] and by Brenner in his wake. Instead, Ahad Ha-Am assumed a fusion of horizons between past and present. The past is the legacy within which individuals find themselves, but they still turn to the legacy of the present in search of their world and their values. The 'individual self' and the 'national self' are not two separate entities. The past that establishes the individual self contains within it the people's past, even though 'Past and Future', which was published in 1892, might give the impression that Ahad Ha-Am makes their relationship merely analogous.[66]

This analysis clearly points to the special status of the past as the central time axis of the people's culture, and as the individual's primal space. Ahad Ha-Am could already say at this stage of his thinking that, in a choice between two alternative and problematic 'sections' – one that abandons the future and sinks into the past and one that abandons the past and turns only to the future – the latter is worse:

Far more dangerous, therefore, is that other section, which seeks salvation in a Future not connected with our Past, and believes that after a history extending over thousands of years a people can begin all over again, like a newborn child...This section forgets that it is the nation – that is, the national Ego in the form given to it by history – that desires to live: not some other nation, but just *this* one, with all its essentials, and all its memories, and all its hopes…and they err who think it possible to lead this also along the path of their own choice. The path of the national Ego is already marked and laid out by its national character, and that character has its foundation in the Past, and its completion in the Future.[67]

Ahad Ha-Am holds that the basic foundation of the people is the past; the past preserves the identity of the people and prevents its collapse. The rebirth of this same nation – the turn to the future – refutes the historical mode in which the people prevails as a specific collective. Ahad Ha-Am, therefore, seeks to fuse past and present in the movement of the tradition *per se*. The point of departure, then, is the people, which preserves its historical continuity through a continued connection of present and future to the past: 'The "national self"… in essence and principle…is nothing but a combination of past and future.'[68] The past and the future contain within them the fundamental ideas of the national Jewish 'self'.

Berdyczewski and Brenner, and in their wake scholars such as Yehkezkel Kaufmann[69] and Brinker,[70] held that Ahad Ha-Am's polemic with Brenner's article, as well as papers that Ahad Ha-Am published later in the 1890s, expose him as retreating from his original positions. From a stance that emphasises liberty and freedom of opinion in the spirit of the *Haskalah*, Ahad Ha-Am went on to deny Jews the right he had assumed for himself to 'speak my mind concerning the beliefs and the opinions which I have inherited from my ancestors'. I will argue, however, that Ahad Ha-Am never retreated as claimed. The article 'Torah from Zion' relies on his previous claims, and his view in the various sources is clear: people can judge and criticize their ancestors' tradition, but they cannot negate tradition *per se* as the constitutive foundation of Jewish existence. Such a negation uproots Jewish existence altogether. What troubled Ahad Ha-Am was Brenner's contempt for Jewish tradition, his view of it as a Christian 'Bible' that hypnotizes successive generations. He viewed this approach as reflecting a detachment from tradition rather than as a critique of views within the tradition that still assume its primacy.

This difference between my interpretation and the prevalent view guides my reading of Ahad Ha-Am's critique of Brenner as he formulated it in 'Torah from Zion'. My interpretation will show that the starting point of Ahad Ha-Am's critique differs from Brenner's in the three aspects noted above, and continues his classic attitudes.

Ahad Ha-Am criticizes Brenner and argues that liberation from the past is impossible – the re-creation of a people is not a viable option:

A national consciousness 'free' from the national past is an 'absurdity' unheard of in any nation or tongue. Nothing can be liberated from the natural conditions of its existence unless it is also 'liberated' from its very existence. Can a tree be liberated from its roots, which are buried deep in the ground and deny it freedom of movement?[71]

The past is the fixed element constraining the movement of the present and the future. This claim of Ahad Ha-Am is not new, since he views the past as a decisive element in the creation of a society and a people. Ahad Ha-Am dismisses the option of shaping national existence through the future as an alternative to the past. In Brenner's perception, as noted, concrete practical action is what brings individuals together to make a people. Ahad Ha-Am's counterclaim is that creating a frame for concrete action is not yet a melting pot for nation building: 'Millions of individuals who have come from all corners of the planet to one country and found in it "a place for productive action" are not yet one nation and do not have a shared national consciousness but only a consciousness of shared interests.'[72] Shared action without assuming a 'shared national consciousness' does not create a nation. Ahad Ha-Am does not deny that, in the long range, interests-driven action will lead to nation-building, if a cultural past is woven in the course of time. In his article, Ahad Ha-Am deals with two such instances. The first is the United States, which is beginning to evolve into a nation although its builders' actions had relied on their shared interests. A long time was required for a gathering of individuals to become a people, 'and several more generations will pass until this new creature reaches full maturity'.[73] The opposite case is the French nation, which tried to disconnect from its past 'but soon after realized its mistake, the roots were not pulled up, and the tree still stands on them'.[74] How, then, can we think about the existence of a Jewish people detached from its past? A Jewish people detached from its past will have failed to shed its Judaism, but will still be unable to become a new people. If Brenner calls for the affirmation of Jewish existence as Jewish existence, he cannot let go of the basis – the past. A 'free national consciousness in the present' entirely detached from the past is thus impossible. National consciousness means the affirmation of Jewish givenness.

Ahad Ha-Am thus pinpointed Brenner's weakness, as I discussed in the previous chapter. Brenner, who affirms Jewish thrownness unconditionally, should have understood that this thrownness cannot shed the cultural past that is constitutive of Jewish existence. To be a Jew means to acknowledge that you are thrown into a Jewish culture and a Jewish tradition, even if you reject certain contents. What remains of being a Jew once the past has been sloughed off?! Brenner wishes to claim one thing and its opposite – to affirm his being a Jew and to remove from it the characteristics of Jewish existence. In truth, Brenner seeks to identify Jewish thrownness with the primary, pre-cultural experience of membership and solidarity with a specific human group – the Jewish group. But what turns this group into a group? What unites all the individuals? According to Ahad Ha-Am, it is the past: without the cultural component (the common memories, the myths, and the practices), without a shared past, even if only imagined, there is no people.

To the past, Brenner counterposes the experience of belongingness, and excels at describing its unconditioned supremacy. But Ahad Ha-Am argues that this supremacy has a cultural-national horizon. Individuals are Jews because they belong to the Jewish people, and the Jewish people is Jewish because it bears a unique Jewish culture. To be a Jew is not only a physical characteristic. Natural reality includes no entity that we can call Jewish. Jewishness is a cultural feature and implies taking part in a network of Jewish meanings, a network that by nature is historical-cultural. From this perspective, Brenner sees the end – the experience of connection between Jews, whereas Ahad Ha-Am presents the archeology or the genealogy of this experience. This, then, is the difference between an existentialist reading of culture and a cultural-historical one.

But Ahad Ha-Am too faces a problem: the past he presents as the stable moorings of Jewish existence is not the past that had been 'there' but the past as interpreted in the present. From this perspective, a crucial difference distinguishes the religious from the secular perception of the past. Ahad Ha-Am's historical interpretation appears to question the religious approach. How can one then speak of the past, if it is so different?

Ahad Ha-Am devotes the bulk of 'Torah from Zion' to a discussion of the past, in various ways. First, he accepts the idea that 'our heritage is pervaded by a religious spirit'.[75] Second, contrary to Brenner, he argues that the religious past has not vanished, it lives on in the present: 'This religious spirit is not only past, but a living force still active in the present too.'[76] In Ahad Ha-Am's perception, this datum confronts secular nationalists with a hard predicament. They are the ones who need to reinterpret the past. The transformation of the religious past that Ahad Ha-Am proposes reflects the full secular reversal, which re-embraces the past.

In the religious perception as Ahad Ha-Am understands it, the past denotes past events. The meaning of such events as the giving of the Torah, God's revelation, the exodus from Egypt and so forth, lies in their nature as events that took place, which assume special status because they happened. By contrast, in the secular perception of the past, past events are not facts that happened 'there' but part of a network of historical-cultural meanings, whose significance rests on their standing in the inner cultural discourse:

> Everything that leaves a mark on life, even if only imagined, really and genuinely 'exists' in a historical sense.[77] Therefore, even one who does not believe in divine reality as such cannot refute its existence as an actual historical force. And a national Jew, even if he is an apostate, cannot say: 'I have no part in the God of Israel,' in the historical power that instilled life into our people and influenced the character of its spirit and the course of its life for thousands of years. One who really has no share in the God of Israel, one who does not feel any spiritual closeness to that 'supernal' world in which our ancestors invested their minds and their hearts over generations and from which they drew moral power – might be a fine person but he is not a national Jew, even if he 'lives in the Land of Israel and speaks the holy tongue.'[78]

This programmatic passage, like the 'Moses' article, reflects an important intuition that, in many ways, has resurfaced in the current critical discourse. Postmodern philosophers are forced to contend with the question of an entity existing 'there'. Those who are committed to religious faith must account for the meaning of the concept 'God': does this concept denote an entity in the world, or is it meaningless since it does not denote such an entity and, therefore, a religion resting on the existence of God has no meaning? The characteristic answer of these thinkers is related to the attempt to understand ontological religious language anew. In their view, religious language is not ontological but expressive. Gordon Kaufman, who is a representative of this approach, argues that when analysing religion we must

> begin with awareness that all talk of God belongs to and has its meaning within a particular symbolical frame of orientation for human life which emerges in a particular strand of human history. The symbol 'God' like the rest ... of religious symbols around the world was created as women and men in that historical movement gradually put together a world-picture which enabled them, with some measure of success, to come to terms with the exigencies of life. This symbol, then (like all others), must be understood as a product of the human imagination.[79]

The transformation in the meaning of religious concepts is clear: from concepts denoting an entity they become concepts within a discourse, whose meaning is internal.

Many years before this new discourse, Ahad Ha-Am set the foundations for a conscious transformational perception of the Jewish past. This past can now be described from two entirely different perspectives: one religious and one secular. Ahad Ha-Am held that national Jews, be they religious or secular, share the same language despite the dramatic difference in their views about the meaning of the past: both have a share in the God of Israel. In his view, the difference between religious and secular national Jews is not so dramatic: 'One says, "I believe," and the other "I feel."'[80]

Brenner disagreed with this approach, and his position appears more plausible. The obvious problem with Ahad Ha-Am's view is that, unlike Brenner, he failed to note that the language was not a shared one. Religious language is referential – it relates to facts and to entities in the world. In Ahad Ha-Am's transformational version, the language is expressive rather than referential – it conveys a network of internal meanings. The apparent resemblance between the two languages is misleading, since the ostensible linguistic similarity conceals the metaphysical gap between them. Religious language is metaphysical, whereas secular language is historical-cultural.[81]

Ahad Ha-Am's stance is problematic, though not because of the transformation he performs, as Baruch Kurzweil had claimed,[82] since it is in the nature of culture to reinterpret its past in new and different modes. Cultures even undergo transformations as part of the dialogue they conduct with their past. Only one assuming that the past is a set and sealed entity that is transmitted through tradition without any option of change might, like Kurzweil, consider Ahad Ha-Am's transformation an improper move. The problem in Ahad Ha-Am's approach lies in the blurring of the transformation and in the creation of a shared field to include anyone who ascribes any significance to the past. Ascribing weight and significance to the past does not necessitate an identical interpretation of the past. Ahad Ha-Am, then, is creating a new type of 'abnormal discourse', involving serious impediments.

The terms 'normal discourse' and its antithesis, 'abnormal discourse', were coined by Richard Rorty. 'Normal discourse' denotes a discourse containing basic agreements for evaluating and judging the participants' views. These agreements enable determinations on what is a good argument, what is a successful critique, and, ultimately, how the discourse is decided. By contrast, an 'abnormal discourse' is one where these agreements have been abandoned or never existed. The absence of agreements precludes the discourse's development as a rational-critical exchange. No resolution exists in this discourse and, instead, so Rorty claims, hermeneutics arises as an attempt to explain the occurrence of an 'abnormal discourse'.[83]

What Ahad Ha-Am proposes is an 'abnormal discourse', though detecting this may not be easy because this discourse assumes a 'normal' garb. In ordinary circumstances, we can quickly detect whether agreements exist or have been abandoned. In the discourse that Ahad Ha-Am suggests, however, disagreements are elusive because he presents key concepts in the discourse as obvious and universally agreed upon when they could not possibly be so. The 'obviousness' of the discourse is meant to blur and hide that this discourse is 'abnormal' and to shape a culture of apparent 'normal discourse'. There are basic agreements, as it were, among the various segments of the Jewish people: all have a share in the God of Israel. Furthermore, the concept of 'Jewish past' indicates something clear and agreed upon by all partners to the discourse, whether secularists or religious.

Believers in the God of Israel and national Jews *à la* Ahad Ha-Am share a basic structural experience: all feel that they face a demand from 'there', from something that is beyond them, that precedes them and demands from them some kind of response. This is also the nature of the shared past that Ahad Ha-Am speaks of. In other words, the past denotes the experience of a primary heteronomous element. Since an experience of heteronomy denotes a relationship with what had been and is unconditioned by the self's judgment, it is interpreted as an element from the past breaking into the present. By contrast, the experience of autonomy begins in the present and turns to the future. According to this analysis, the past is a formal element without any particular content. Rather, it endows with special value contents interpreted as past, a value based precisely on the status of human beings as creatures on whom demands are placed, who do not create themselves *ex nihilo*.

But precisely the shared formal aspect – the experience of demands placed on the individual by a 'there' that preceded the present – sheds light on the profound difference between the meaning that believers and secular Jews assign to the past: believers assign metaphysical-theological meaning to the past, and secular Jews – cultural meaning. Believers also know that a critical component of the present plays a vital role in the practice and the significance of the religious normative system – the nature of Jewish tradition as a renewing tradition, which turns to the past and reinterprets it from a new perspective.[84] The believers' view of the present, however, is unique: just as the meaning they ascribe to past contents is metaphysical-theological rather than cultural, they perceive in the same terms their creative and interpretive activity in the present – through this action, they realize God's will. Different segments of the Jewish people, then, interpret in conflicting ways the two fundamental components – past and present – crucial to the shaping of culture. Ahad Ha-Am blurred this difference.

Brenner refused to take part in this conceptual blur and proposed a clean approach that preserves the distance between the partners to the discourse. The world of religion is sealed to secularists. Brenner, who understands the inner meaning of religious language and the nature of secular Jewish existence in the present, knows that consensus on the past (as religious Jews had perceived it in the past and perceive it in the present) is not feasible through a transformation of the past, and suggests abandoning it instead.

Ultimately, the dispute focuses on whether the transformation is necessary for national existence. Ahad Ha-Am's position is clear: only through a transformation shifting from religious to historical-cultural language can the secular world once again appropriate the cultural texts. This appropriation is necessary because the 'national self' is not a renewed creation of the Jewish people. The Jewish people has constitutive texts, which bear Jewish national existence. Ahad Ha-Am therefore states that liberation from Scripture is impossible because, unlike the New Testament, which is the 'historical tombstone' of a particular period, Scripture is the 'historical force of all times', 'a part of our national "self" that is inconceivable without it'.[85]

Unlike Brenner, then, Ahad Ha-Am claims that secularists do not view Scripture as only a historical text or solely as the bearer of national memory. Scripture is the constitutive text of Jewish existence throughout its history, and applying aesthetic criteria to it is therefore inappropriate. In order to clarify this point, Ahad Ha-Am returns to the parental analogy and states: 'Have you ever heard of a child turning its back on its mother because it has found a fairer one?'[86] As the relationship with a parent is primary and unconditioned, so the relationship with Scripture. It is not conditioned by its contents or by the extent to which it is the bearer of the national memory. The relationship with Scripture must be based on the idea that this is a foundational text for the Jewish people, as the mother (and the father in Ahad Ha-Am's original analogy) is primal to her children.

Ahad Ha-Am's stance, however, is not free of problems. The fundamental question is: is the Jewish people founded on a text, such as Scripture, or is this text one of the institutions of the Jewish people? This question, which Ahad Ha-Am does not explicitly address, is crucial to this discussion. The possibility that the Jewish people is constituted by a particular text emerges in Jewish literature throughout its history, but this perception is incomprehensible: if we assume that the people became one through the book and it is not a people without it, the first constitutive act becomes impossible. According to this presumption, there was no subject to precede the book, embrace it, and turn it into a cultural asset. The book is meant to create the people. But barring a people, how exactly does the book create it? The book's standing is contingent on the existence of a readership that does not depend on it, that is ready to appreciate it and evaluate it. In other words, the very act of judging the book as a holy book, as a special text in the life of the nation, must assume the existence of a nation that does not depend on the book and relates to it in the hierarchical fashion of a judge to the object of judgment. The view that the book is one of the institutions of the people appears more plausible. The Jewish people adopted the Scriptures and ascribes special status to them. This view assumes that the existence of the Jewish people does not depend on any particular text; rather, the Jewish people creates and confers meaning on various texts in the course of history, and has also ascribed special status to Scripture.

And yet, the judging stance typical of the attitude towards cultural institutions clarifies the extent to which Ahad Ha-Am's view is problematic. Indeed, believers see the Bible as the book attesting to their unique relationship with God, the legislator of the Torah and the ruler of history. For believers, even if Scriptures are not constitutive of the very existence of the Jewish people as a people, its existence 'is inconceivable without it', just as Jewish existence is inconceivable without the covenant between the Jewish people and God. But why assume such a necessity from a secular perspective? This is indeed the point that Brenner emphasises.

Brenner and Ahad Ha-Am are thus resorting to different languages of discourse. As an existentialist, Brenner looks for the two necessary axes that determine the borders of human existence: the necessary datum imposed on human beings on the one hand, and freedom on the other. Scriptures are not part of the factual datum, but Brenner is not willing to see them as an object of free choice either. The individuals joining together to form the Jewish people are neither thrown into the texts nor do they need to embrace them. Their existence as Jews is not conditioned by culture but by primal thrownness on the one hand, and by the decision to embrace it and act within it on the other. Historical continuity, the 'national self' in Ahad Ha-Am's terms, is not part of thrownness. The individual is not born into a stable and fixed 'national self'. For the individual and for the multitude, life is actually woven in the flux between thrownness, meaning the specific Jewish destiny, and the decision to act within its context. The text of Scripture is not a cornerstone in the unfolding web of life.

Ahad Ha-Am, by contrast, assumes that the existence of the individual is contingent upon the existence of a Jewish 'national self'. The existence of this self is stable and continuous, made up of a cultural historical network of meaning in which the Scriptural text plays a decisive role. He rejects the possibility that language, detached from its historical dimension, could shape communication networks for Jews:

> Hebrew? When stripped from the 'hypnosis' of the past – what is it to us? Cut off from us for millennia, how would its literary merit stand it in good stead if its very literature, if all the 'Judaism' included in it, if even its 'Book of Books' – none has any hold on us now, neither on our mind nor on our feelings? And why should we not turn our back on it as well if we were to find – and we certainly could! – a fairer one?[87]

At this juncture, Ahad Ha-Am detects the most vulnerable spot in Brenner's approach: Hebrew, like all languages, obviously has a cultural-historical sediment and Brenner, as noted, was aware of that. If liberation from the historical-cultural baggage is indeed possible, it is pointless to assume that language cannot be liberated from the individual's reflective voyage. If culture can be shed, so can the Hebrew language. Why then grant it special status? Brenner wishes to adopt a synchronic language and ignore its diachronic character, and Ahad Ha-Am discerned the problematic entailed in this view.

Clearly, the range of issues, arguments, and counter-arguments conveys deep and fundamental differences in the approach to Jewish existence and to human existence in general: the status of the individual, the relationship between the individual and the people, the standing of culture, and the attitude to religion. These basic differences lead to different conclusions: Brenner turns to practice, to the action that sets the foundation for the connection with the people, whereas Ahad Ha-Am recurrently directs us to culture. Despite the differences between them, both share one basic experience: the affirmation of Jewish existence as unconditioned. Ahad Ha-Am is not the only one who writes from the perspective of this primary connection, and Brenner conveys this approach no less convincingly. Brenner may be expressing this affirmation more transparently, since it is not mediated by religion, tradition, or past culture. The affirmation of Jewish existence is a 'Here I am!' 'I am a Jew' declaration, as a primal fundamental fact that will become concretely manifest in the future through a whole gamut of concrete actions. Within this existentialist approach, Judaism is not a solid system of contents but 'an empirical stance maintaining Judaism or

Jewishness to be basically a reflection of what the Jews do and implying that whether or not Judaism bears any intrinsic values, such values are irrelevant to the issues at hand'.[88]

To conclude this point, the positions outlined by both Ahad Ha-Am and Brenner are worth contrasting with that of Ber Borochov. Borochov confronted the question of the past in the present:

> The return to the past only because it is the past is reactionary, because through this aspiration the past becomes a fetish, something of absolute value that one is obliged to return to. No less reactionary, however, is the fear to return to the past only because it is the past. This fear too causes the fetishization of the past, turns it into a kind of taboo, forbidden to touch, bearing disaster, from which one must keep away at all costs.[89]

Borochov pointed out the two dangers lurking on the path of the relationship with the past – plunging into it on the one hand, and negating it entirely on the other. Borochov discerned that the tension between the affirmation of the past and a stance of freedom towards it is a disposition that releases us from the trap of the fetish. Both Ahad Ha-Am and Brenner, each in his own way, contended with the problem of the past. Ahad Ha-Am held that the past is a primary element in the creation of identity, but the individual faces the past as a free being. He thereby liberated the Jew from the problem of past as a fetish. In many senses, however, Ahad Ha-Am distanced the secular Jew from the believer, who assigns a central role to the past precisely because it is the past. Ahad Ha-Am was unaware of this difference, although he did establish the core of identity through the connection with the past.

Brenner chose the present as his starting point. Although he would appear to be close to what Borochov calls the 'fetishization of the past', its fixation as a 'taboo, forbidden to touch', this is not the case. Brenner also assumes an unfolding relationship with the past but, contrary to Ahad Ha-Am, he did not hold it to be vital in the creation of identity. It is not the past as such that is the anchor of identity but rather some of its contents, which can be adopted in the present. Whereas Ahad Ha-Am disregarded the difference between secularists and believers, Brenner disregarded the centrality of the association with the past, the 'there' imposing demands on the self in the constitution of identity. The implications of this disregard could be a deepening detachment between parents and children, potentially leading to an absolute negation of the parents as parents – their real faces are lost; their concrete existence and their cultural fullness vanishes, and an abstract biological element is all that is left. Berl Katzenelson voiced this concern with great sensitivity when he spoke of the 'curse' affecting a generation that does not know 'what it has inherited and against what it has rebelled'.[90] Is it indeed possible to join Jewish existence and to affirm Jewish destiny when the kernel of identity is estrangement from the real world of Jews? Could Jews of Brenner's generation, or of any other, be Jews while ignoring their past? These are the questions at the centre of an unresolved dialectic, the experience of an inner tear in Brenner's Jewish-existentialist world view.

Epilogue

The clash between Brenner and Ahad Ha-Am is a critical moment in the reflection on Jewish identity. The two partners to this confrontation present the two ends that delineate the field of discourse on the subject. At one end is Ahad Ha-Am, who emphasises culture as the constitutive element of identity, and at the other is Brenner, who searches for a primordial, pre-cultural element that constitutes Jewish identity.

Both continue the historical Jewish discourse that recurrently returned to deal with the question of Jewish identity, particularly in crisis situations demanding a decision. Instances include determining the status of Jews who converted, be it forcibly or voluntarily,[91] or who are guilty of a serious transgression, such as breaking the Sabbath in public,[92] or, by contrast, the status of converts to Judaism.[93] At any such moment, the relevant question was and is: what is the fundamental premise of Jewish identity – genealogical ascription or commitment to the Torah and the commandments, that is, commitment to cultural contents.

Mainstream Jewish tradition made the genealogical rather than the normative-cultural component the basis of Jewish identity: a Jew is one who is born to a Jewish mother. A convert to Judaism is born into the Jewish-ethnic collective. Beside the tradition that emphasised the ethnic original component, however, another trend based Jewish existence on a normative foundation and on personal commitment to the Torah and the commandments.[94] This approach gained further strength with emancipation and growing secularization. Primary ethnic belongingness was no longer sufficient for some segments within the community of believers, who faced the rise of a social stratum that deviated from the mainstream and offered an alternative to Jewish existence that is not based on the Torah and the commandments. In these circumstances, a demand emerged requiring Jewish identity to be constituted on the Torah. The normative element and commitment to it were perceived as the glass screen separating those included in the collective and those deviating and excluded from it.

This historical tale appears to be unrelated to the dispute between Brenner and Ahad Ha-Am, since both were already working within a secular culture, but this is not so. Precisely because he recognizes secularism and its implications, Ahad Ha-Am seeks to make canonic texts once again the linchpin of Judaism. In this sense, he is close to the position of tradition, which founded Jewish existence on a commitment to cultural contents – the Torah and its commandments. Ahad Ha-Am and this tradition differ concerning the nature and the meaning of Jewish contents, but they agree on the premise that the deep meaning of Judaism is cognitive and content-oriented. In the traditional field of discourse, then, Ahad Ha-Am supports the less popular approach, which emphasises Jewish content.

Brenner appears to support the classic approach, whereby being a Jew is unconditioned by ideas and beliefs. To be a Jew is a primary genealogical datum. And yet, the picture becomes more complex here because, as noted, Brenner does not unequivocally support this view. Herzl, in his view, is not a Jew, even though genealogically he is one. Brenner demands a decision on the primary datum, a decision that is to be concretized in actual work. The decision and its nature actually draw him closer to the tradition that Ahad Ha-Am supports. This analysis shows that, even if both these thinkers continue some directions of the traditional discourse, they redraw the boundaries of the field of discourse on Jewish identity and stand at two opposing ends.

Jewish identity, however, cannot be realized at one of these two extremes. The Jewish life experience shows that solidarity is not conditioned by normative sharing but by a sense of a common fate. This commonality imposes responsibility and an obligation that establishes the network of cultural and practical ties within the Jewish collective.

Remaining within this common fate, however, impoverishes existence. People live within culture, myth, ethos, and memory, and a life without them is an empty one. When Jewish existence relies entirely on the fate component, it withers. Living a human life obligates the individual to transcend givenness and to seek cultural realization.

But making culture the sole constitutive element of Jewish identity could emasculate the primal sense of connection and attachment. This primal sense is present in our life in various modes, beginning with the family and up to interpersonal relations, which are not necessarily based on conceptual consensus but on an experience of mutual presence and unmediated mutual fullness. Overemphasis on the cultural element could trivialize basic human connections and remove the reason for a communal life.

Brenner and Ahad Ha-Am together, then, delineate the field of a Jewish identity constituted by the dialectic between primary bonds and culture. The role of these two elements is to balance each other so as not to detract from human life, making it shallow and dull. The relationship between the views of Brenner and Ahad Ha-Am is thus like a relationship between two opposite elements that nurture and enrich one another, while they also preclude the fall into the unidimensional trap represented by each one of them separately.

Notes

1   *Writings*, vol.3, 476–87.
2   For an account of this event, see Nurit Govrin, ed., *The Brenner Affair* (in Hebrew) (Jerusalem: Yad Yitzhak Ben-Zvi, 1985).
3   Hillel Zeitlin, 'Contents, Forms, and Ways of Life' in *The Brenner Affair*, ed. Nurit Govrin (Jerusalem: Yad Yitzhak Ben-Zvi, 1985), 153.
4   Fischel Shneursohn, a psychologist and Habad follower, wrote a famous novel describing the world of the 'fallen'. See Fischel Shneursohn, *Hayyim Gravitser* (in Hebrew), trans. (from Yiddish) Abraham Schlonsky (Tel Aviv: Abraham Zioni, 1956). Shneursohn was also close to Zeitlin. See Jonathan Meir, ed., 'Hasidism in the World to Come: Neo-Romanticism, Hasidism, and Messianic Longings in the Writings of Hillel Zeitlin' (in Hebrew), introduction to *Rabbi Nachman of Bratslav: His Life and Work*, by Hillel Zeitlin, *Yeri'ot: Essays and Papers in Jewish Studies Bearing on the Humanities and the Social Sciences*, 5 (2006), 30.
5   Zeitlin, 'Contents, Forms', 155.
6   See, for instance, Joseph Klausner 'Freedom and Heresy', in *The Brenner Affair*, ed. Nurit Govrin (Jerusalem: Yad Yitzhak Ben-Zvi, 1985), 149–52.
7   *Ibid.*
8   Samuel Schneider, *The Traditional Jewish World in the Writings of Joseph Hayim Brenner* (in Hebrew) (Tel Aviv: Reshafim, 1994), 81.
9   *Ibid.*, 83.
10   On identity discourse, see Avi Sagi, *The Jewish-Israeli Voyage: Culture and Identity* (in Hebrew) (Jerusalem: Shalom Hartman Institute, 2006),135–54, 209–12.
11   *Writings*, vol.3, 485.
12   *Ibid.*, 478.
13   *Ibid.*, 480.
14   *Ibid.*, 481.
15   Cited in Yosef Hayim Yerushalmi, *Freud's Moses: Judaism Terminable and Interminable* (New Haven: Yale University Press, 1991), 14.
16   *Ibid.*
17   See also Eran Rolnik, *Freud in Zion: History of Psychoanalysis in Jewish Palestine/Israel 1918–1948* (in Hebrew) (Tel Aviv: Am Oved: 2007), 85.
18   *Writings*, vol. 3, 478.
19   *Ibid.*
20   *Ibid.*, 481
21   *Ibid.*, 480.
22   *Ibid.*, 478.

23   *Ibid.*, 479.

24   *Ibid.*

25   *Ibid.*, 483.

26   On the element of religiosity among Second and Third Aliyah pioneers, see Moti Zeira, *Rural Collective Settlement and Jewish Culture in Eretz Israel during the 1920s* (in Hebrew) (Jerusalem: Yad Yitzhak Ben Zvi, 2002), index, under '*religiosiut*'. See also David Horowitz, *My Yesterday* (in Hebrew) (Jerusalem: Schocken, 1970), who describes this element as the force driving *Hashomer ha-Tsa'ir* members. In pp.136–7, Horowitz quotes Meir Ya'ari, who expresses increasing reservations about the element of religiosity and refers to it as 'deceptions of "bleeding hearts" and the product of a bourgeois mentality'. See also David Maletz, *The Gate is Locked* (in Hebrew) (Tel Aviv: Am Oved, 1959), 86.

27   *Writings*, vol.3, 479.

28   *Ibid.*, 481.

29   *Ibid.*, 486.

30   *Ibid.*, 482–3.

31   Ahad Ha-Am , 'Two Domains', in *Selected Essays of Ahad-Ha-Am*, trans. Leon Simon (Philadelphia: Jewish Publication Society, 1912), 91–2.

32   *Writings*, vol.3, 483. Note in this context that the figure of Yehezkel in *Breakdown and Bereavement*, as Gershon Shaked showed, epitomizes Christian elements drawn from the Jesus archetype. See Gershon Shaked, 'Reflections on *Breakdown and Bereavement* by Y. H. Brenner' (in Hebrew), in *Yosef Haim Brenner: A Selection of Critical Essays on his Literary Prose*, ed. Yitzhak Bakon (Tel Aviv: Am Oved, 1972), 207–208.

33   *Writings*, vol.3, 484.

34   *Ibid.*, 480.

35   *Ibid.*

36   *Ibid.*, 480–81.

37   *Ibid.*

38   Govrin, *The Brenner Affair*, 32.

39   *Writings*, vol.3, 487.

40   *Ibid.*

41   Menachem Brinker, *Normative Art and Social Thought in Y. H. Brenner's Work* (in Hebrew) (Tel Aviv: Am Oved, 1990), 175.

42   *Ibid.*, 161,

43   David Canaani, *The Second Aliyah and its Attitude to Religion and Tradition* (in Hebrew) (Tel Aviv: Sifriat Hapoalim, 1976).

44   *Writings*, vol.3, 487.

45   Iris Parush, *National Ideology and Literary Canon* (Jerusalem: Bialik Institute, 1992), 287–8 (in Hebrew).

46   Hayyim Nahman Bialik, *Spoken Words* (in Hebrew), vol.1 (Tel Aviv: Dvir, 1935), 15.

47   *Ibid.* See also *ibid.*, vol.2, 137, 142–57.

48   The Gospel of St John, 1:1.

49   See Larry W. Hurtado, *How on Earth Did Jesus Become a God? Historical Questions about Earliest Devotion to Jesus* (Grand Rapids, MI: W. B. Eerdmans, 2005), 50.

50   Ahad Ha-Am, *Collected Writings* (in Hebrew) (Tel Aviv: Dvir, 1965), 406–409.

51   *Writings*, vol.2, 1279–80

52   Micha Josef Berdyczewski, *Collected Works* (in Hebrew), ed. Avner Holtzman and
      Yitzhak Kafkafi (Tel Aviv: Hakibbutz Hameuchad, 1996–2009), vol.5, 28, 184–5;
      vol.6, 69–74.

53   Ahad Ha-Am, *Selected Essays*, 194.

54   Ahad Ha-Am, *Collected Writings*, 151.

55   *Ibid.*

56   Rina Hevlin, *Coping with Jewish Identity: A Study of Ahad Ha-Am's Thought* (in
      Hebrew) (Tel Aviv: Hakibbutz Hameuchad, 2001), 39–40.

57   Ahad Ha-Am, *Selected Essays*, 91–2.

58   On this point of departure, see also Clifford Geertz, *The Interpretation of Cultures:
      Selected Essays* (New York: Basic Books, 1973), 56, 61. See also Sagi, *The Jewish-Israeli
      Voyage*, 212–18.

59   Ahad Ha-Am, *Selected Essays*, 93.

60   See Avi Sagi, *Tradition vs. Traditionalism: Contemporary Perspectives in Jewish Thought*,
      trans. Batya Stein (Amsterdam and New York: Rodopi, 2008), ch.1; Sagi, *The
      Jewish-Israeli Voyage*, ch.4.

61   Ahad Ha-Am, *Selected Essays*, 44.

62   *Ibid.*

63   On this question see Sagi, *Tradition vs. Traditionalism*, ch.1; *idem, The Jewish-Israeli
      Voyage*, ch.4.

64   On this question see, at length, Hevlin, *Coping with Jewish Identity*, ch.3.

65   See, for instance, Berdyczewski, *Collected Works*, vol.6, 69–74

66   Ahad Ha-Am, *Selected Essays*, 80.

67   *Ibid.*, 89–90.

68   *Ibid.*, 82.

69   See Yehezkel Kaufmann, *Exile and Estrangement: A Socio-Historical Study on the Fate of
      the Nation of Israel from Antiquity until the Present* (in Hebrew), vol.2 (Tel Aviv: Dvir,
      1961), 408; *idem*, 'Ahad Ha-Am's Main Ideas' (in Hebrew), in *Selected National
      Writings* (Jerusalem: WZO, 1995), 140–59

70   Brinker, *Normative Art*, 161–4.

71   Ahad Ha-Am, *Collected Writings*, 407.

72   *Ibid.*

73   *Ibid.*

74   *Ibid.*

75   *Ibid.*

76   *Ibid.*

77   Ahad Ha-Am refers here to his article 'Moses', in *Selected Essays*, 306.

78   Ahad Ha-Am, *Collected Writings*, 408.

79   Gordon Kaufman, *In Face of Mystery: A Constructive Theology* (Cambridge, MA:
      Harvard University Press, 1995), 39–40.

80   Ahad Ha-Am, *Collected Writings*, 408.

81   Yosef Hayim Yerushalmi noted this in *Zakhor: Jewish History and Jewish Memory*
      (Seattle and London: University of Washington Press, 1982), 81–103. For
      an extensive discussion of this position, see Roni Miron, 'Past, Linkage, and

Interpretation: Y. H. Yerushalmi and A. Funkenstein on *Wissenschaft des Judentums'* (in Hebrew), *Alpayim*, 31 (2007).

82 See Baruch Kurzweil, 'Judaism as the Discovery of the National-Biological Will to Live' (in Hebrew), in *Our New Literature: Continuity or Revolution* (Jerusalem: Schocken, 1960), 190–224.

83 See Richard Rorty, *Philosophy and the Mirror of Nature* (Princeton: Princeton University Press, 1980), 320.

84 On this question, see Moshe Halbertal, *Interpretive Revolutions in the Making: Values as Interpretative Considerations in Midrashei Halakhah* (in Hebrew) (Jerusalem: Magnes Press, 1997).

85 Ahad Ha-Am, *Collected Writings*, 408.

86 *Ibid.*

87 *Ibid.*

88 Shmuel Almog, 'The Role of Religious Values in the Second Aliyah', in *Zionism and Religion*, ed. Shmuel Almog, Jehuda Reinharz and Anita Shapira (Hanover: Brandeis University Press with the Zalman Shazar Center for Jewish History, 1998), 243.

89 Dov Ber Borochov, *Collected Writings* (in Hebrew), vol.1 (Tel Aviv: Hakibbutz Hameuchad and Sifriat Hapoalim, 1956), 90.

90 Berl Katzenelson, *Writings* (in Hebrew) (Tel Aviv: Mapai, 1949), 163.

91 See, for instance, Simha Assaf, *In the Tents of Jacob* (in Hebrew) (Jerusalem: Mosad Harav Kook, 1943), 145–80; Jacob Katz, *Halakhah and Kabbalah: Studies in the History of Jewish Religion, Its Various Faces, and Social Relevance* (in Hebrew) (Jerusalem: Magnes Press, 1984), 255–69.

92 Avi Sagi and Zvi Zohar, *Circles of Jewish Identity, A Study in Halakhic Literature* (in Hebrew) (Jerusalem and Tel Aviv: Hakibbutz Hameuchad and Shalom Hartman Institute, 2000).

93 Avi Sagi and Zvi Zohar, *Transforming Identity: The Ritual Transition from Gentile to Jew – Structure and Meaning* (London: Continuum, 2007).

94 See *ibid.*; see also Sagi and Zohar, *Circles of Jewish Identity*.

Bibliography

Abrams, M. H. *The Mirror and the Lamp: Romantic Theory and the Critical Tradition*. Oxford: Oxford University Press, 1971.

Agnon, S. Y. *Only Yesterday*. Translated by Barbara Harshav. Princeton: Princeton University Press, 2000.

Ahad Ha-Am. *Selected Essays of Ahad-Ha-Am*. Translated by Leon Simon. Philadelphia: Jewish Publication Society, 1912.

——. 'Slavery in Freedom'. In *Contemporary Jewish Thought: A Reader*, edited by Simon Noveck. London: Vision Press Limited, 1964.

——. *Collected Writings* (Hebrew). Tel Aviv: Dvir, 1965.

Almog, Shmuel. 'The Role of Religious Values in the Second Aliyah' (Hebrew). In *Zionism and Religion*, edited by Shmuel Almog, Jehuda Reinharz, and Anita Shapira. Hanover: Brandeis University Press, with the Zalman Shazar Center for Jewish History, 1998.

Améry, Jean. *At the Mind's Limits: Contemplations by a Survivor of Auschwitz and Its Realities*. Translated by Sidney Rosenfeld and Stella P. Rosenfeld. Bloomington, ID: Indiana University Press, 1980.

Anton, Corey. *Selfhood and Authenticity*. Albany, NY: SUNY Press, 2001.

Appelfeld, Aharon. *First Person Essays* (Hebrew). Jerusalem: WZO, 1979.

Aristotle. *Poetics*. Edited and translated by Stephen Halliwell. Cambridge, MA: Harvard University Press, 1995.

Arpali, Boaz. *The Negative Principle: Ideology and Poetics in Two Stories by Y. H. Brenner* (Hebrew). Tel Aviv: Hakibbutz Hameuchad, 1992.

——. '*Ba-Horef* by Brenner: An Existential-Psychological Point of View' (Hebrew). *Eleventh World Congress of Jewish Studies*, Division C, Vol. III. Jerusalem: World Union of Jewish Studies, 1994, 151–8.

——. 'Asymmetrical Contrasts – Between the Truth of Death and a Life of Falsehood: Ideological, Existential, and Psychological Crossroads in Y. H. Brenner's *Misaviv la-Nekudah*' (Hebrew). *Sadan: Studies in Hebrew Literature at the Outset of the Twentieth Century*, 4 (2000): 211–65.

——. 'Ideology and Anti-Ideology in "Around the Point" by Y. H. Brenner' (Hebrew). In *Literature and Society in Modern Hebrew Culture: Papers in Honor of Gershon Shaked*, edited by Judith Bar-El, Yigal Schawartz, and Tamar S. Hess (Tel Aviv: Hakibbutz Hameuchad, 2005).

Assaf, Simha. *In the Tents of Jacob* (Hebrew). Jerusalem: Mosad Harav Kook, 1943.

Bakon, Yitzhak. *The Young Brenner* (Hebrew). Tel Aviv: Hakibbutz Hameuchad, 1975.

———. *The Lonely Young Man in Hebrew Literature 1899–1908* (Hebrew). Tel Aviv: Tel Aviv University, 1978.

———. *In the One Year* (Hebrew). Papyrus: Tel Aviv University, 1981.

———. *Brenner in London: The Me'orer Period – 1905–1907* (Hebrew). Beer Sheva: Ben-Gurion University, 2000.

Barash, Asher. 'On Y. H. Brenner' (Hebrew). *Notebooks on Literature, Philosophy and Criticism* 30 (1954): 237–8.

Barrett, William. *Irrational Man: A Study in Existential Philosophy.* Garden City: NY: Doubleday, 1962.

Bartana, Ortsion. *Caution, Israeli Literature: Trends in Israeli Fiction* (Hebrew). Tel Aviv: Tel Aviv University, 1989.

Bartonov, Shlomo, ed. *Micha Josef Berdyczewsky, Yosef Haim Brenner: Letters* (Hebrew). Tel Aviv: Hakibbutz Hameuchad, 1962.

Bar-Yosef, Hamutal. *Decadent Trends in Hebrew Literature: Bialik, Berdyczewski, Brenner* (Hebrew). Beer Sheva: Ben-Gurion University, 1997.

Ben-Aharon, Yariv. 'The Roots of Prayer in Y. H. Brenner' (Hebrew). *Amudim* 429 (September 1981): 336–40.

Ben-Nahum, Daniel. 'Y. H. Brenner through a Contemporary Perspective' (Hebrew). *Orlogin* 4 (1951): 32–47.

Ben-Or (Orinovsky), Aaron. *The History of Modern Hebrew Literature* (Hebrew) vol.2. Tel Aviv: Yizre'el, 1959.

Berdyczewski, Micha Josef. *Collected Works* (Hebrew), vols.5–6, edited by Avner Holtzman and Yitzhak Kafkafi. Tel Aviv: Hakibbutz Hameuchad, 1996–2009.

Berger, Peter. *The Heretical Imperative: Contemporary Possibilities of Religious Affirmation.* New York: Anchor Press, 1979.

Berlin, Isaiah. *Four Essays on Liberty.* Oxford and New York: Oxford University Press, 1969.

———. 'The Hedgehog and the Fox: An Essay on Tolstoy's View of History'. In *The Proper Study of Mankind: An Anthology of Essays,* edited by Henry Hardy and Roger Hausheer. London: Pimlico, 1998.

Beylin, Asher. *Brenner in London* (Hebrew). Tel Aviv: Hakibbutz Hameuchad, 2006.

Bialik, Hayyim Nahman. *Spoken Words* (Hebrew), vol.1. Tel Aviv: Dvir, 1935.

Boelen, Bernard J. *Existential Thinking.* New York: Herder and Herder, 1971.

Booth, Wayne C. *The Rhetoric of Fiction,* 2nd edn. Chicago: University of Chicago Press, 1983.

Borochov, Dov Ber. *Collected Writings* (Hebrew), vol.1. Tel Aviv: Hakibbutz Hameuchad and Sifriat Hapoalim, 1956.

Brenner, Yosef Haim. *Collected Writings* (Hebrew), 3 vols. Tel Aviv: Hakibbutz Hameuchad, 1967.

——. *Breakdown and Bereavement.* Translated by Hillel Halkin. Philadelphia: Jewish Publication Society of America, 1971.

——. *Writings* (Hebrew), 4 vols. Tel Aviv: Hakibbutz Hameuchad, 1978–85.

——. *The Yiddish Writings* (in Yiddish and Hebrew), edited by Yitzhak Bakon. Beer-Sheva: Ben-Gurion University, 1985.

Breuer, Yitzhak. *Moriyah* (Hebrew). Jerusalem: Mosad Harav Kook, 1982.

Brinker, Menachem. 'Brenner and the Workers' Movement: A Critic from Within' (Hebrew). In *Hebrew Literature and the Labour Movement*, edited by Pinhas Ginossar. Beer Sheva: Ben-Gurion University Press, 1989.

——. *Normative Art and Social Thought in Y. H. Brenner's Work* (Hebrew). Tel Aviv: Am Oved, 1990.

——. 'Epilogue' (Hebrew). In *Breadown and Bereavement.* Tel Aviv: Hakibbutz Hameuchad, 2006.

Buber, Martin. *Paths in Utopia.* Translated by R. F. C. Hull. New York: Macmillan, 1958.

Camus, Albert. *The Rebel: An Essay on Man in Revolt*, Translated by Anthony Bower. London: H. Hamilton, 1953.

——. *The Plague.* Translated by Stuart Gilbert. Harmondsworth, Essex: Penguin Books, 1960.

——. *The Myth of Sisyphus.* Translated by Justin O'Brien. Harmondsworth, Essex: Penguin Books, 1975.

——. *The First Man.* Translated by David Hapgood. New York: Random House, 1996.

Canaani, David. *The Second Aliyah and its Attitude to Religion and Tradition* (Hebrew). Tel Aviv: Sifriat Hapoalim, 1976.

Cohen, Adir. *Brenner's Literary Oeuvre* (Hebrew). Tel Aviv: Gome, 1972.

Dagan, Hagai. 'Homeland and the Jewish Ethos: An Ongoing Dissonance' (Hebrew). *Alpayim* 18 (1999): 9–23.

Ewen, Josef. 'Cathartic and Anti-Cathartic Elements in Brenner's Work' (Hebrew). In *On Poetry and Prose: Studies in Hebrew Literature*, edited by Zvi Malachi. Tel Aviv: Tel Aviv University, 1977.

——. *Y. H. Brenner's Craft of Fiction* (Hebrew). Jerusalem: Bialik Institute, 1977.

Feierberg, Mordecai Ze'ev. *Whither? and Other Stories*, Translated by Hillel Halkin, Philadelphia: Jewish Publication Society of America, 1973.

Friedman, David Aryeh. 'Bereaved' (Hebrew). *Ha-Tekufah* 10 (1921).

———. *Y. H. Brenner: The Man and his Work* (Hebrew). Berlin: Judischer Verlag, 1923.

———. *Prose Studies: Essays and Articles on Narrators and Literature* (Hebrew). Tel Aviv: Mahbarot le-Sifrut, 1966.

———. 'The Cellar Man or the Hebrew Apostate' (Hebrew). In *Yosef Haim Brenner: A Selection of Critical Essays on his Literary Prose*, edited by Yitzhak Bakon. Tel Aviv: Am Oved, 1972.

Friend, Robert. *Found in Translation: Modern Hebrew Poets – A Bilingual Edition*. New Milford, CT: The Toby Press, 2006.

Frye, Northrop. *Anatomy of Criticism*. Princeton: Princeton University Press, 1957.

Gadamer, Hans-George. *Truth and Method*. Translated by Joel Weinscheimer and Donald G. Marshall. New York: Crossroad, 1989.

Geertz, Clifford. *The Interpretation of Cultures: Selected Essays*. New York: Basic Books, 1973.

Gorny, Yosef. 'Hope in Anguish: On the Zionist Views of Y. H. Brenner' (Hebrew). *Assufoth: A Publication Devoted to the Study of the Jewish Labor Movement* 2 (1971): 5–30.

———. 'There is no Messiah: To Work!' (Hebrew). In *Notebooks for the Study of the Work and Endeavor of Y. H. Brenner*, ed. Israel Levin, vol.2. Tel Aviv: Tel Aviv University and Workers' Federation, 1977.

Goultschin, Moshe. *Baruch Kurzweil as a Commentator of Culture* (Hebrew). Ramat-Gan: Bar-Ilan University Press, 2009.

Govrin, Nurit. *Roots and Tops: The Imprint of the First Aliyah on Hebrew Literature* (Hebrew). Tel Aviv: Papyrus, 1981.

———. *From Horizon to Horizon: The Life and Work of G. Shofman* (Hebrew), vol.2 (Tel Aviv: Tel Aviv University and Yahdav, 1982).

———. *The Brenner Affair* (Hebrew). Jerusalem: Yad Yitzhak Ben-Zvi, 1985.

———. *Alienation and Regeneration*. Translated by John Glucker. Tel Aviv: MOD, 1989.

Gurevitch, Zali. *On Israeli and Jewish Place* (Hebrew). Tel Aviv: Am Oved, 2007.

Halbertal, Moshe. *Interpretive Revolutions in the Making: Values as Interpretative Considerations in Midrashei Halakhah* (Hebrew). Jerusalem: Magnes Press, 1997.

Halkin, Simon. *Introduction to Hebrew Literature: Lecture Notes* (Hebrew). Jerusalem: Students Association at Hebrew University, 1960.

Hegel, G. W. F. *Phenomenology of Spirit*. Translated by A. V. Miller. Oxford: Clarendon Press, 1979.

Heidegger, Martin. *Being and Time*. Translated by John Macquarrie and Edward Robinson. New York: Harper and Row, 1962.

——. 'The Origin of the Work of Art'. In *Poetry, Language, Thought.* Translated by Albert Hofstadter. New York: Harper and Row, 1971.

——. *Martin Heidegger Basic Writings.* London: Routledge and Kegan Paul, 1978.

——. *The Basic Problems of Phenomenology.* Translated by Albert Hofstadter. Bloomington, ID: Indiana University Press, 1988.

Hevlin, Rina. *Coping with Jewish Identity: A Study of Ahad Ha-Am's Thought* (Hebrew). Tel Aviv: Hakibbutz Hameuchad, 2001.

Hirschfeld, Ariel. 'On "Nerves" by Y. H. Brenner' (Hebrew). In *Literature and Society in Modern Hebrew Culture: Papers in Honor of Gershon Shaked,* edited by Judith Bar-El, Yigal Schawartz and Tamar S. Hess. Tel Aviv: Hakibbutz Hameuchad, 2005.

Holtzman, Avner. *Hebrew Fiction in the Early Twentieth Century, Unit 1* (Hebrew). Tel Aviv: Open University, 1993.

——. *Literature and Life: Essays on M. J. Berdyczewsky* (Hebrew). Jerusalem: Carmel, 2003.

——. *Loves of Zion: Studies in Modern Hebrew Literature* (Hebrew). Jerusalem: Carmel, 2006.

Horowitz, David. *My Yesterday* (Hebrew) Jerusalem: Schocken, 1970.

Hubben, William. *Dostoevsky, Kierkegaard, Nietzsche and Kafka: Four Prophets of Our Destiny.* New York: Macmillan, 1952.

Hurtado, Larry W. *How on Earth Did Jesus Become a God? Historical Questions about Earliest Devotion to Jesus.* Grand Rapids, MI: W. B. Eerdmans, 2005.

Ibsen, Henrik. *Peer Gynt: A Dramatic Poem.* Translated by Christopher Fry and Johan Fillinger. Oxford: Oxford University Press, 1989.

Kabak, Aharon Avraham. *Between the Sea and the Desert* (Hebrew), vol.1. Tel Aviv: Shtibel, 1933.

——. *The Empty Space* (Hebrew). Tel Aviv: Am Oved, 1953.

Karin-Frank, Shyli. *Utopia Reconsidered* (Hebrew). Tel Aviv: Hakibbutz Hameuchad, 1986.

Katz, Jacob. *Halakhah and Kabbalah: Studies in the History of Jewish Religion, Its Various Faces, and Social Relevance* (Hebrew). Jerusalem: Magnes Press, 1984.

——. 'Though He Sinned, He Remains an Israelite'. In *Halakhah and Kabbalah: Studies in the History of Jewish Religion, its Various Faces and Social Relevance* (Hebrew). Jerusalem: Magnes Press, 1986.

Katzenelson, Berl. *Writings* (Hebrew). Tel Aviv: Mapai, 1949.

Kaufman, Gordon. *In Face of Mystery: A Constructive Theology.* Cambridge, MA: Harvard University Press, 1995.

Kaufmann, Yehezkel. *Exile and Estrangement: A Socio-Historical Study on the*

Fate of the Nation of Israel from Antiquity until the Present (Hebrew), vol.2. Tel Aviv: Dvir, 1961.

——. 'Ahad Ha-Am's Main Ideas' (Hebrew). In *Selected National Writings* (Jerusalem: WZO, 1995).

Keshet, Yeshurun (Yaakov Koplewitz). *In Bialik's Times: Essays* (Hebrew). Tel Aviv: Dvir, 1943.

——. *In Brenner's Generation* (Hebrew). Jerusalem: Bialik Institute, 1943.

——. 'On Y. H. Brenner: A Profile' (Hebrew). *Anthology of Literature, Criticism, and Thought* 3 (1963): 146–75.

Kierkegaard, Søren. *The Point of View for My Work as an Author.* Translated by Walter Lowrie. New York: Harper and Row, 1962.

——. *Søren Kierkegaard's Journals and Papers.* Edited and translated by Howard V. Hong and Edna Hong, 2 vols. Bloomington, IN: Indiana University Press, 1967.

——. *The Sickness unto Death.* Translated by H. V. Hong and E. Hong. Princeton: Princeton University Press, 1980.

——. *Fear and Trembling: Repetition.* Edited and translated by Howard V. Hong and Edna H. Hong. Princeton: Princeton University Press, 1983.

——. *Concluding Unscientific Postcript to Philosophical Fragments*, vol.1. Translated by Howard V. Hong and Edna Hong. Princeton: Princeton University Press, 1992.

Kimhi, Dov. *Brief Essays* (Hebrew). Jerusalem: Reuven Mass, 1984.

Klausner, Joseph. 'Freedom and Heresy' (Hebrew). In *The Brenner Affair.* Edited by Nurit Govrin. Jerusalem: Yad Yitzhak Ben-Zvi, 1985.

Kook, Abraham Yitzhak Hacohen. *Orot ha-Rehaya* (Hebrew). Jerusalem: Mosad Harav Kook, 1970.

Krieger, Murray. *The Tragic Vision: Variations on a Theme in Literary Interpretation.* Chicago: University of Chicago Press, 1966.

Kundera, Milan. *The Art of the Novel.* Translated by Linda Asher. New York: Harper and Row, 1988.

Kurzweil, Baruch. 'Judaism as the Discovery of the National-Biological Will to Live' (Hebrew). In *Our New Literature: Continuity or Revolution* (Jerusalem: Schocken, 1960).

——. *Our New Literature: Continuity or Revolution* (Hebrew). Jerusalem: Schocken, 1965.

——. *Between Vision and the Absurd: Chapters in the Path of Our Literature in the Twentieth Century* (Hebrew). Jerusalem: Schocken, 1966.

——. 'Between Brenner, Weinninger, and Kafka'. In *Yosef Haim Brenner: A Selection of Critical Essays on his Literary Prose* (Hebrew), edited by Yitzhak Bakon. Tel Aviv: Am Oved, 1972.

——. 'Breakdown and Bereavement: The Last Stop of an Absurd Jewish Existence' (Hebrew). In *Breakdown and Bereavement, with an Essay by Baruch Kurzweil*. Tel Aviv: Am Oved, 1972.

Kushnir, Mordechai, ed. *Yosef Haim Brenner: Selected Memories* (Hebrew). Tel Aviv: Hakibbutz Hameuchad, 1944.

Kymlicka, Will. *Liberalism, Community and Culture*. Oxford, Clarendon Press, 1991.

Laing, R. D. *The Divided Self: An Existential Study in Sanity and Madness*. New York: Pantheon Books, 1960.

Lavi, Shlomo. *The Aliyah of Shalom Layish* (Hebrew). Tel Aviv: Ayanot, 1957.

Lichtenbaum, Yosef. *Yosef Haim Brenner: His Life and Work*. Tel Aviv: Niv, 1967.

Macquarrie, John. *Existentialism*. Harmonsdsworth: Middlesex: Penguin Books, 1973.

Maletz, David. *The Gate is Locked* (Hebrew). Tel Aviv: Am Oved, 1959.

Mannheim, Karl. *Ideology and Utopia*. London: Routedge and Kegan Paul, 1979.

Maritain, Jacques. 'From Existential Existentialism To Academic Existentialism'. *Sewanee Review* 26 (1948): 210–29.

May, Rollo. *The Discovery of Being: Writings in Existential Psychology*. New York: Norton, 1983.

Megged, Matti. 'Y. H. Brenner: Two Episodes' (Hebrew). In *Anaf: An Anthology of Young Literature*. Edited by Dan Miron. Jerusalem: Schocken, 1964.

——. 'The Tragic "Self" as Reality and as Ideal' (Hebrew). In *Yosef Haim Brenner: A Selection of Critical Essays on his Literary Prose*. Edited by Yitzhak Bakon. Tel Aviv: Am Oved, 1972.

——. 'Reality and Holiness' (Hebrew). *On Poetry and Prose: Studies in Hebrew Literature*. Edited by Zvi Malachi. Tel Aviv: Tel Aviv University, 1977.

Meir, Jonatan. 'Longing of Souls for the *Shekhinah*: Relations between Rabbi Kook, Zeitlin, and Brenner' (Hebrew). In *The Path of the Spirit: The Eliezer Schweid Jubilee Volume*, vol.2. Edited by Yehoyada Amir. Jerusalem: Hebrew University of Jerusalem, 2005.

——. 'Hasidism in the World to Come: Neo-Romanticism, Hasidism, and Messianic Longings in the Writings of Hillel Zeitlin' (in Hebrew), introduction to *Rabbi Nachman of Bratslav: His Life and Work*, by Hillel Zeitlin, *Yeri'ot: Essays and Papers in Jewish Studies Bearing on the Humanities and the Social Sciences*, 5 (2006).

Miron, Dan. 'Hebrew Literature at the Beginning of the Twentieth Century' (Hebrew). *Anthology of Literature, Criticism and*

Philosophy, vol.2. Jerusalem: The Hebrew Writers Association in Israel, 1961.

Miron, Roni. 'Past, Linkage, and Interpretation: Y. H. Yerushalmi and A. Funkenstein on *Wissenschaft des Judentums*' (Hebrew). *Alpayim* 31 (2007): 169–223.

——. *Karl Jaspers: From Selfhood to Being*. Atlanta, GA-New York: Rodopi, in press.

Murdoch, Iris. *Existentialists and Mystics: Writings on Philosophy and Literature*. New York: Allen Lane, 1998.

Nabokov, Vladimir. *Speak, Memory*. New York: Pyramid Books, 1968.

Naveh, Hannah. *The Confessional Narrative : A Description of Genre and Its Practice in Modern Hebrew Literature* (Hebrew). Tel Aviv: Papyrus, 1988.

Nietzsche, Friedrich. *Thus Spoke Zarathustra: A Book for Everyone and No One*. Translated by R. J. Hollingdale. Harmondsworth, Middlesex: Penguin Books, 1961.

——. *The Will to Power*. Translated by Walter Kaufman. New York: Vintage, 1968.

——. *Twilight of the Idols and the Anti-Christ*. Translated by R. J. Hollingdale. Harmondsworth, Middlesex: Penguin Books, 1968.

——. *The Gay Science*. Edited by Bernard Williams. Translated by Josefine Nauckhoff. Cambridge: Cambridge University Press, 2001.

——. *The Genealogy of Morals*. New York: Dover Thrift Editions, 2003.

Olafson, Frederick A. *What is a Human Being? A Heideggerian View*. Cambridge: Cambridge University Press, 1995.

Olson, Alan M. and Rouner, Leroy S., eds. *Transcendence and the Sacred*. Notre Dame, IN: University of Notre Dame Press, 1981.

Ophir, Adi. *The Order of Evils: Toward an Ontology of Morals*. Translated by Rela Mazali and Havi Karel. New York: Zone Books, 2005.

Parush, Iris. *National Ideology and Literary Canon* (Hebrew). Jerusalem: Bialik Institute, 1992.

——. 'The Conception of Literary Canon in Brenner's Criticism'. In *Yitzhak Bakon Volume: Belles-Lettres and Literary Studies*. Edited by Aharon Komem (Beer Sheva: Ben-Gurion University, 2002).

Penueli, S. I. *Stages in Modern Hebrew Literature* (Hebrew). Tel Aviv: Dvir, 1953.

——.   *Brenner and Gnessin in Early Twentieth-Century Hebrew Fiction* (Hebrew). Tel Aviv: Students' Association at Tel Aviv University, 1965.

Philips, D. Z. *Faith after Foundationalism*. London: Routledge and Kegan Paul, 1988.

Plato. *Great Dialogues.* Translated by W. H. D. Rouse. New York: New American Library, 1956.

Popper, Karl R. *The Open Society and Its Enemies,* vol.1. London: Routledge and Kegan Paul, 1974.

Poznansky, Menachem. 'Y. H. Brenner: An Exchange of Letters' (Hebrew). *Mi-Bifnim* 29, 1–2 (1967): 86–95.

Rabinovich, Isaiah. *Yezer Vyezirah* (Hebrew). Jerusalem: Bialik Institute, 1951.

——. *Hebrew Narrative Seeks a Hero: Directions in the Artistic Development of Modern Hebrew Fiction* (Hebrew). Ramat-Gan: Hebrew Writers Association in Israel, 1967.

Ramraz-Rauch, Gila. *Y. H. Brenner and Modern Literature* (Hebrew). Tel Aviv: Aked, 1970.

Rolnik, Eran. *Freud in Zion: History of Psychoanalysis in Jewish Palestine/Israel 1918–1948* (Hebrew) Tel Aviv: Am Oved: 2007.

Rorty, Richard. *Philosophy and the Mirror of Nature.* Princeton: Princeton University Press 1980.

——. *Contingency, Irony and Solidarity.* Cambridge: Cambridge University Press, 1989.

Rosenzweig, Franz. *The Star of Redemption.* Translated by William W. Hallo. Boston: Beacon Press, 1964.

——. '"The New Thinking": A Few Supplementary Remarks to The Star [of Redemption]'. In *Franz Rosenzweig's 'The New Thinking'.* Edited and translated by Alan Udoff and Barbara E. Galli. Syracuse, NY: University of Syracuse Press, 1999.

Russell, Frances Theresa. *Touring Utopia: The Realm of Constructive Humanism.* New York: Dial Press, 1932.

Sadan, Dov. *A Psychoanalytic Midrash: Studies in Brenner's Psychology* (Hebrew). Jerusalem: Magnes Press, 1996.

Sagi, Avi. *Kierkegaard, Religion, and Existence: The Voyage of the Self.* Translated by Batya Stein. Amsterdam-Atlanta, GA: Rodopi, 2000.

——. *Circles of Jewish Identity, A Study in Halakhic Literature* (Hebrew). Tel Aviv and Jerusalem: Hakibbutz Hameuchad and Shalom Hartman Institute, 2000.

——. *Albert Camus and the Philosophy of the Absurd.* Translated by Batya Stein. Amsterdam and New York: Rodopi, 2002.

——. *The Jewish-Israeli Voyage: Culture and Identity* (Hebrew). Jerusalem: Shalom Hartman Institute, 2006.

——. *Tradition vs. Traditionalism: Contemporary Perspectives in Jewish Thought.* Translated by Batya Stein. Amsterdam-New York: Rodopi, 2008.

——. *Jewish Religion after Theology.* Translated by Batya Stein. Boston: Academic Studies Press, 2009.

Sagi, Avi and Yedidia Stern. 'Exiling Identity: *Altneuland* and *Der Judenstaat*' (Hebrew). *Alpayim* 30 (2007): 46–70.

Sagi, Avi and Zvi Zohar. *Circles of Jewish Identity, A Study in Halakhic Literature* (Hebrew). Jerusalem and Tel Aviv: Hakibbutz Hameuchad and Shalom Hartman Institute, 2000.

——. *Transforming Identity: The Ritual Transition from Gentile to Jew – Structure and Meaning*. London: Continuum, 2007.

Sagiv, Asaf. 'Zionism and the Myth of Motherland'. *Azure* 5 (Autumn 5759/1998): 98–112.

Sartre, Jean-Paul. *Nausea*. Translated by Lloyd Alexander. Norfolk: CT: New Directions, 1959.

——. *Anti-Semite and Jew*. Translated by George J. Becker. New York: Schocken, 1970.

Schechter, Nathan. 'Truth from the Land of Israel: Post-Zionism and "Mi-Kan U-Mi-Kan"' (Hebrew). *Keshet ha-Hadashah* 9 (2004): 160–78.

Schleiermacher, Friedrich. *Hermeneutics: The Handwritten Manuscripts*. Edited by Heinz Kimmerle. Translated by James Duke and Jack Forstman. Missoula, MT: Scholars' Press, 1977.

Schneider, Samuel. *The Traditional Jewish World in the Writings of Joseph Hayim Brenner* (Hebrew). Tel Aviv: Reshafim, 1994.

Schrag, Calvin O. *Existence and Freedom, Towards an Ontology of Human Finitude*. Evanston, IL: Northwestern University Press, 1983.

Schweid, Eliezer. *Judaism and the Solitary Jew* (Hebrew). Tel Aviv: Am Oved, 1974.

Shaked, Gershon. 'Reflections on *Breakdown and Bereavement* by Y. H. Brenner' (Hebrew). In *Yosef Haim Brenner: A Selection of Critical Essays on his Literary Prose*. Edited by Yitzhak Bakon. Tel Aviv: Am Oved, 1972.

——. *Dead End: Studies in Y. H. Brenner, M. J. Berdyczewski, G. Schoffman and U. N. Gnessin* (Hebrew). Tel Aviv: Hakibbutz Hameuchad, 1973.

——. *Hebrew Narrative Fiction 1880–1980*, vol.1, *In Exile* (Hebrew). Tel Aviv: Hakibbutz Hameuchad, 1978.

Shapira, Anita. *The Bible and Israeli Identity* (Hebrew). Jerusalem: Magnes Press, 2005.

Shimoni, Gideon. *The Zionist Ideology*. Hanover and London: Brandeis University Press and University Press of New England, 1995.

Shinan, Abraham. *Trends in Modern Hebrew Literature* (Hebrew), vol.4. Ramat-Gan: Massada, 1967.

Shmueli, Ephraim. *Wondering and Thinking in a Techno-Scientific World* (Hebrew). Jerusalem: Bialik Institute, 1985.

Shneursohn, Fischel. *Hayyim Gravitser* (Hebrew). Translated by Abraham Schlonsky from Yiddish. Tel Aviv: Abraham Zioni, 1956.

Smolenskin, Peretz. *Story without Heroes* (Hebrew). Tel Aviv: Am Oved, 1953.

Soloveitchik, Joseph B. *The Lonely Man of Faith*. Northvale, NJ: Jason Aronson, 1965.

——. *Kol Dodi Dofek: Listen – My Beloved Knocks*. Translated by David Z. Gordon. New York: Yeshiva University, 2006.

Tabenkin, Yitzhak. 'Brenner in the Perception of his Contemporaries' (Hebrew). *Notebooks for the Study of the Work and Endeavor of Y. H. Brenner*, ed. Israel Levin, vol.2. Tel Aviv: Tel Aviv University and Workers' Federation, 1977.

Talmon, J. L. *The Origins of Totalitarian Democracy*. London: Secker and Warburg, 1952.

Taylor, Charles. *Hegel and Modern Society*. Cambridge: Cambridge University Press 1996.

Tennen, Hanoch. *The Conception of an Existential Ethics in Karl Jaspers' Philosophy* (Hebrew). Ramat-Gan: Massada, 1977.

Thiselton, Anthony C. *New Horizons in Hermeneutics*. Grand Rapids, MI: Zondervan, 1992.

Thompson, John. 'Tradition and Self in a Mediated World'. In *Detraditionalization: Critical Reflections on Authority and Identity*. Edited by Paul Heelas, Scott Lash and Paul Morris. Cambridge, MA: Blackwell, 1996.

Tillich, Paul, *Dynamics of Faith*. New York: Harper and Row, 1957.

——. *Systematic Theology*, vol.2. Chicago: University of Chicago Press, 1967.

——. *What is Religion?* New York: Harper, 1973.

Tolstoy, Leo. *The Death of Ivan Ilyich*. Translated by Aylmer Maude. In *Classics of Modern Fiction*. Edited by Irving Howe. New York: Harcourt, Brace, Jovanovich, 1980.

Troisfontaines, Roger. *Existentialism and Christian Thought*. Translated by Martin Jarret-Kerr. London: Adam and Charles Black, 1949.

Tzemah, Ada. *A Movement at the Spot: Joseph Chaim Brenner and His Novels* (Hebrew). Tel Aviv: Hakibbutz Hameuchad, 1984.

Tzemah, Shlomo. 'Y. H. Brenner' (Hebrew). *Ha-Shiloah* 28 (1912): 465–6.

Tzur, Muki. *Doing It the Hard Way [Le-lo Kutonet Passim]* (Hebrew). Tel Aviv: Am Oved, 1978.

Wellek, Rene and Warren Austin. *Theory of Literature*. New York: Hartford Brace, 1949.

Winquist, Charles E. *Homecoming: Interpretation, Transformation, and Individuation*. Missoula, MT: Scholars Press, 1978.

Wittgenstein, Ludwig. *On Certainty*. Translated by Dennis Paul and G. E. M. Anscombe. Oxford: Basil Blackwell, 1969.

——. *Lectures and Conversation on Aesthetic, Psychology, and Religious Belief.* Edited by Cyril Barrett. Oxford: Basil Blackwell, 1970.

Yerushalmi, Yosef Hayim. *Zakhor: Jewish History and Jewish Memory.* Seattle and London, University of Washington Press: 1982.

——. *Freud's Moses: Judaism Terminable and Interminable.* New Haven: Yale University Press, 1991.

Yitzhaki, Moshe. 'From Apostasy to Prayer: Religious Elements in Breakdown and Bereavement by Y. H. Brenner' (Hebrew). *Alei Siah* 55 (2006): 24–37.

Zach, Nathan. 'Sickness and the Allure of the Concealed' (Hebrew). In *Yosef Haim Brenner: A Selection of Critical Essays on his Literary Prose.* Edited by Yitzhak Bakon. Tel Aviv: Am Oved, 1972.

Zeira, Moti. *Rural Collective Settlement and Jewish Culture in Eretz Israel during the 1920s* (Hebrew). Jerusalem: Yad Yitzhak Ben Zvi, 2002.

Zeitlin, Hillel. 'Contents, Forms, and Ways of Life' (Hebrew). In *The Brenner Affair.* Edited by Nurit Govrin. Jerusalem: Yad Yitzhak Ben-Zvi, 1985.

Zimerman, Shoshana. *From Thee to Thee: The Underlying Principle in H. N. Bialik's Poetry* (Hebrew). Tel Aviv: Tag, 1998.

Zimmerman, Michael E. *Eclipse of the Self, The Development of Heidegger's Concept of Authenticity.* Athens, OH: Ohio University Press, 1982.

Zweig, Stefan. *Beware of Pity.* Translated by Phyllis and Trevor Blewitt. Harmondsworth, Middlesex: Penguin Books, 1982.

Index